FOWL LANGUAGE
TWEENAGE WASTELAND

BRIAN GORDON

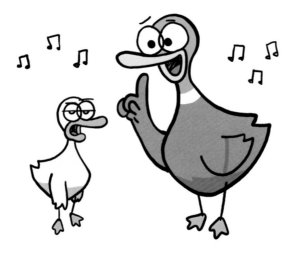

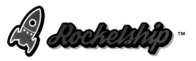

Rocketship Entertainment, LLC
rocketshipent.com

Tom Akel, CEO & Publisher • **Rob Feldman,** CTO • **Jeanmarie McNeely,** CFO
Brandon Freeberg, Dir. of Campaign Mgmt. • **Phil Smith,** Art Director • **Aram Alekyan,** Designer
Jimmy Deoquino, Designer • **Jed Keith,** Social Media • **Jerrod Clark,** Publicity

FOWL LANGUAGE volume 1 | Softcover Edition ISBN: 978-1-952126-99-4 | Hardcover Edition ISBN: 978-1-962298-00-1

For my ducklings,
Max, Phoebe, Ike and Millie,
and for my sweet girl, Cat.
I love you all so much.
Thanks for all the inspiration
and for putting up with me.

B. Gordon

INTRODUCTION

"May you live in interesting times" is an old expression that sounds like a blessing but meant as a curse—the understanding being that uninteresting times are marked by tranquility, while interesting times are full of turmoil and constant upheaval.

We were warned well ahead of time that the tween and teen years would be a ridiculous shit-show, and yet we continued raising them in spite of this knowledge. Technically, yes, it IS the law, but we also loved them. And hey, maybe they would be the exception to the rule?

Well, no. Sadly all the cliches are true. All the crying, drama, and ceaseless arguing arrived as promised—and that was just me. Not to be outdone, the kids are doing their best to give as good as they get. It's loads of fun.

To add to the challenge, each of our four kids are challenging (read: torturing) us in their own unique and contradictory ways. At any given moment, one of our kids may have taken a vow of silence, while another speaks only in screams. We've simultaneously faced resentment for somehow holding one back from their true scholastic potential, while the others are furious that we ask that they complete any of their schoolwork.

Just to make things extra-interesting, all of this drama happened to kick off around the same time as the Covid lockdowns. As if living with four hormonal kids wasn't challenging enough, fate decided to lock us indoors together for a couple years. For the record, I've excluded nearly all my quarantine-related cartoons from this collection as a courtesy to the reader. I'm as nostalgic as the next guy, but no one needs a reminder of the days when we thought we had to bleach our groceries before hunting and gathering for toilet paper.

In collecting these cartoons, I'm reminded of a mom and her teenage daughter who came up to me outside of a sandwich shop shortly after my first child was born. It was the first time I had left the house since he was born and I was sleep-deprived, demoralized and questioning if I was even up to the task of being a parent.

She fawned over him for a moment and then added bitterly "Enjoy this time. It only gets worse." I remain dumbstruck by her assholery. Not only was this the exact-wrong pep talk I needed at the time, but in hindsight, she was dead wrong. As hard as the kids are now, I would never trade this time for the days of sleepless nights and getting thrown up on after every meal.

So, while this book is dedicated to my family, who, despite all my teasing, I love with every ounce of my being, I also dedicate this book to that woman. I can only hope you had a dozen more babies since the day we met, and I pray they are all interesting as fuck.

To everyone else, I hope you get a laugh and maybe some comfort from this collection of cartoons. If I can do this, surely you can, too.

(I *can* do this, right??)

B. Gordon

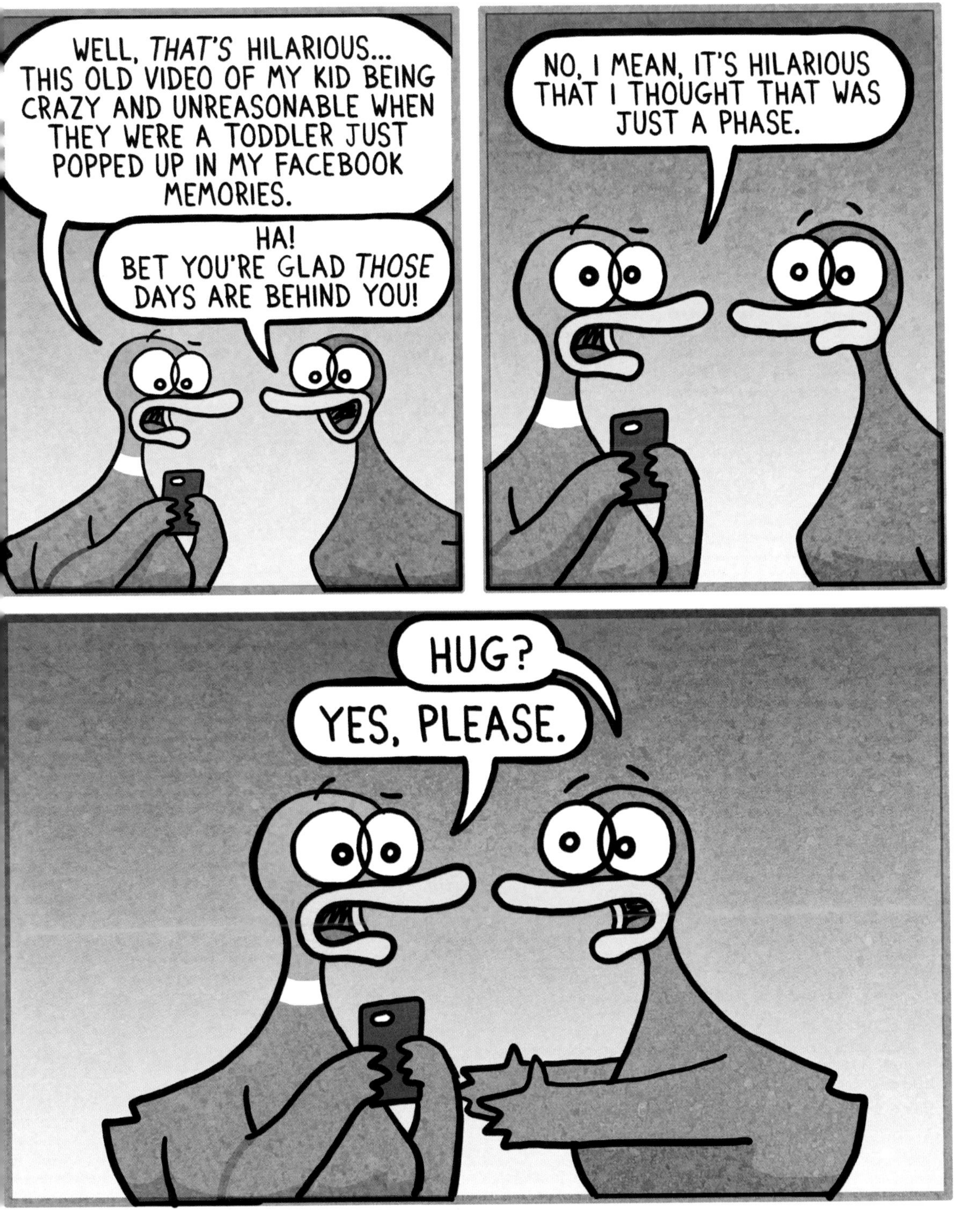
WELL, *THAT'S* HILARIOUS... THIS OLD VIDEO OF MY KID BEING CRAZY AND UNREASONABLE WHEN THEY WERE A TODDLER JUST POPPED UP IN MY FACEBOOK MEMORIES.
HA! BET YOU'RE GLAD *THOSE* DAYS ARE BEHIND YOU!
NO, I MEAN, IT'S HILARIOUS THAT I THOUGHT THAT WAS JUST A PHASE.
HUG?
YES, PLEASE.

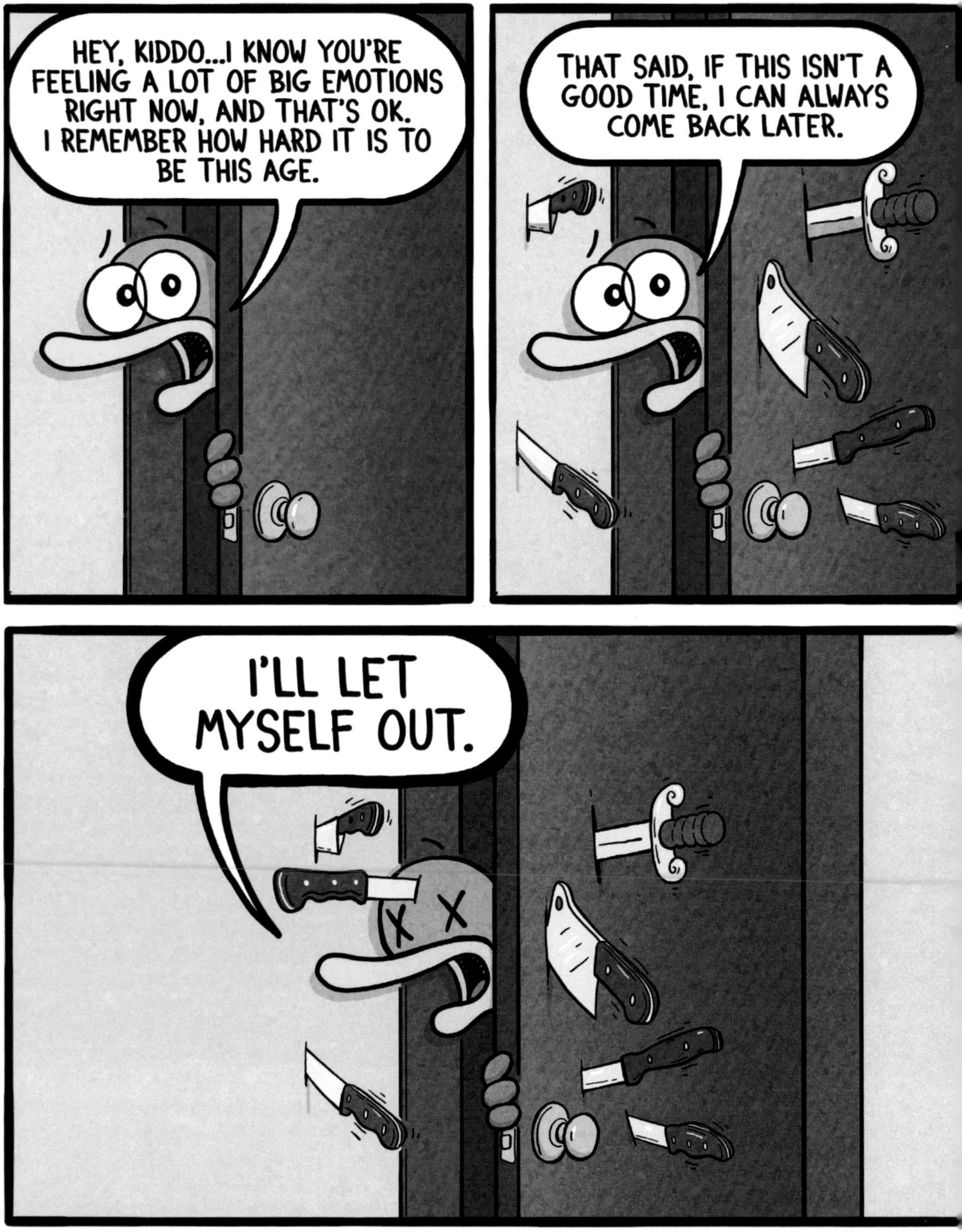
HEY, KIDDO...I KNOW YOU'RE FEELING A LOT OF BIG EMOTIONS RIGHT NOW, AND THAT'S OK. I REMEMBER HOW HARD IT IS TO BE THIS AGE.
THAT SAID, IF THIS ISN'T A GOOD TIME, I CAN ALWAYS COME BACK LATER.
I'LL LET MYSELF OUT.

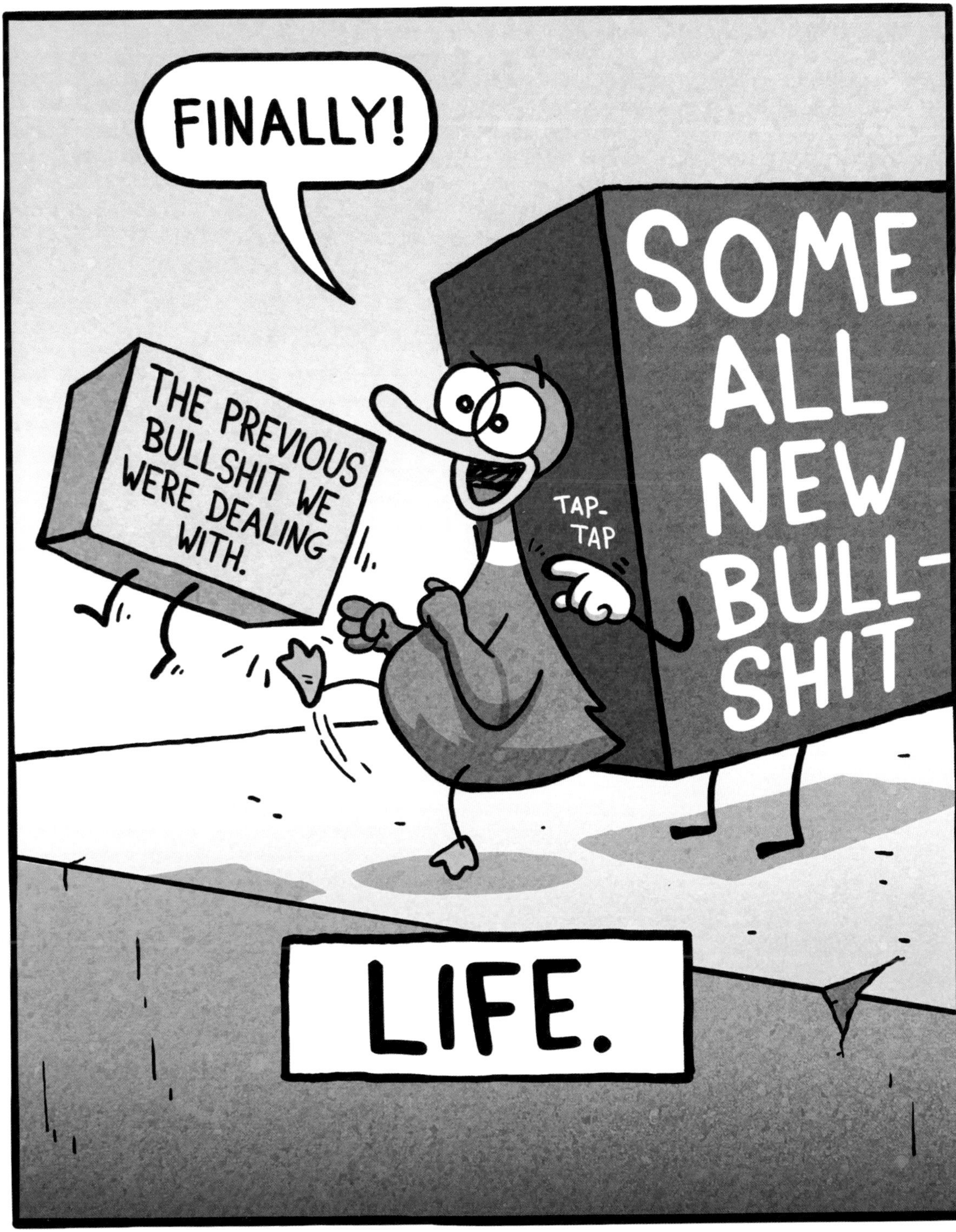
FINALLY!
THE PREVIOUS BULLSHIT WE WERE DEALING WITH.
TAP-TAP
SOME ALL NEW BULL-SHIT
LIFE.

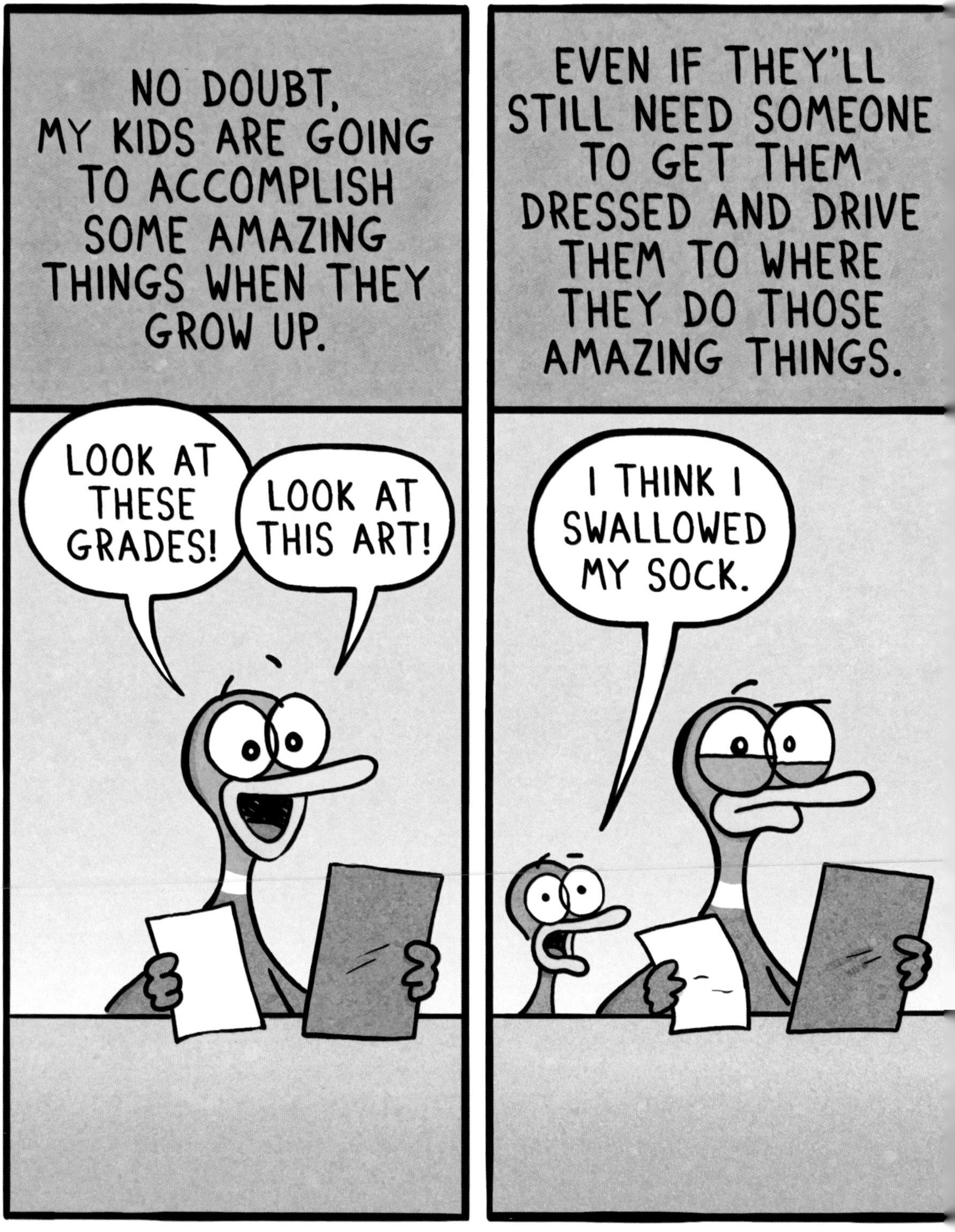
NO DOUBT, MY KIDS ARE GOING TO ACCOMPLISH SOME AMAZING THINGS WHEN THEY GROW UP.
LOOK AT THESE GRADES!
LOOK AT THIS ART!
EVEN IF THEY'LL STILL NEED SOMEONE TO GET THEM DRESSED AND DRIVE THEM TO WHERE THEY DO THOSE AMAZING THINGS.
I THINK I SWALLOWED MY SOCK.

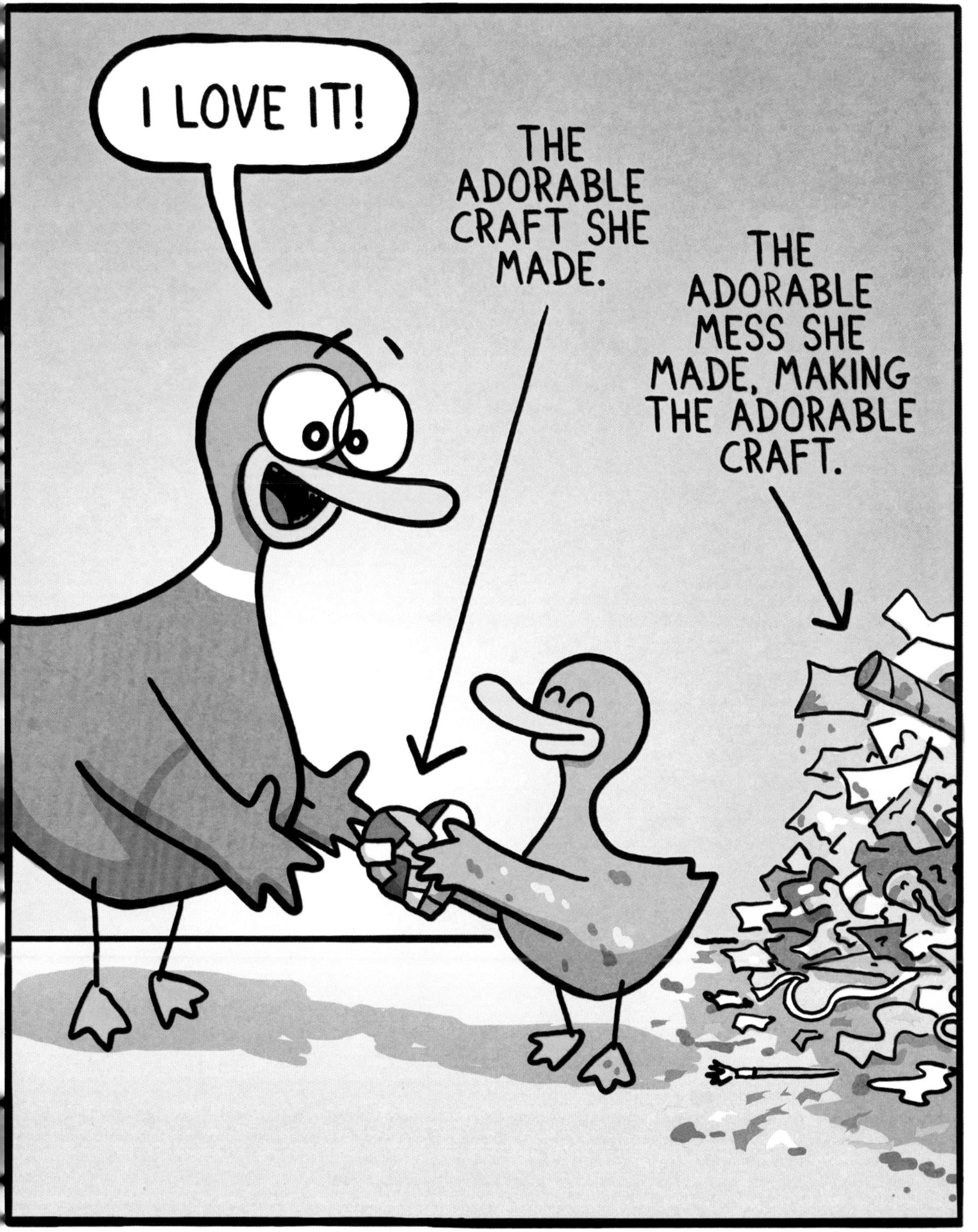
I LOVE IT!
THE ADORABLE CRAFT SHE MADE.
THE ADORABLE MESS SHE MADE, MAKING THE ADORABLE CRAFT.

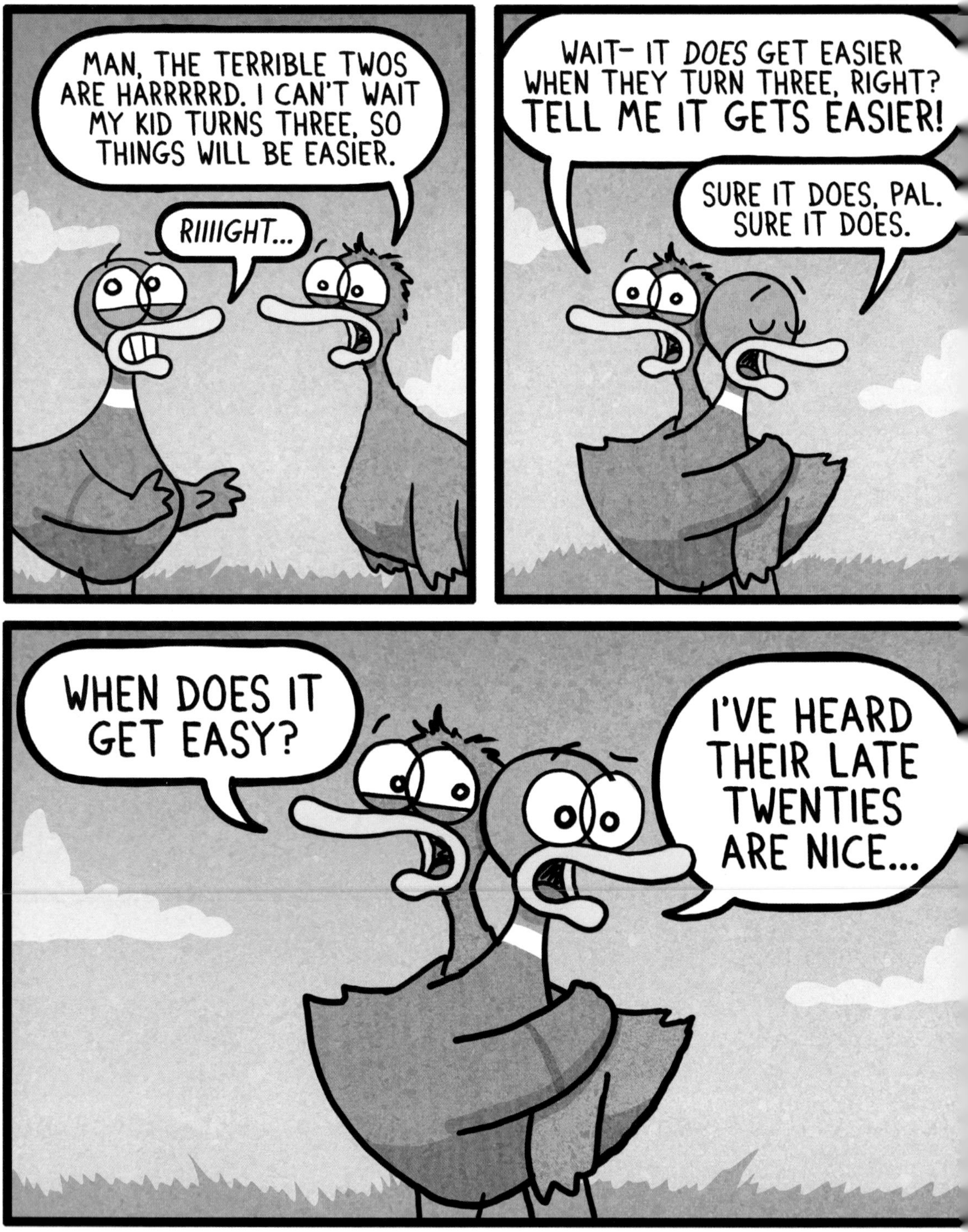
MAN, THE TERRIBLE TWOS ARE HARRRRRD. I CAN'T WAIT MY KID TURNS THREE, SO THINGS WILL BE EASIER.
RIIIIGHT...
WAIT– IT DOES GET EASIER WHEN THEY TURN THREE, RIGHT? TELL ME IT GETS EASIER!
SURE IT DOES, PAL. SURE IT DOES.
WHEN DOES IT GET EASY?
I'VE HEARD THEIR LATE TWENTIES ARE NICE...

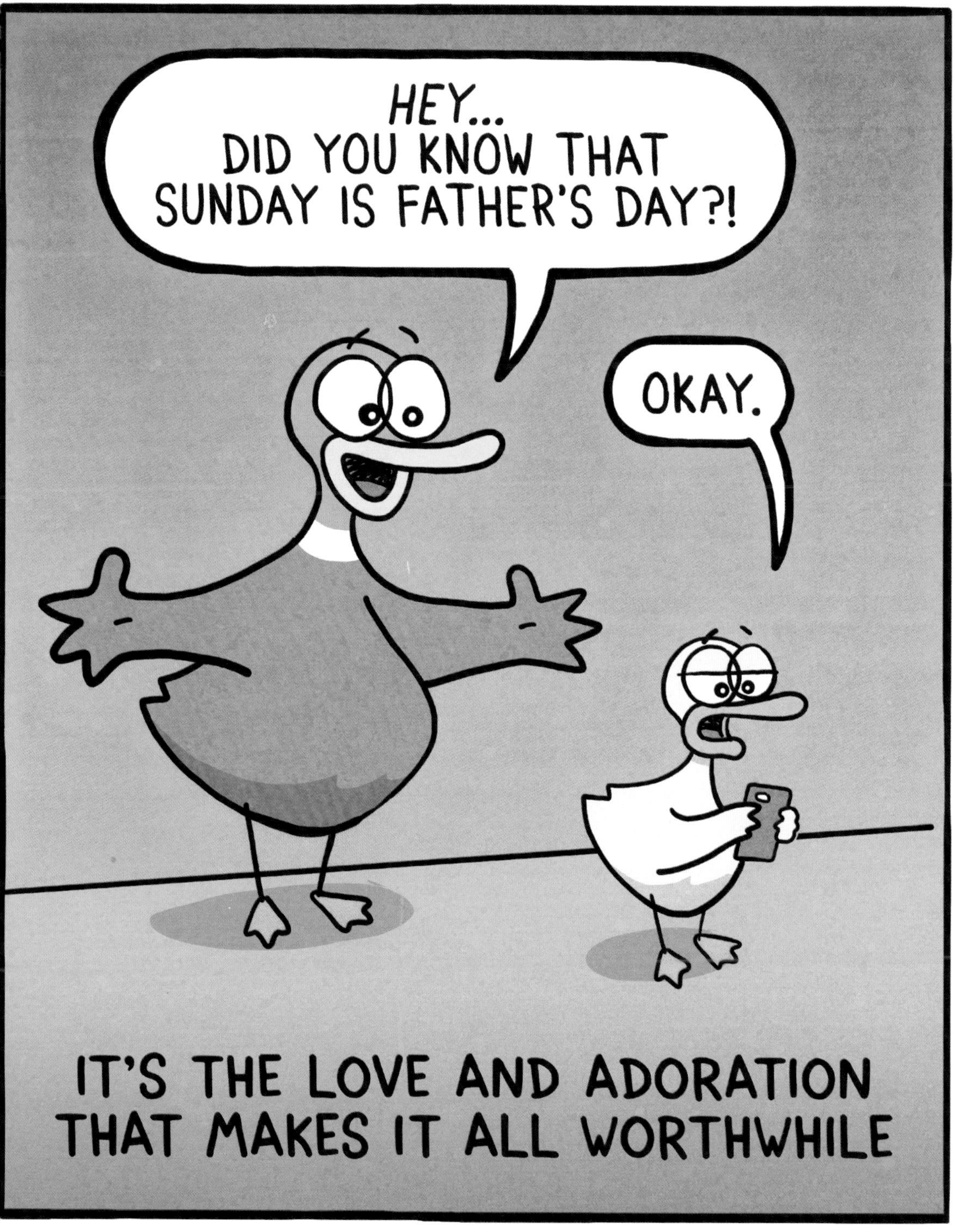
HEY...
DID YOU KNOW THAT
SUNDAY IS FATHER'S DAY?!
OKAY.
IT'S THE LOVE AND ADORATION
THAT MAKES IT ALL WORTHWHILE

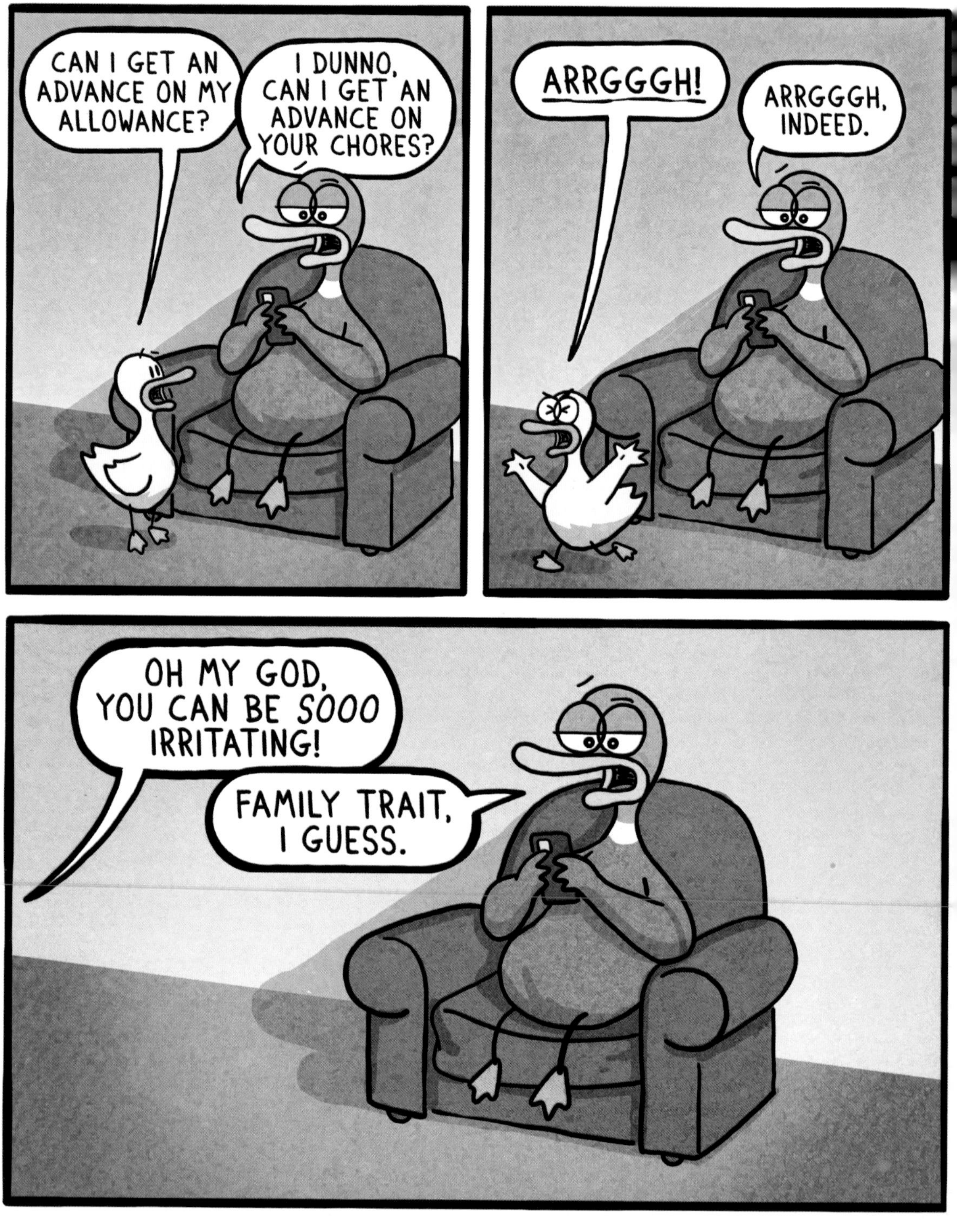
CAN I GET AN ADVANCE ON MY ALLOWANCE?
I DUNNO, CAN I GET AN ADVANCE ON YOUR CHORES?
ARRGGGH!
ARRGGGH, INDEED.
OH MY GOD, YOU CAN BE SOOO IRRITATING!
FAMILY TRAIT, I GUESS.

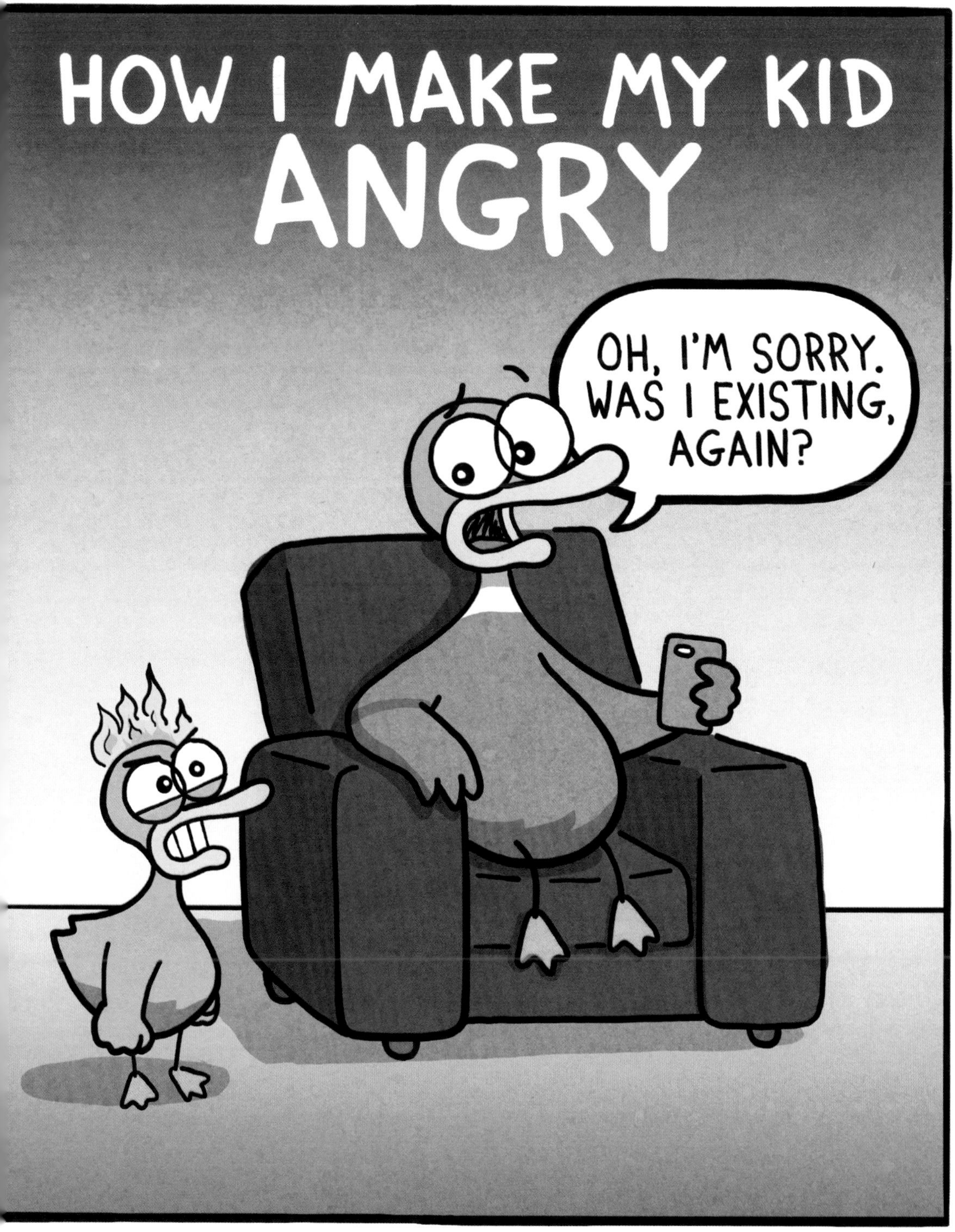
HOW I MAKE MY KID ANGRY
OH, I'M SORRY. WAS I EXISTING, AGAIN?

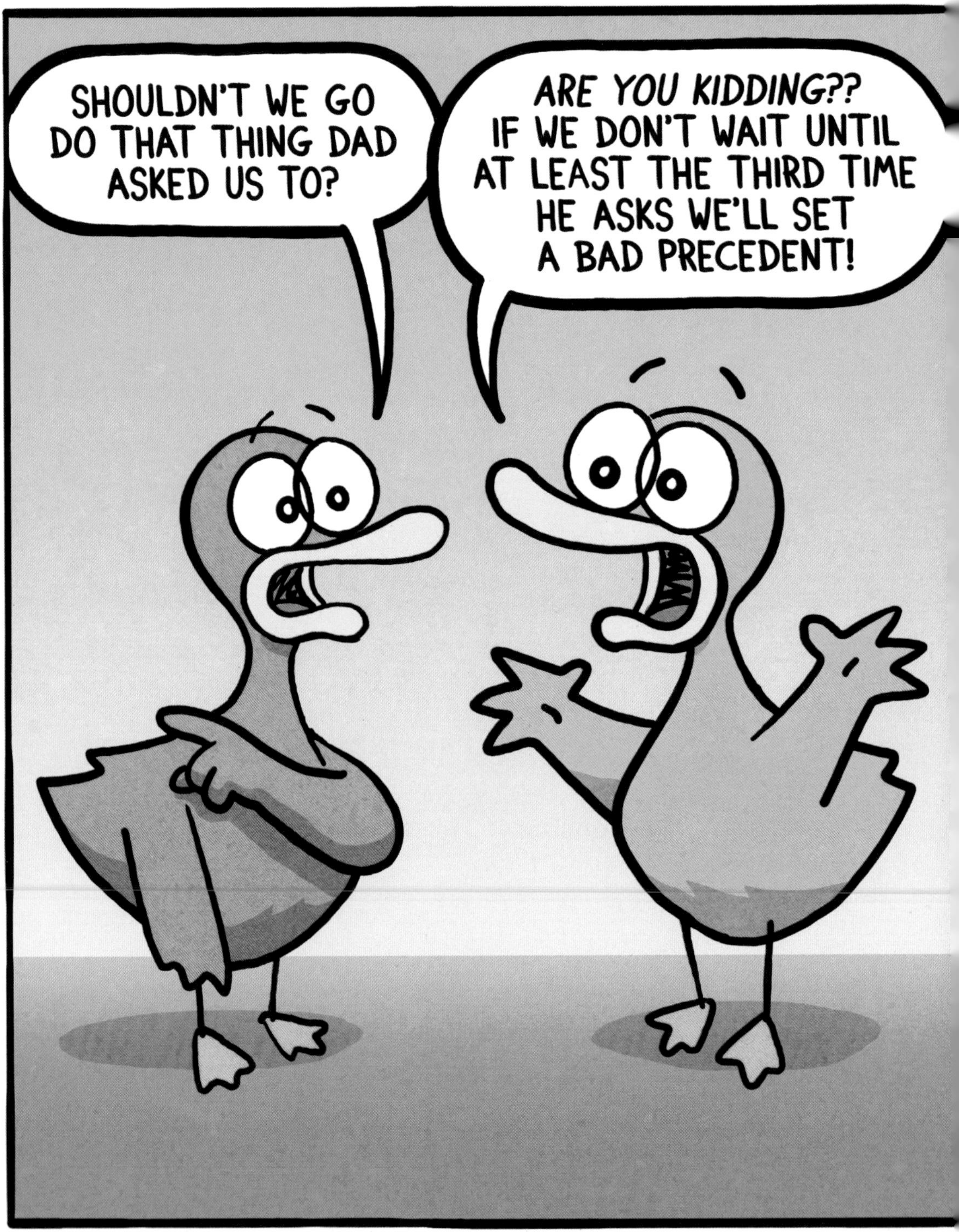
SHOULDN'T WE GO DO THAT THING DAD ASKED US TO?
ARE YOU KIDDING?? IF WE DON'T WAIT UNTIL AT LEAST THE THIRD TIME HE ASKS WE'LL SET A BAD PRECEDENT!

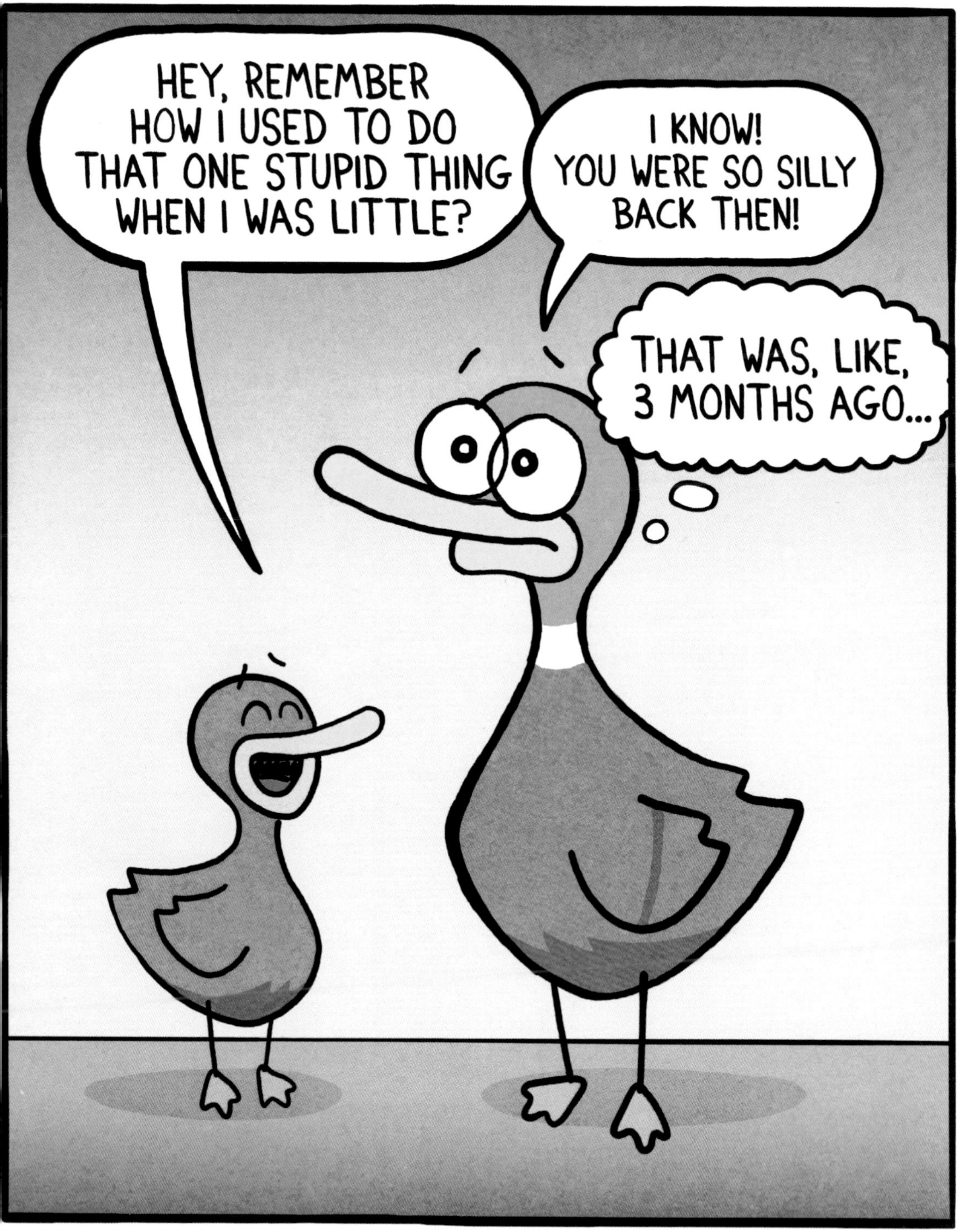
HEY, REMEMBER HOW I USED TO DO THAT ONE STUPID THING WHEN I WAS LITTLE?
I KNOW! YOU WERE SO SILLY BACK THEN!
THAT WAS, LIKE, 3 MONTHS AGO...

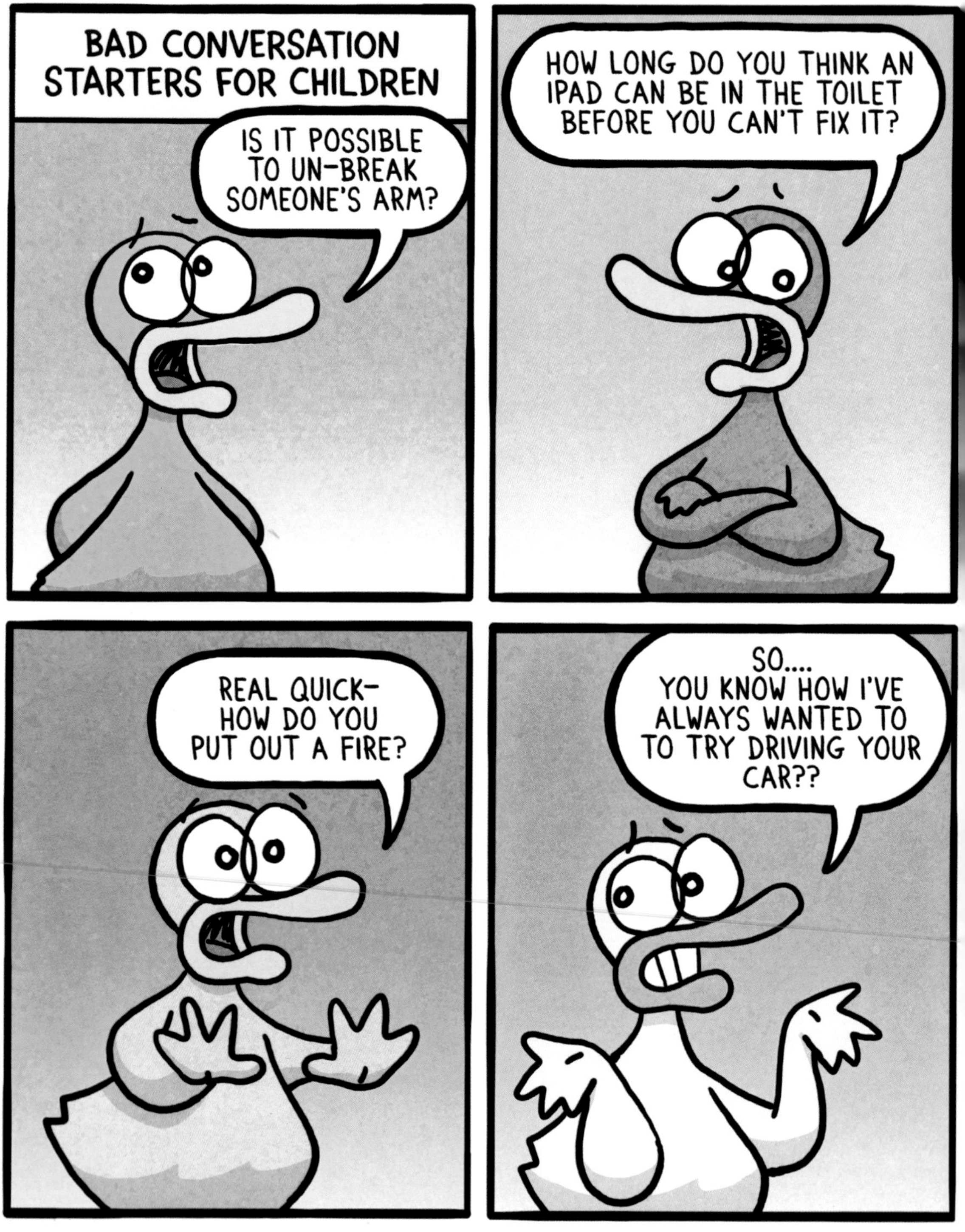
BAD CONVERSATION STARTERS FOR CHILDREN
IS IT POSSIBLE TO UN-BREAK SOMEONE'S ARM?
HOW LONG DO YOU THINK AN IPAD CAN BE IN THE TOILET BEFORE YOU CAN'T FIX IT?
REAL QUICK- HOW DO YOU PUT OUT A FIRE?
SO.... YOU KNOW HOW I'VE ALWAYS WANTED TO TO TRY DRIVING YOUR CAR??

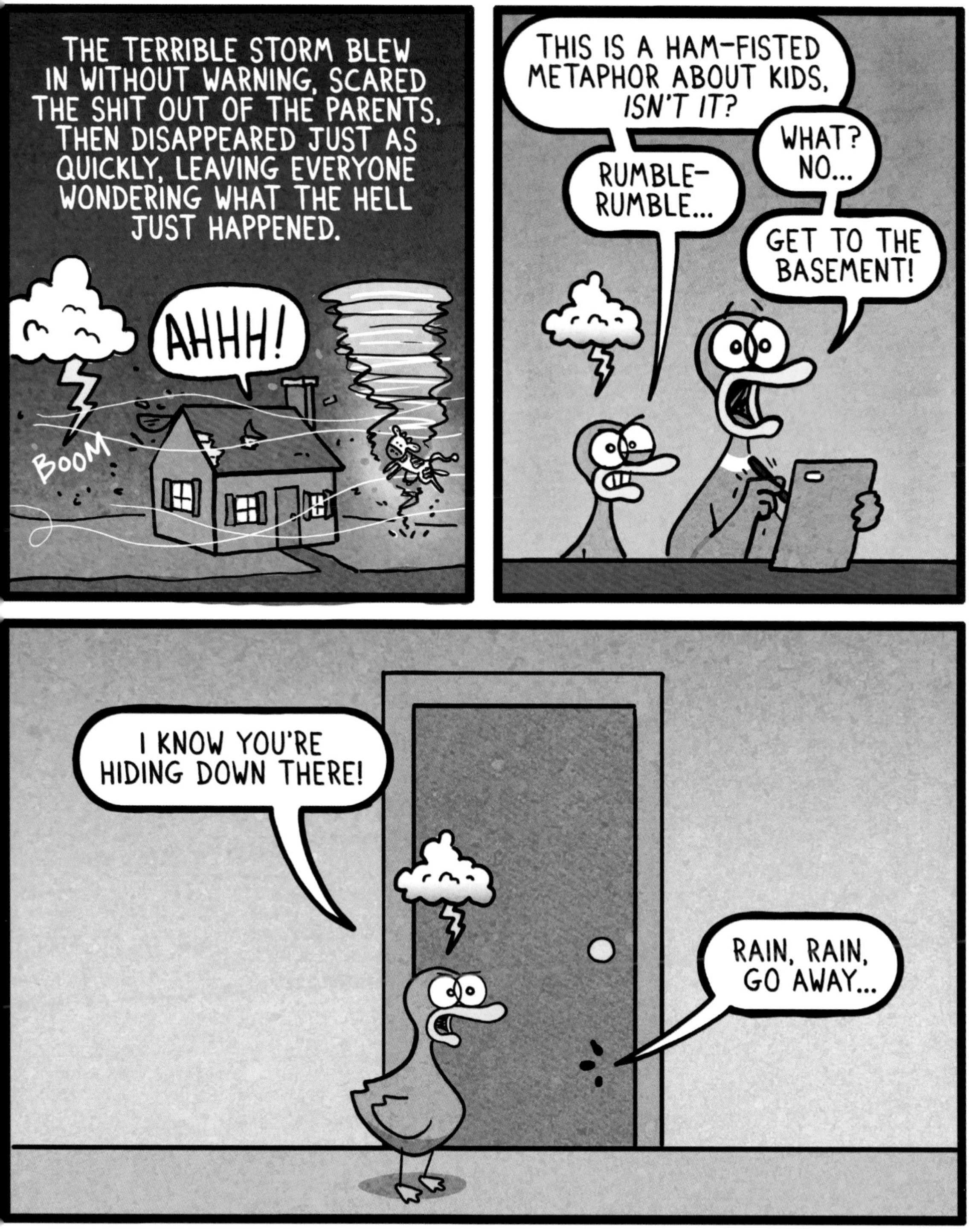
THE TERRIBLE STORM BLEW IN WITHOUT WARNING, SCARED THE SHIT OUT OF THE PARENTS, THEN DISAPPEARED JUST AS QUICKLY, LEAVING EVERYONE WONDERING WHAT THE HELL JUST HAPPENED.
AHHH!
BOOM
THIS IS A HAM-FISTED METAPHOR ABOUT KIDS, *ISN'T IT?*
RUMBLE-RUMBLE...
WHAT? NO...
GET TO THE BASEMENT!
I KNOW YOU'RE HIDING DOWN THERE!
RAIN, RAIN, GO AWAY...

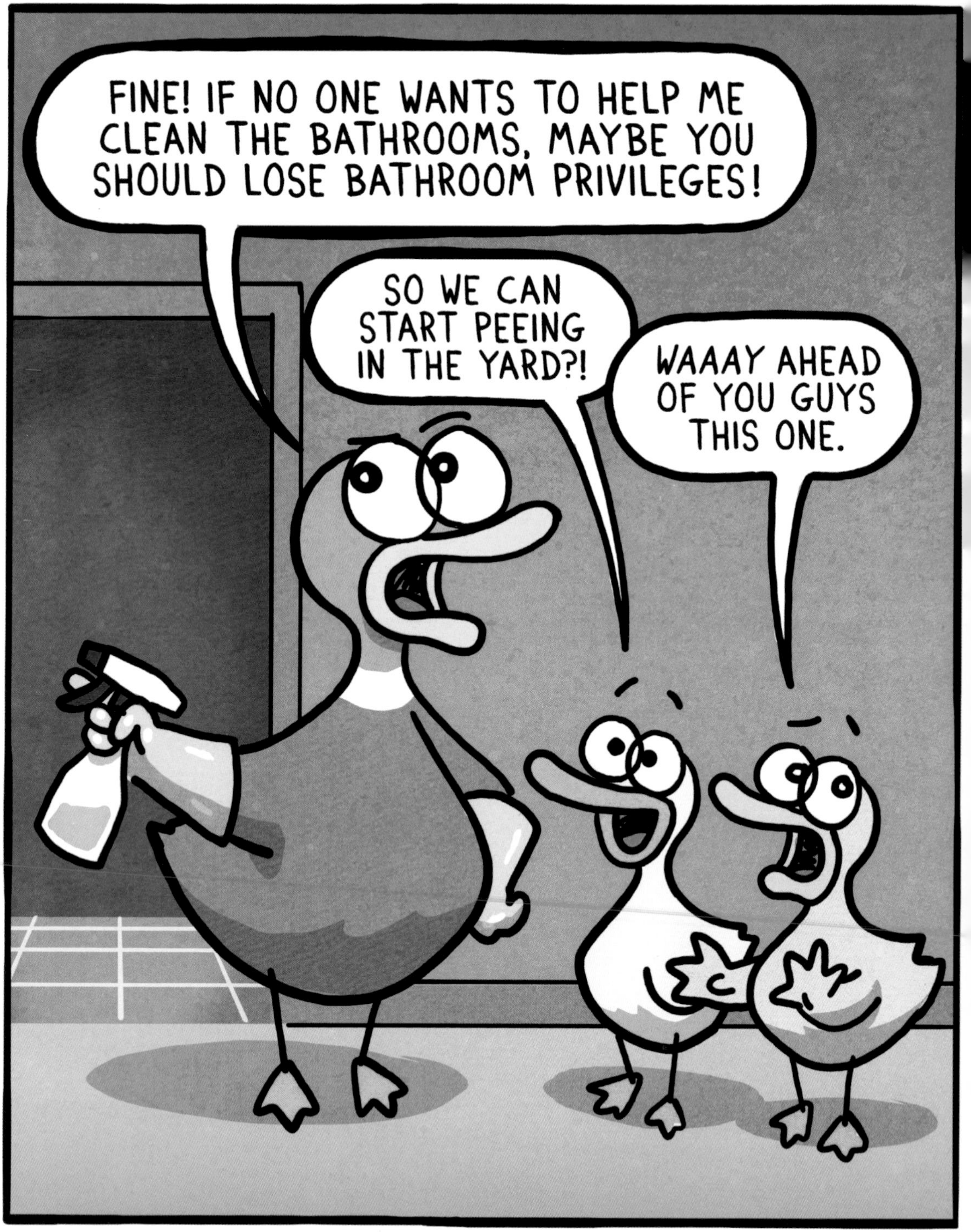
FINE! IF NO ONE WANTS TO HELP ME CLEAN THE BATHROOMS, MAYBE YOU SHOULD LOSE BATHROOM PRIVILEGES!
SO WE CAN START PEEING IN THE YARD?!
WAAAY AHEAD OF YOU GUYS THIS ONE.

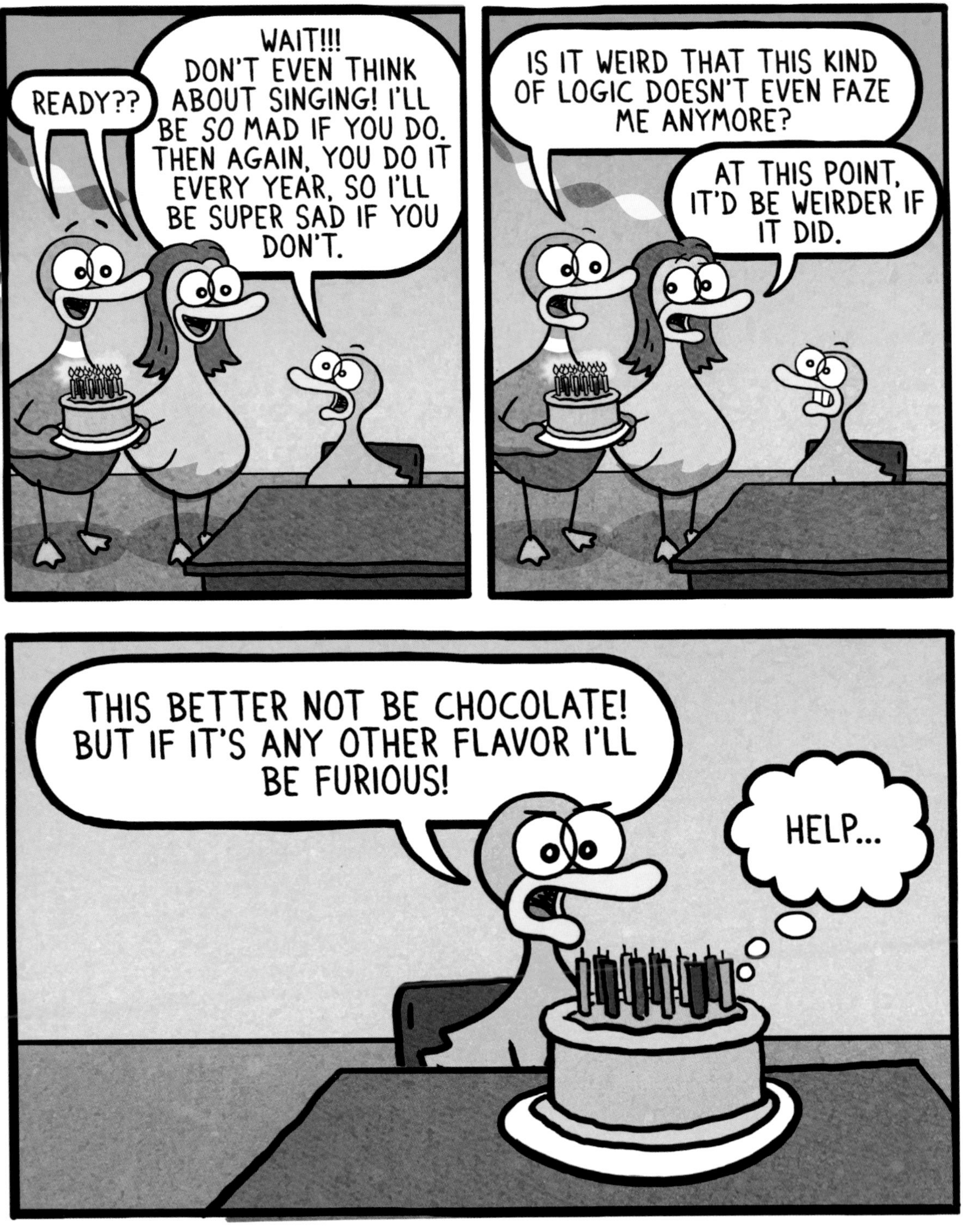
READY??
WAIT!!! DON'T EVEN THINK ABOUT SINGING! I'LL BE *SO* MAD IF YOU DO. THEN AGAIN, YOU DO IT EVERY YEAR, SO I'LL BE SUPER SAD IF YOU DON'T.
IS IT WEIRD THAT THIS KIND OF LOGIC DOESN'T EVEN FAZE ME ANYMORE?
AT THIS POINT, IT'D BE WEIRDER IF IT DID.
THIS BETTER NOT BE CHOCOLATE! BUT IF IT'S ANY OTHER FLAVOR I'LL BE FURIOUS!
HELP...

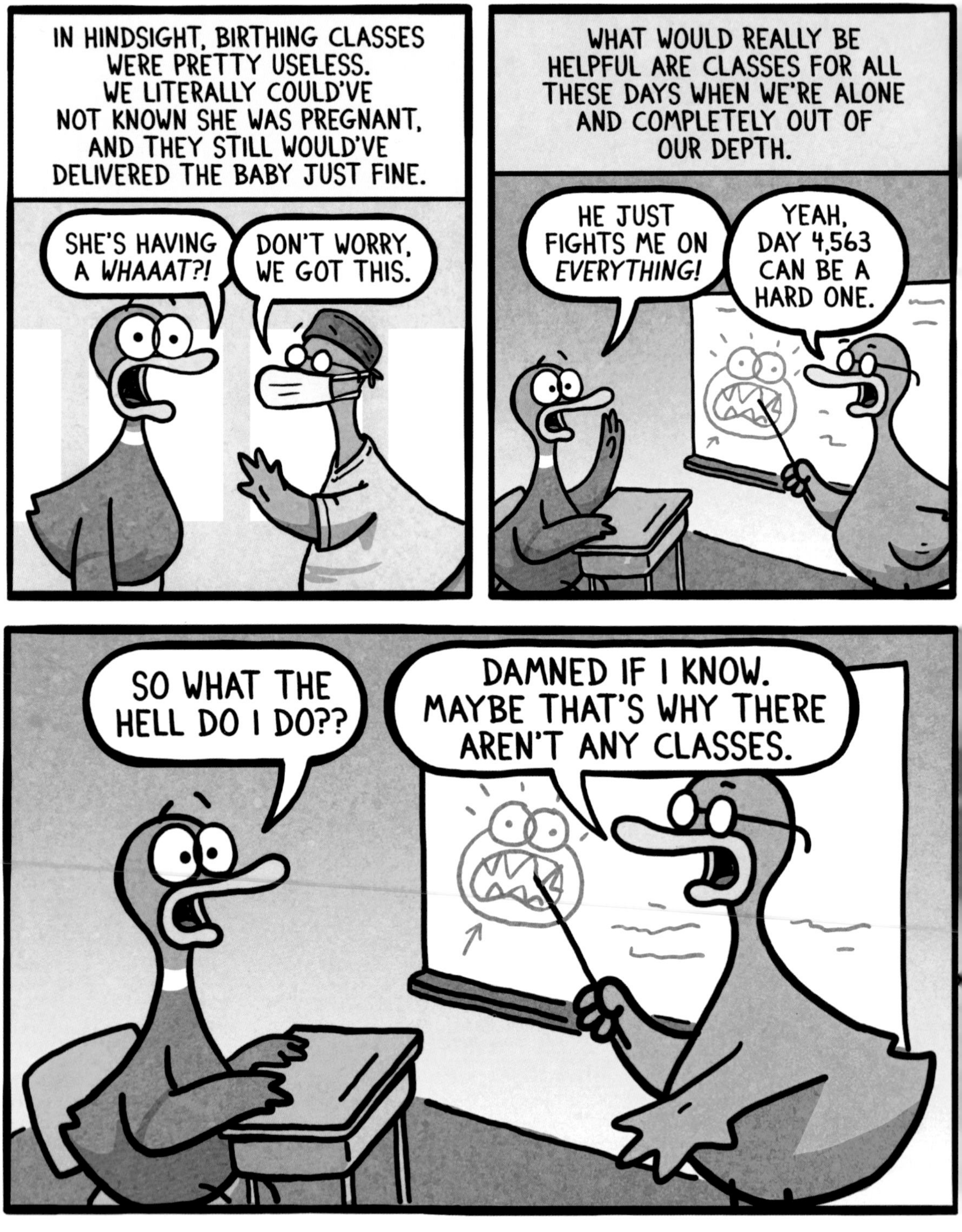
IN HINDSIGHT, BIRTHING CLASSES WERE PRETTY USELESS. WE LITERALLY COULD'VE NOT KNOWN SHE WAS PREGNANT, AND THEY STILL WOULD'VE DELIVERED THE BABY JUST FINE.
SHE'S HAVING A *WHAAAT?!*
DON'T WORRY, WE GOT THIS.
WHAT WOULD REALLY BE HELPFUL ARE CLASSES FOR ALL THESE DAYS WHEN WE'RE ALONE AND COMPLETELY OUT OF OUR DEPTH.
HE JUST FIGHTS ME ON *EVERYTHING!*
YEAH, DAY 4,563 CAN BE A HARD ONE.
SO WHAT THE HELL DO I DO??
DAMNED IF I KNOW. MAYBE THAT'S WHY THERE AREN'T ANY CLASSES.

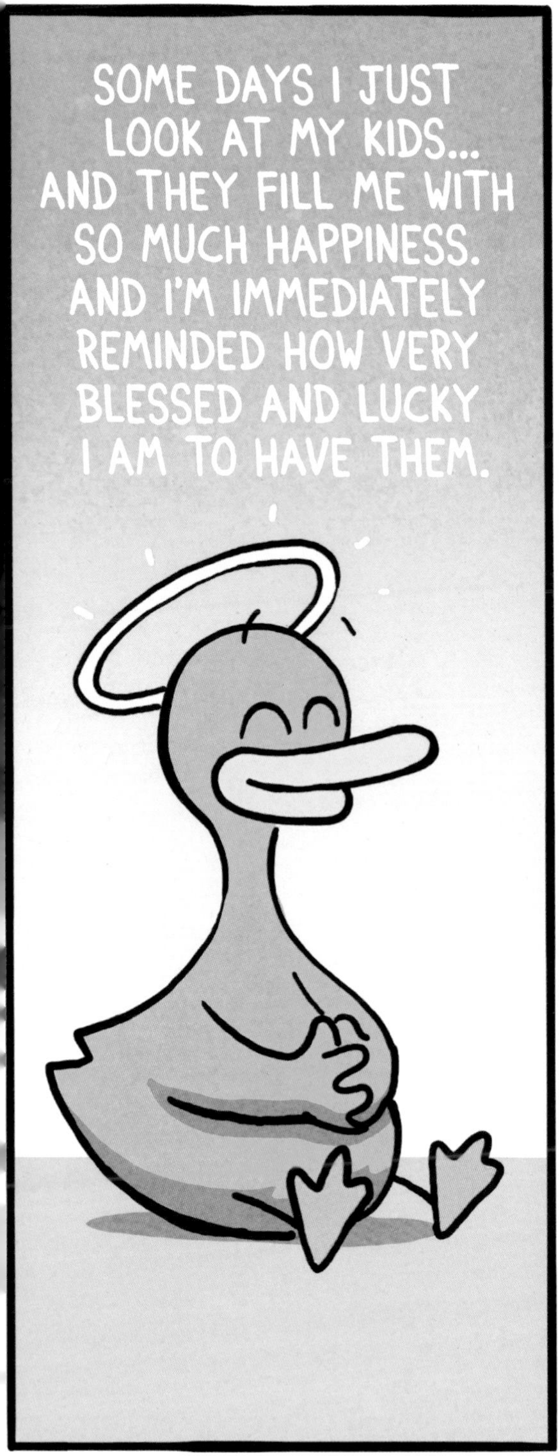
SOME DAYS I JUST LOOK AT MY KIDS... AND THEY FILL ME WITH SO MUCH HAPPINESS. AND I'M IMMEDIATELY REMINDED HOW VERY BLESSED AND LUCKY I AM TO HAVE THEM.

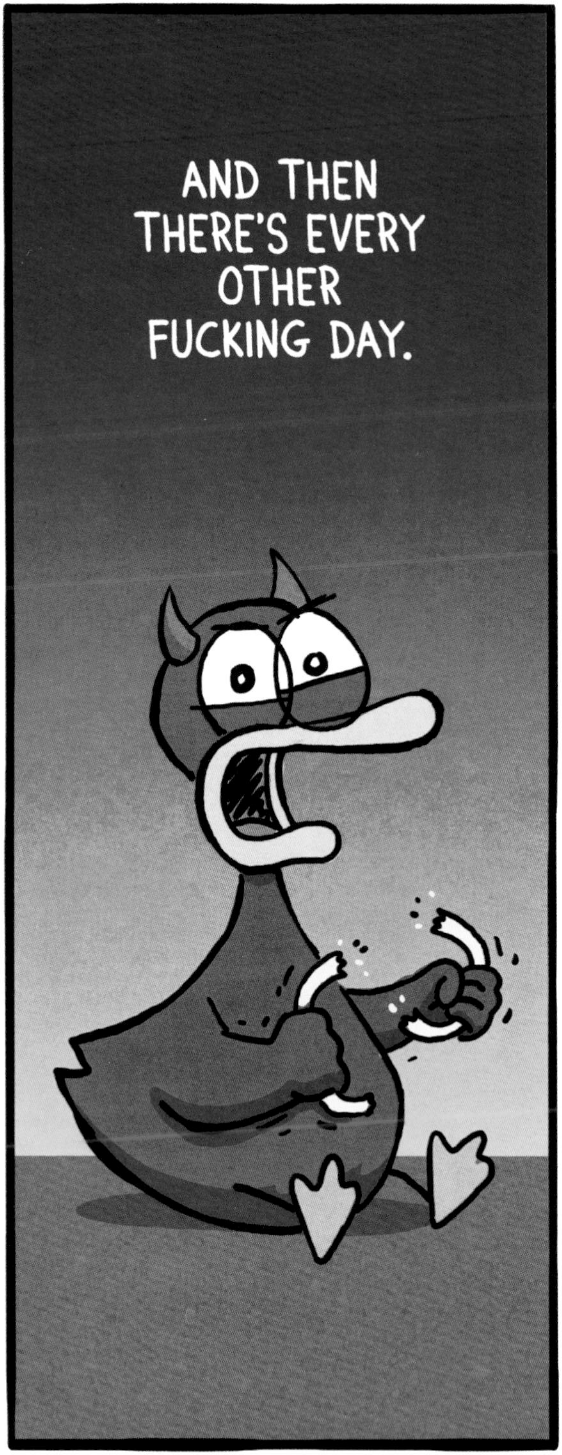
AND THEN THERE'S EVERY OTHER FUCKING DAY.

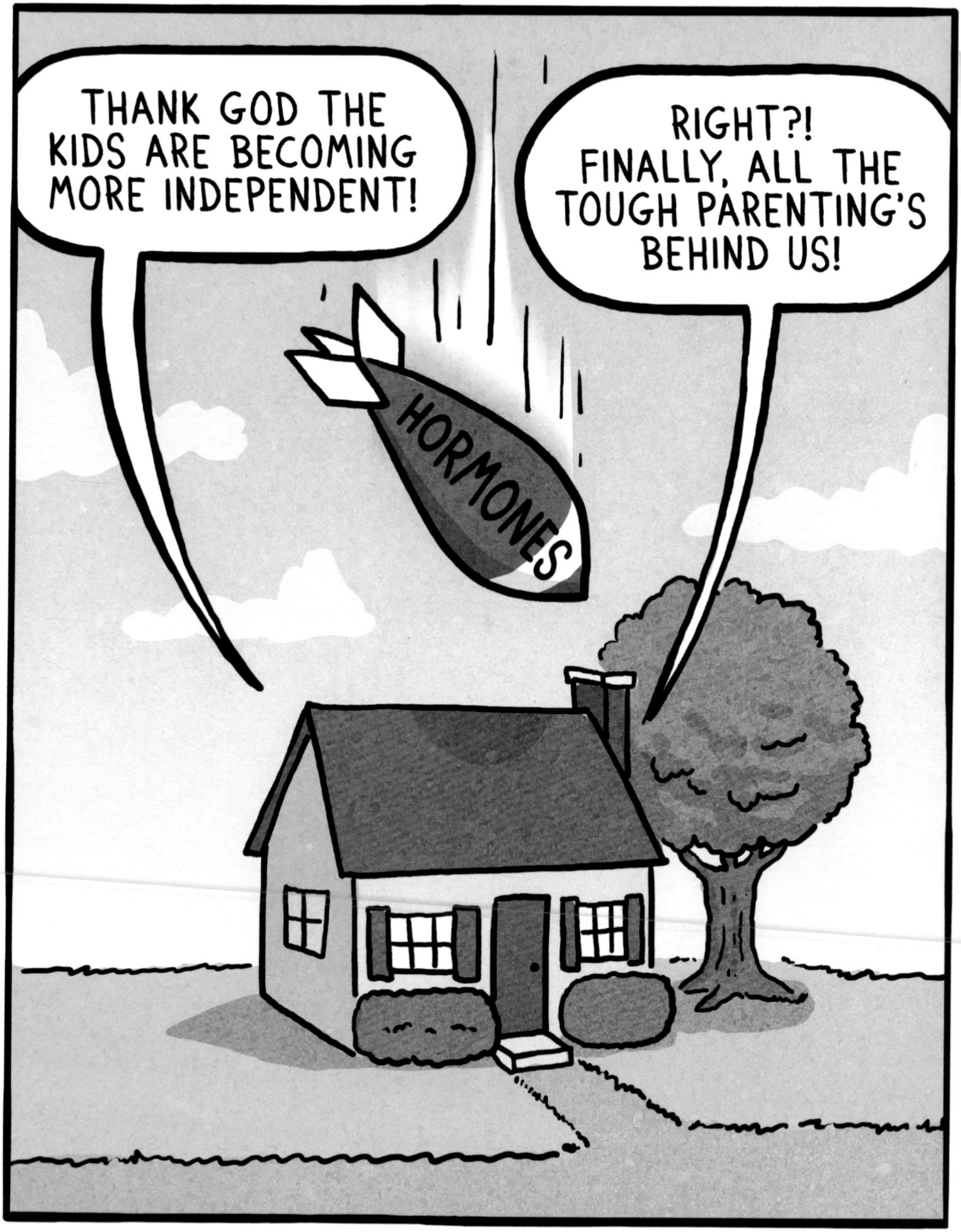
THANK GOD THE KIDS ARE BECOMING MORE INDEPENDENT!
RIGHT?! FINALLY, ALL THE TOUGH PARENTING'S BEHIND US!
HORMONES

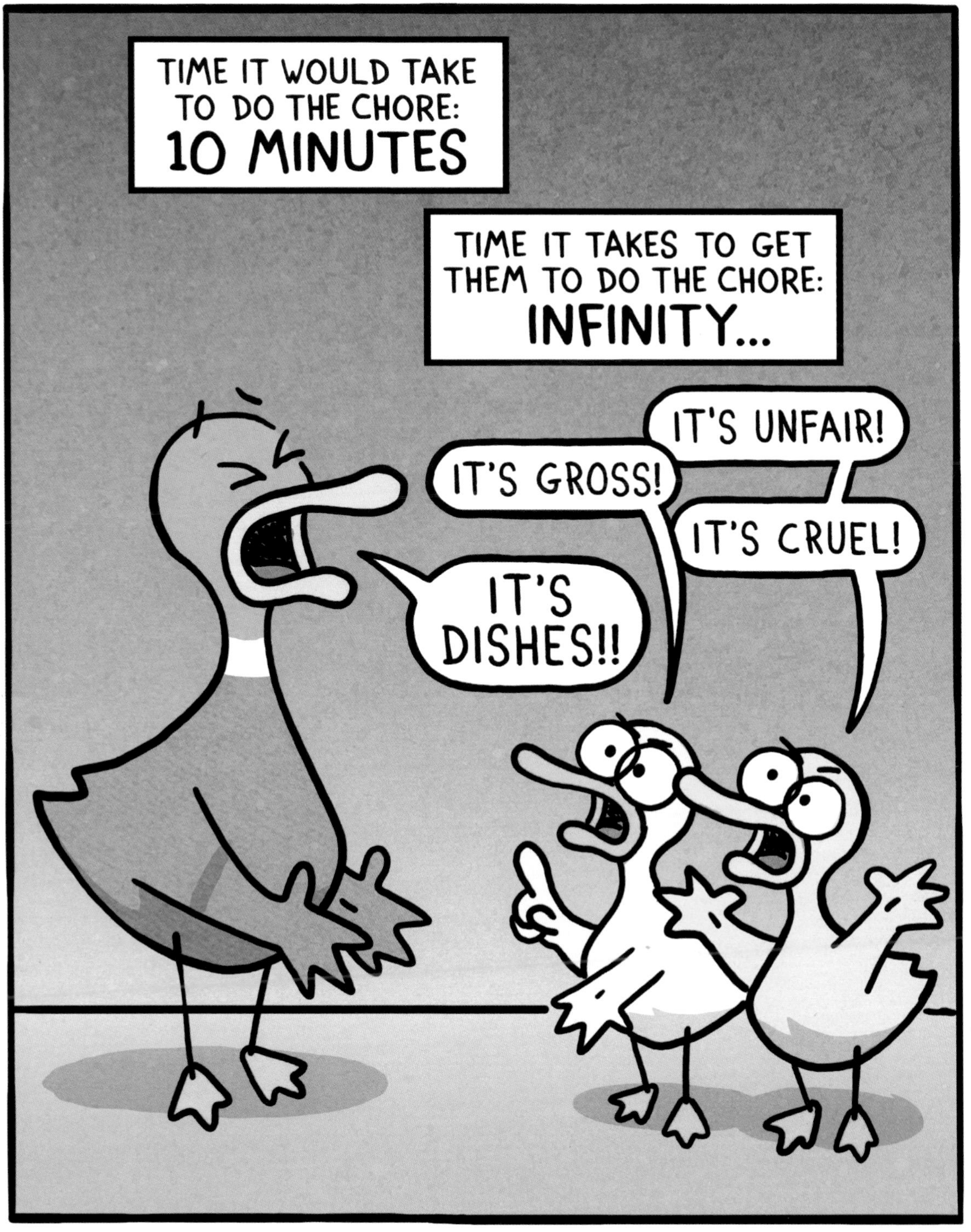
TIME IT WOULD TAKE TO DO THE CHORE: 10 MINUTES
TIME IT TAKES TO GET THEM TO DO THE CHORE: INFINITY...
IT'S DISHES!!
IT'S GROSS!
IT'S UNFAIR!
IT'S CRUEL!

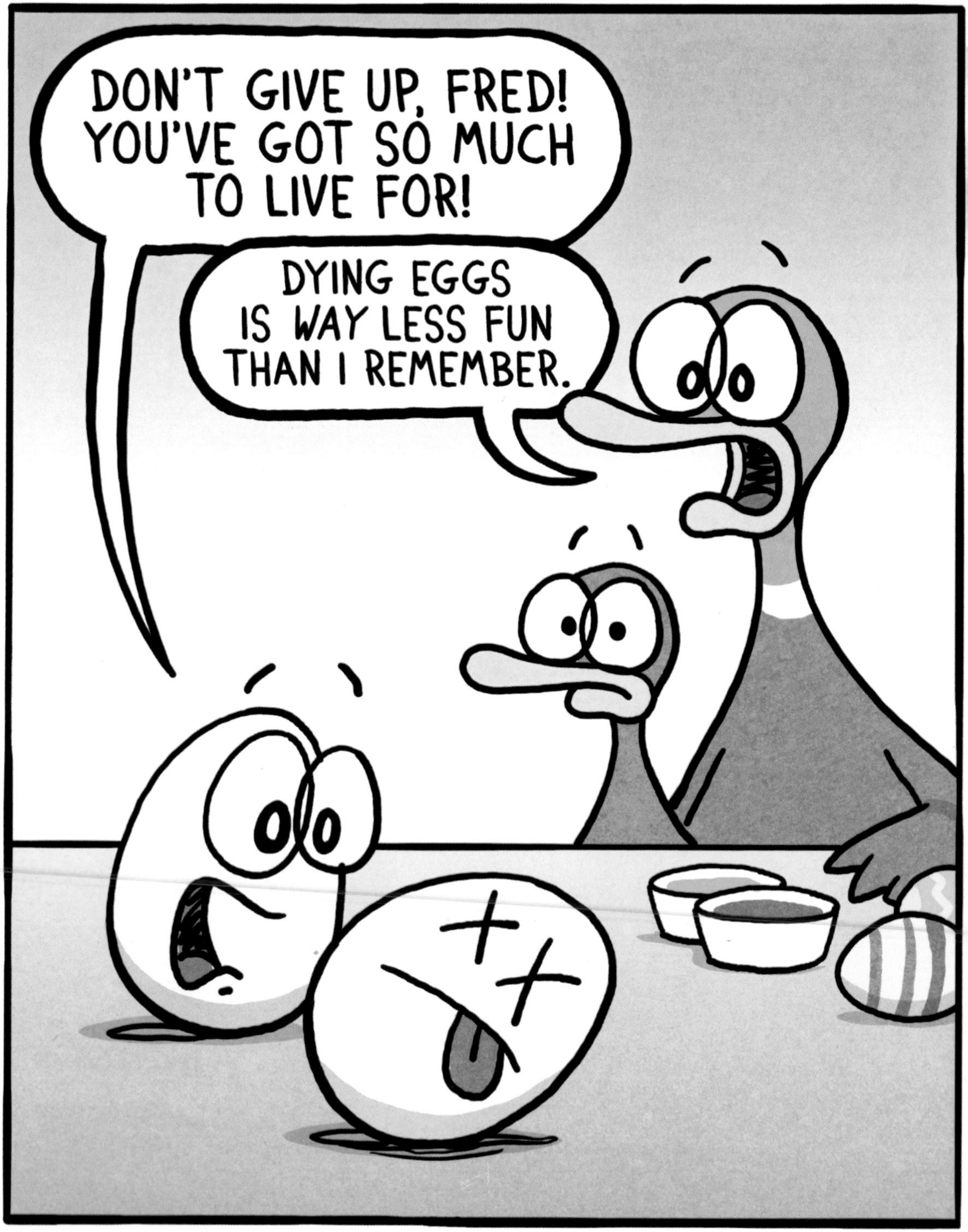
DON'T GIVE UP, FRED! YOU'VE GOT SO MUCH TO LIVE FOR!
DYING EGGS IS WAY LESS FUN THAN I REMEMBER.

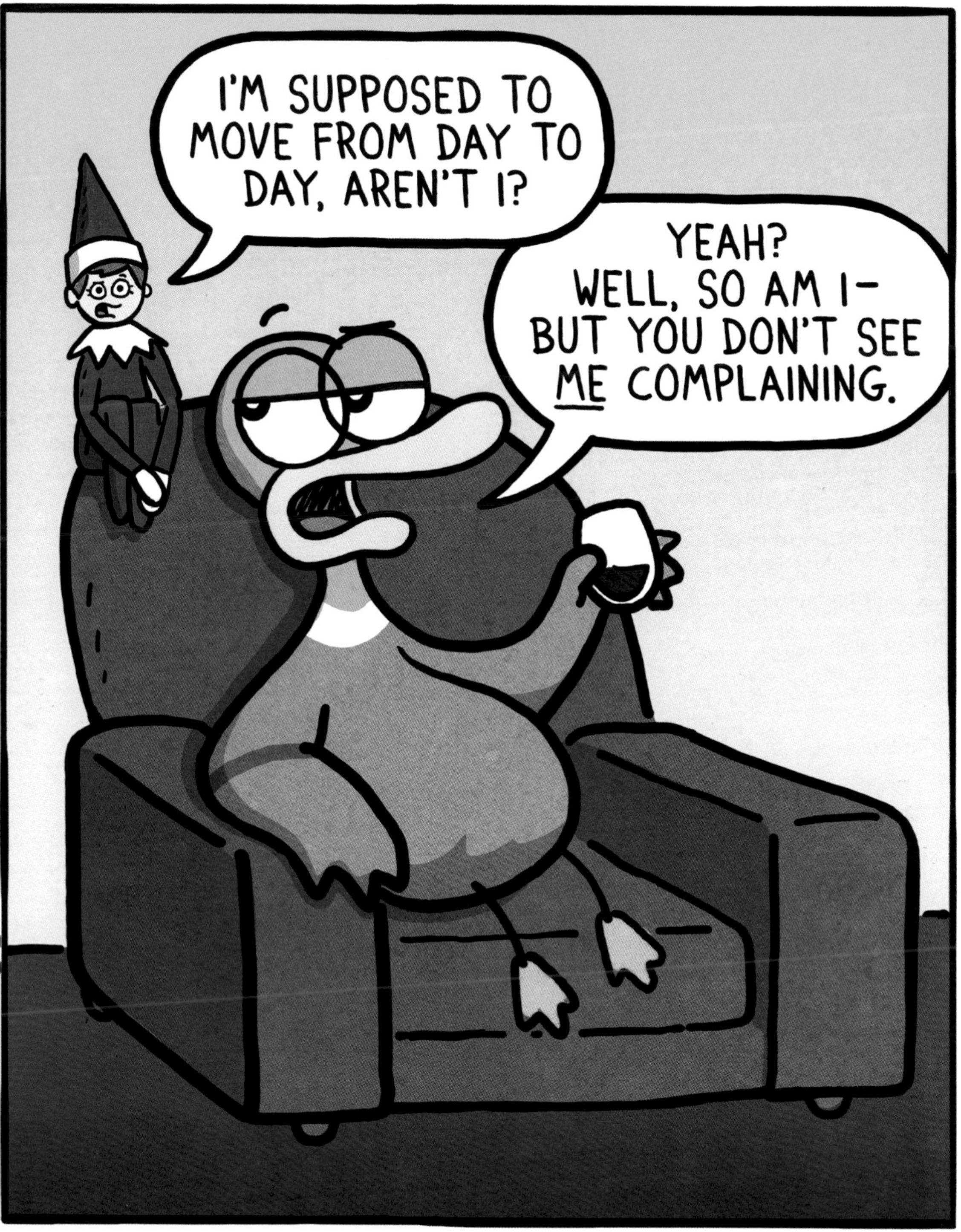
I'M SUPPOSED TO MOVE FROM DAY TO DAY, AREN'T I?
YEAH? WELL, SO AM I– BUT YOU DON'T SEE ME COMPLAINING.

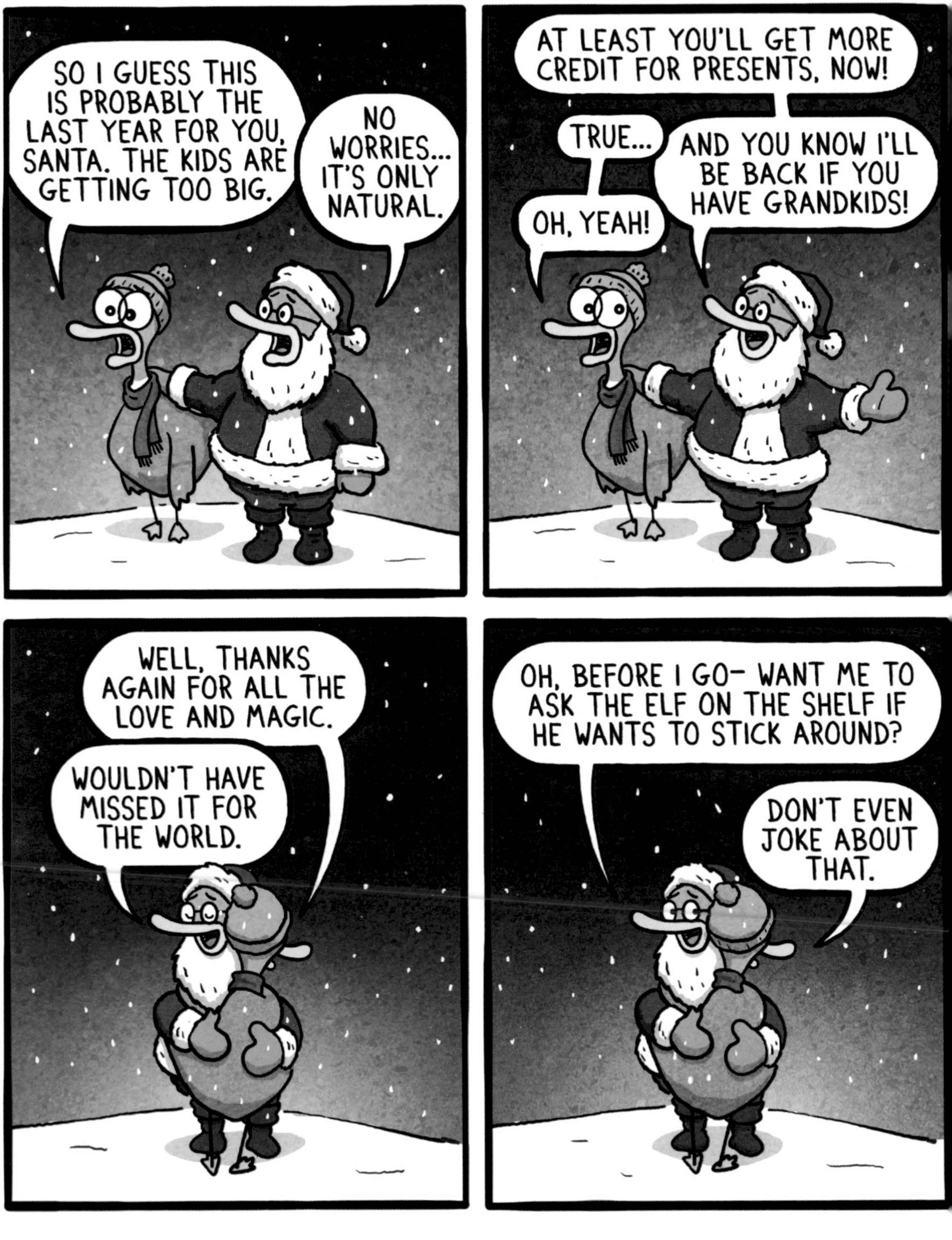
SO I GUESS THIS IS PROBABLY THE LAST YEAR FOR YOU, SANTA. THE KIDS ARE GETTING TOO BIG.
NO WORRIES... IT'S ONLY NATURAL.
AT LEAST YOU'LL GET MORE CREDIT FOR PRESENTS, NOW!
TRUE...
OH, YEAH!
AND YOU KNOW I'LL BE BACK IF YOU HAVE GRANDKIDS!
WELL, THANKS AGAIN FOR ALL THE LOVE AND MAGIC.
WOULDN'T HAVE MISSED IT FOR THE WORLD.
OH, BEFORE I GO— WANT ME TO ASK THE ELF ON THE SHELF IF HE WANTS TO STICK AROUND?
DON'T EVEN JOKE ABOUT THAT.

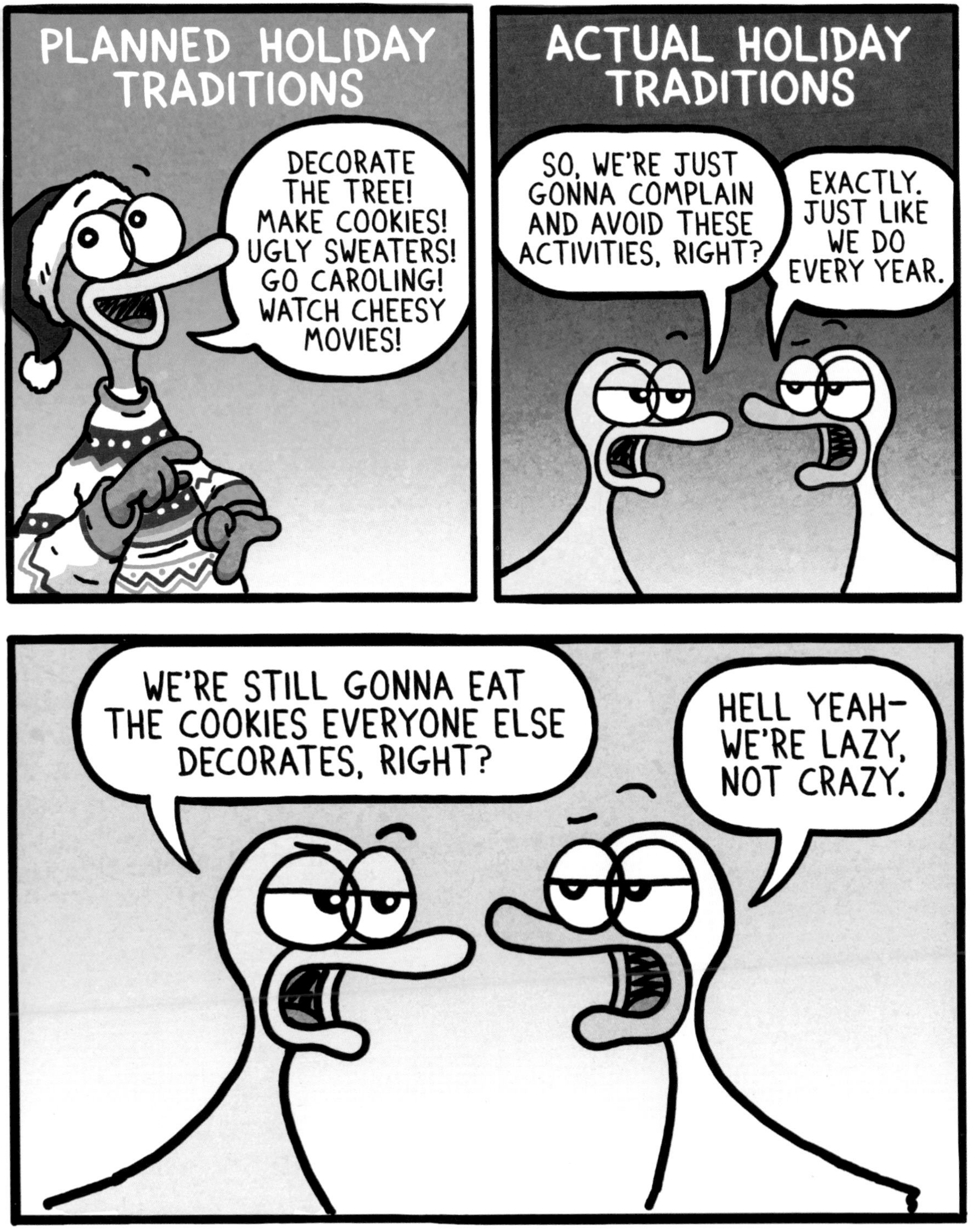
PLANNED HOLIDAY TRADITIONS
DECORATE THE TREE! MAKE COOKIES! UGLY SWEATERS! GO CAROLING! WATCH CHEESY MOVIES!
ACTUAL HOLIDAY TRADITIONS
SO, WE'RE JUST GONNA COMPLAIN AND AVOID THESE ACTIVITIES, RIGHT?
EXACTLY. JUST LIKE WE DO EVERY YEAR.
WE'RE STILL GONNA EAT THE COOKIES EVERYONE ELSE DECORATES, RIGHT?
HELL YEAH— WE'RE LAZY, NOT CRAZY.

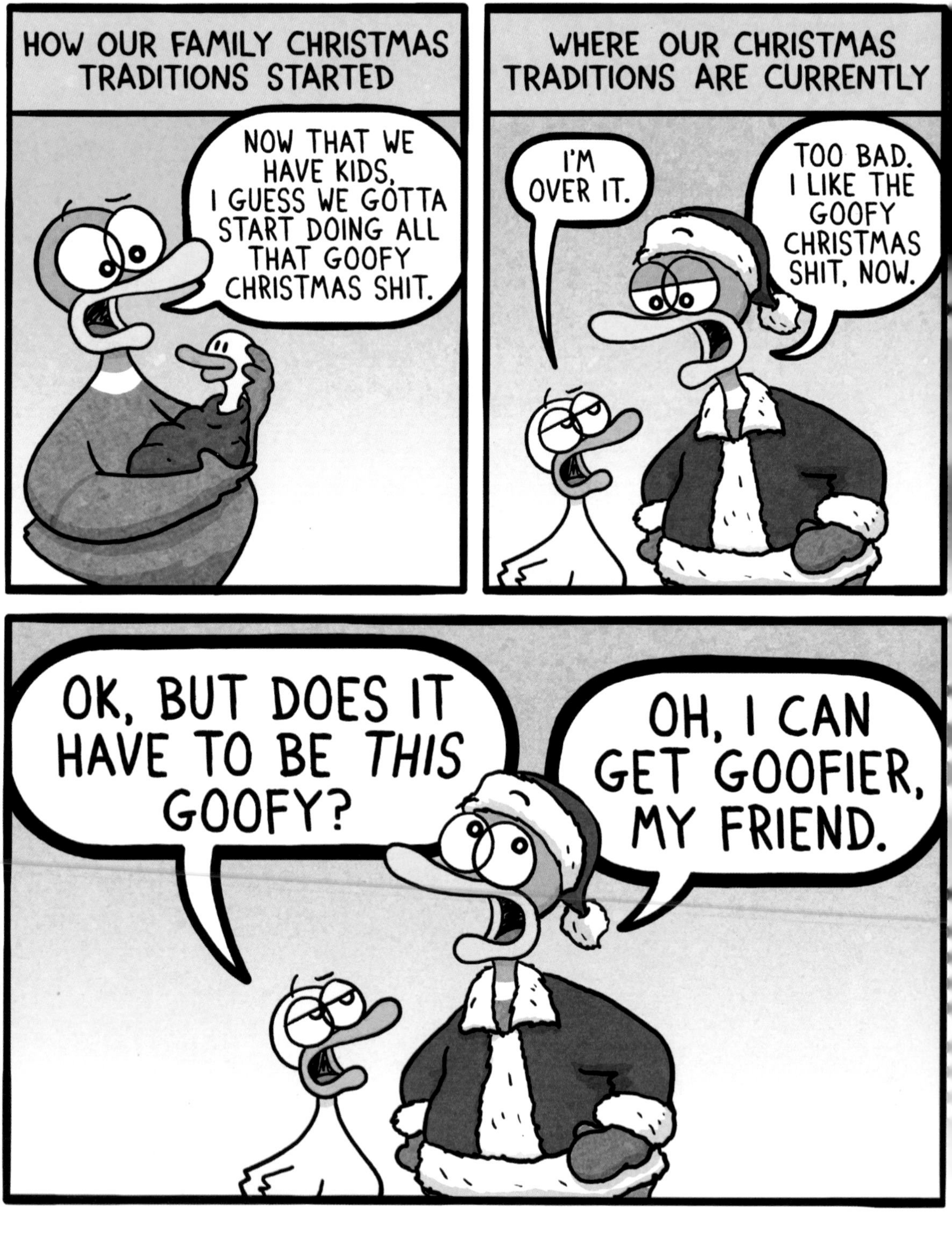
HOW OUR FAMILY CHRISTMAS TRADITIONS STARTED
NOW THAT WE HAVE KIDS, I GUESS WE GOTTA START DOING ALL THAT GOOFY CHRISTMAS SHIT.
WHERE OUR CHRISTMAS TRADITIONS ARE CURRENTLY
I'M OVER IT.
TOO BAD. I LIKE THE GOOFY CHRISTMAS SHIT, NOW.
OK, BUT DOES IT HAVE TO BE *THIS* GOOFY?
OH, I CAN GET GOOFIER, MY FRIEND.

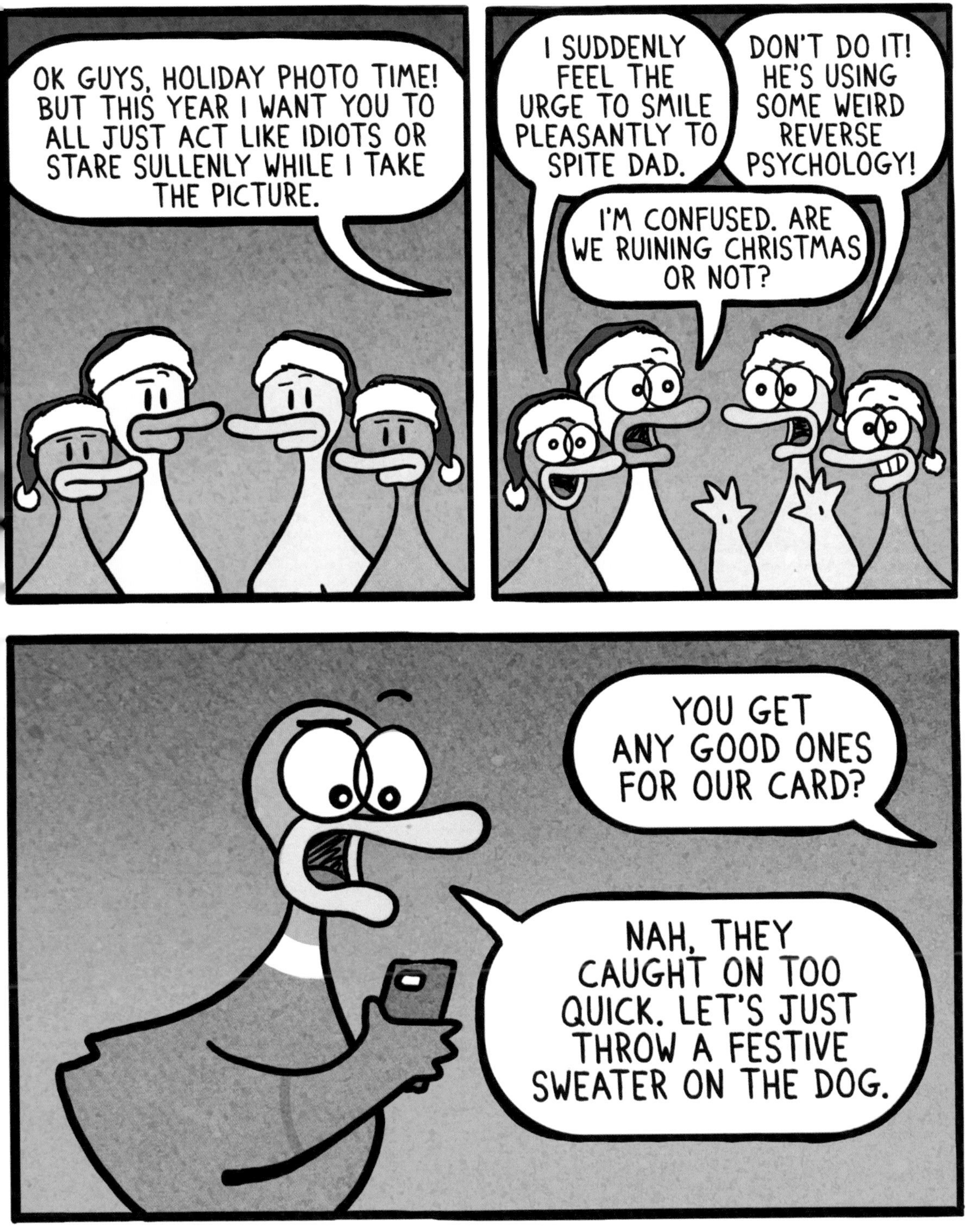
OK GUYS, HOLIDAY PHOTO TIME! BUT THIS YEAR I WANT YOU TO ALL JUST ACT LIKE IDIOTS OR STARE SULLENLY WHILE I TAKE THE PICTURE.
I SUDDENLY FEEL THE URGE TO SMILE PLEASANTLY TO SPITE DAD.
DON'T DO IT! HE'S USING SOME WEIRD REVERSE PSYCHOLOGY!
I'M CONFUSED. ARE WE RUINING CHRISTMAS OR NOT?
YOU GET ANY GOOD ONES FOR OUR CARD?
NAH, THEY CAUGHT ON TOO QUICK. LET'S JUST THROW A FESTIVE SWEATER ON THE DOG.

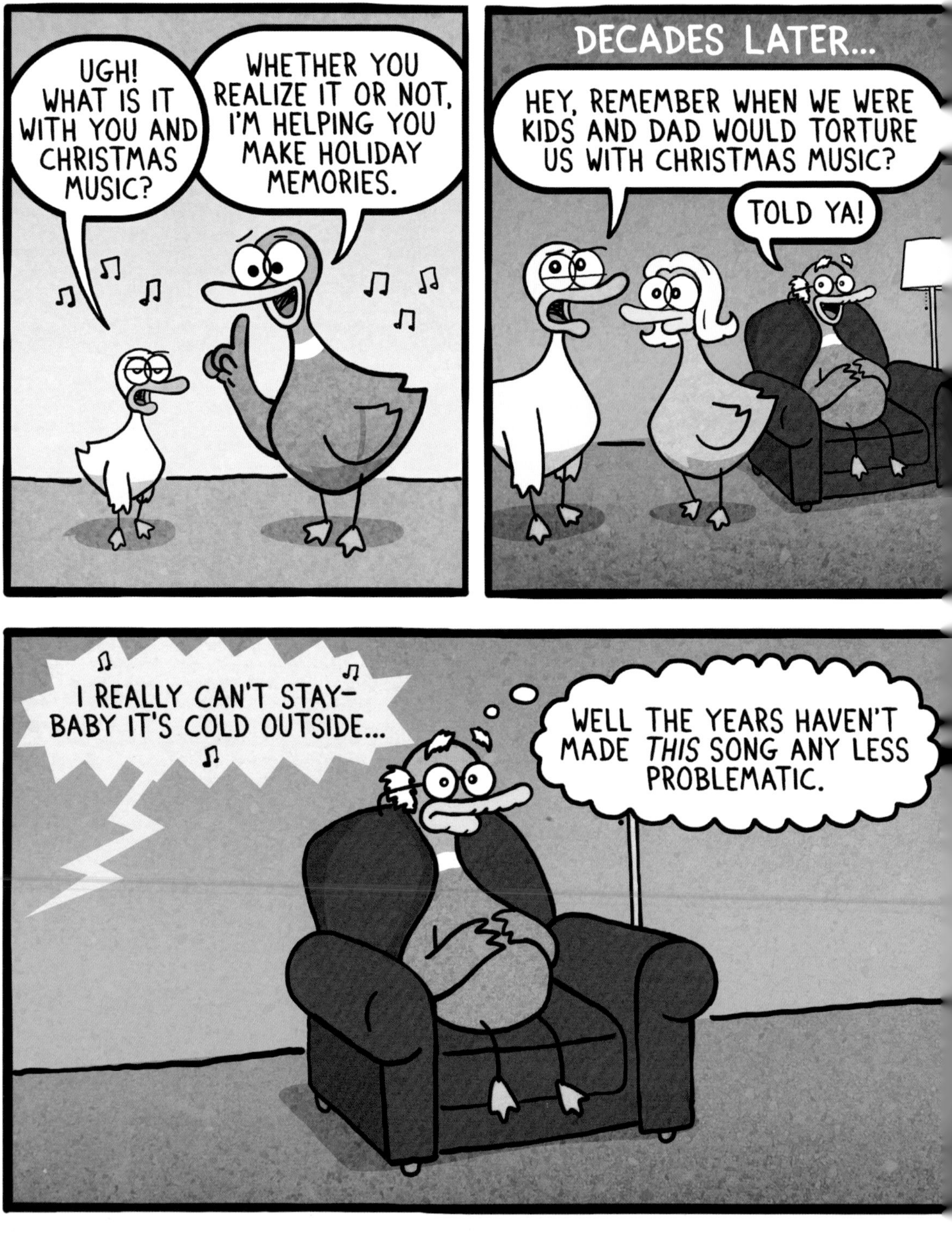
UGH! WHAT IS IT WITH YOU AND CHRISTMAS MUSIC?
WHETHER YOU REALIZE IT OR NOT, I'M HELPING YOU MAKE HOLIDAY MEMORIES.
DECADES LATER...
HEY, REMEMBER WHEN WE WERE KIDS AND DAD WOULD TORTURE US WITH CHRISTMAS MUSIC?
TOLD YA!
I REALLY CAN'T STAY– BABY IT'S COLD OUTSIDE...
WELL THE YEARS HAVEN'T MADE *THIS* SONG ANY LESS PROBLEMATIC.

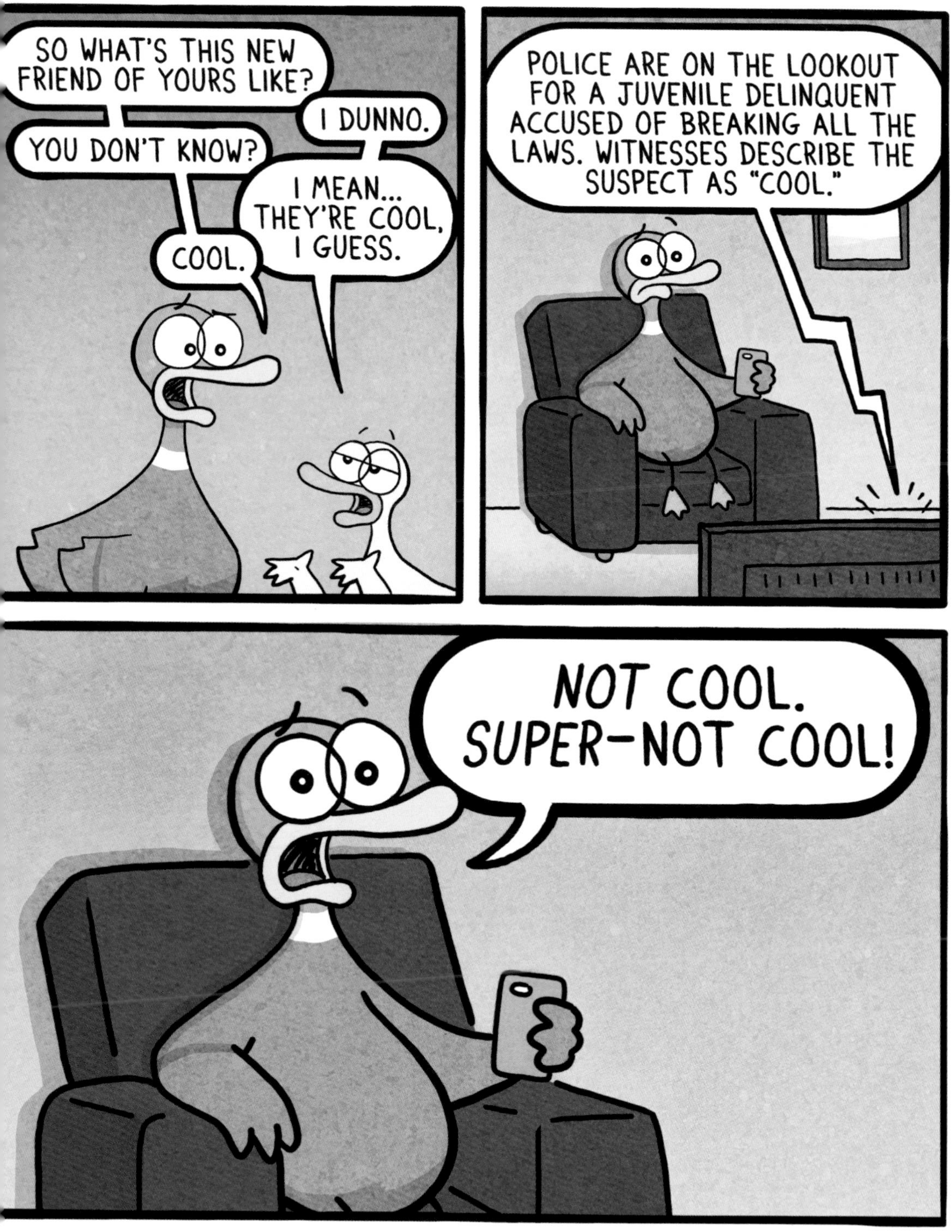
SO WHAT'S THIS NEW FRIEND OF YOURS LIKE?
I DUNNO.
YOU DON'T KNOW?
I MEAN... THEY'RE COOL, I GUESS.
COOL.
POLICE ARE ON THE LOOKOUT FOR A JUVENILE DELINQUENT ACCUSED OF BREAKING ALL THE LAWS. WITNESSES DESCRIBE THE SUSPECT AS "COOL."
NOT COOL. *SUPER*-NOT COOL!

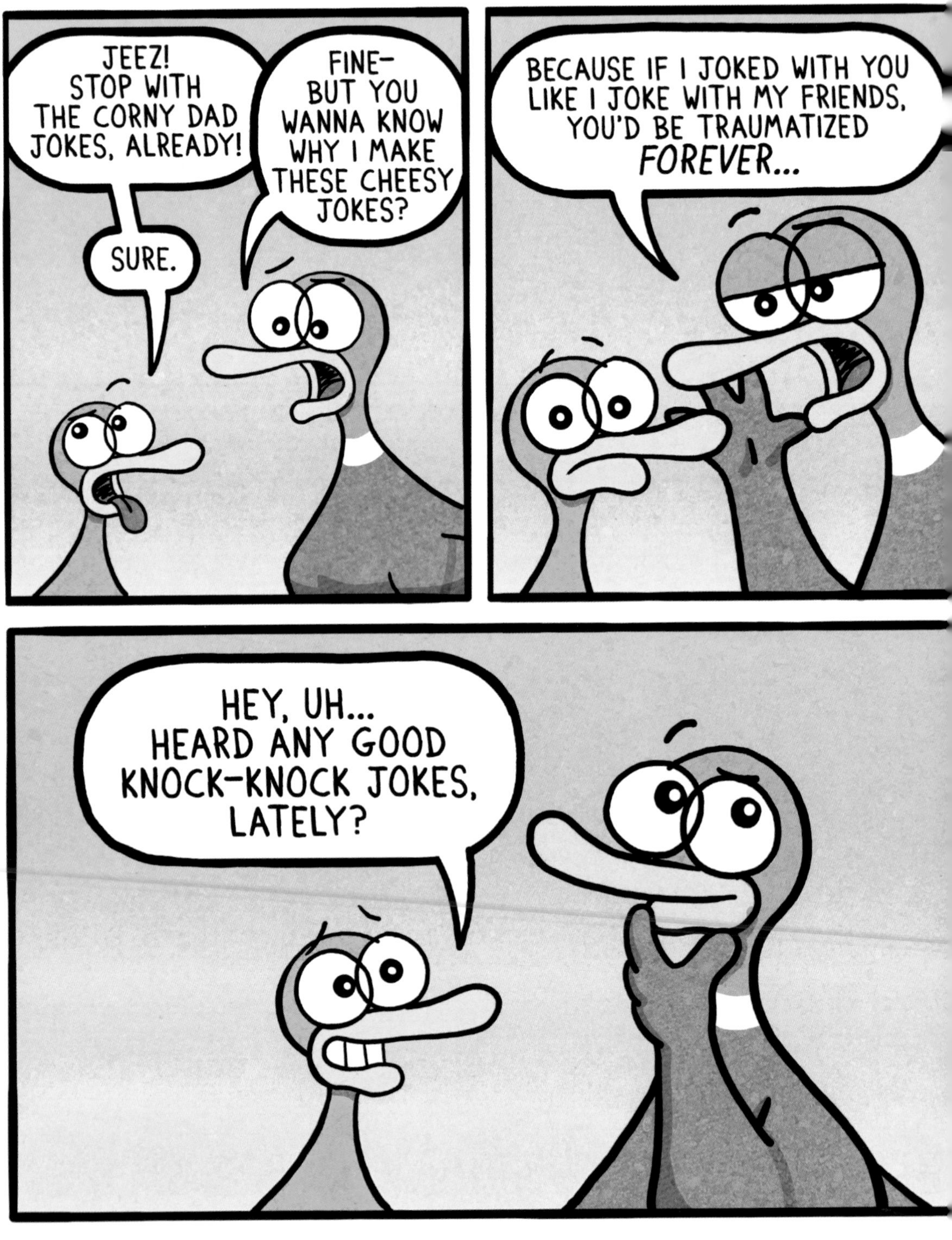

JEEZ! STOP WITH THE CORNY DAD JOKES, ALREADY!
SURE.
FINE– BUT YOU WANNA KNOW WHY I MAKE THESE CHEESY JOKES?
BECAUSE IF I JOKED WITH YOU LIKE I JOKE WITH MY FRIENDS, YOU'D BE TRAUMATIZED *FOREVER...*
HEY, UH... HEARD ANY GOOD KNOCK-KNOCK JOKES, LATELY?

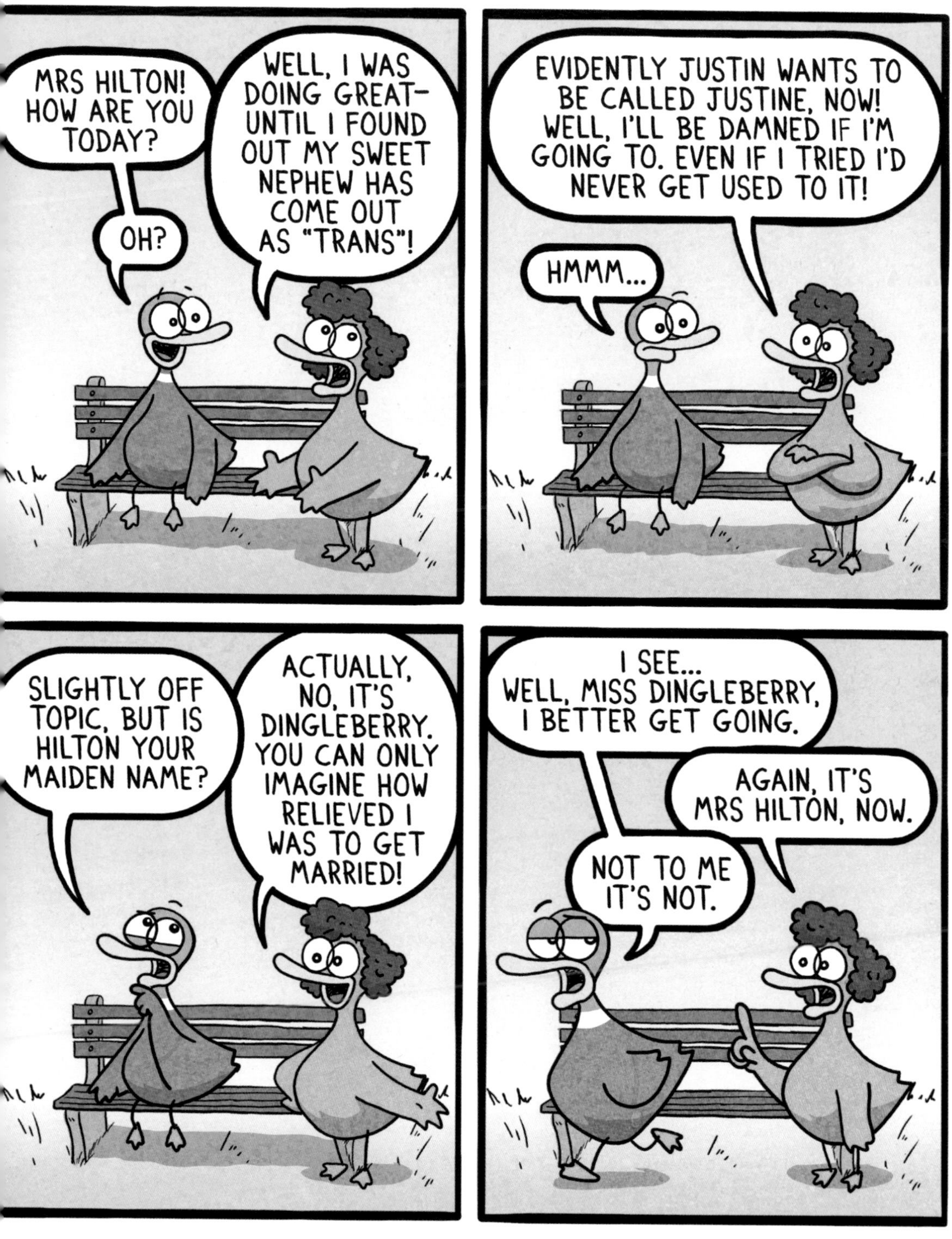
MRS HILTON! HOW ARE YOU TODAY?
OH?
WELL, I WAS DOING GREAT-UNTIL I FOUND OUT MY SWEET NEPHEW HAS COME OUT AS "TRANS"!
EVIDENTLY JUSTIN WANTS TO BE CALLED JUSTINE, NOW! WELL, I'LL BE DAMNED IF I'M GOING TO. EVEN IF I TRIED I'D NEVER GET USED TO IT!
HMMM...
SLIGHTLY OFF TOPIC, BUT IS HILTON YOUR MAIDEN NAME?
ACTUALLY, NO, IT'S DINGLEBERRY. YOU CAN ONLY IMAGINE HOW RELIEVED I WAS TO GET MARRIED!
I SEE... WELL, MISS DINGLEBERRY, I BETTER GET GOING.
AGAIN, IT'S MRS HILTON, NOW.
NOT TO ME IT'S NOT.

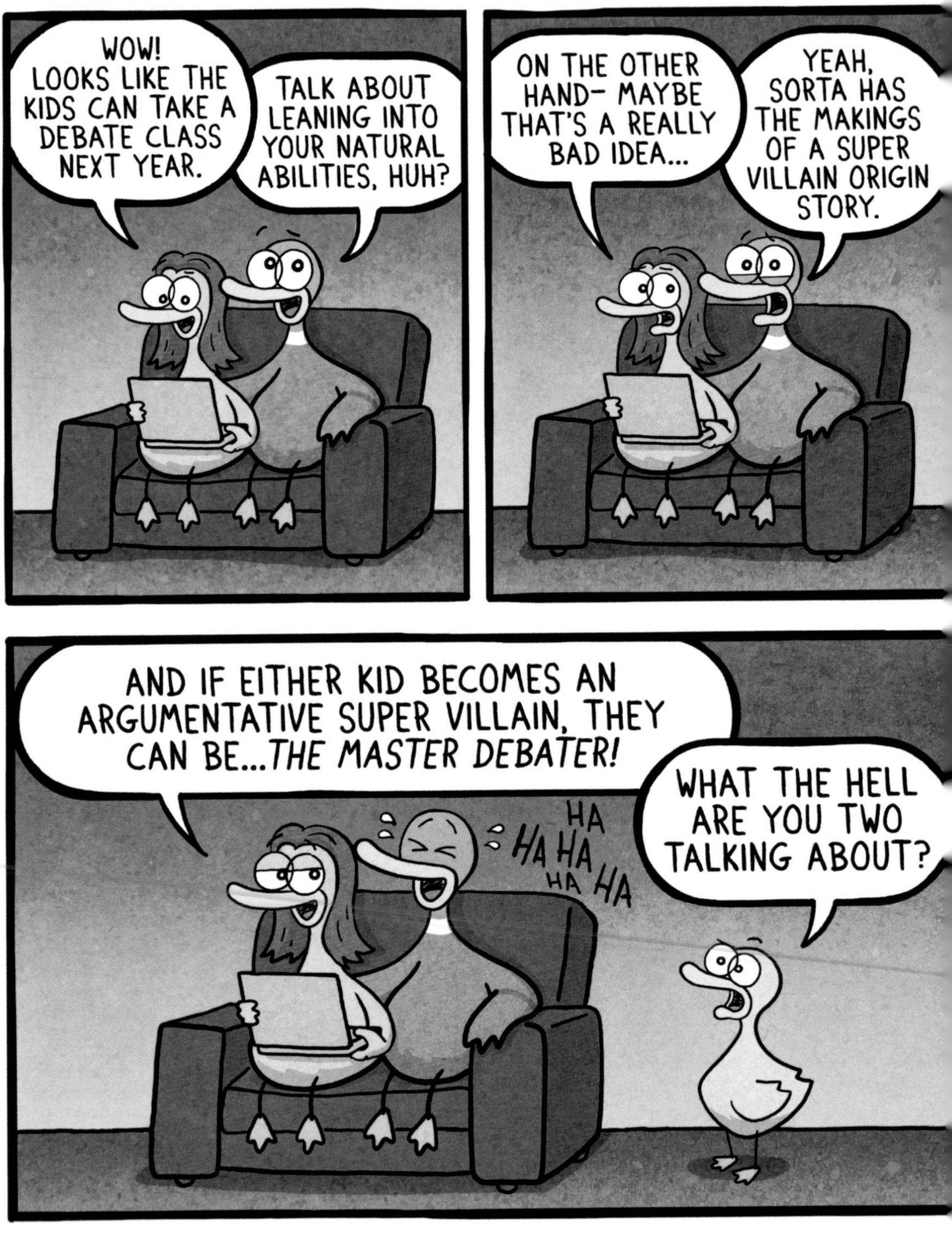
WOW! LOOKS LIKE THE KIDS CAN TAKE A DEBATE CLASS NEXT YEAR.
TALK ABOUT LEANING INTO YOUR NATURAL ABILITIES, HUH?
ON THE OTHER HAND– MAYBE THAT'S A REALLY BAD IDEA...
YEAH, SORTA HAS THE MAKINGS OF A SUPER VILLAIN ORIGIN STORY.
AND IF EITHER KID BECOMES AN ARGUMENTATIVE SUPER VILLAIN, THEY CAN BE...*THE MASTER DEBATER!*
HA HA HA HA HA
WHAT THE HELL ARE YOU TWO TALKING ABOUT?

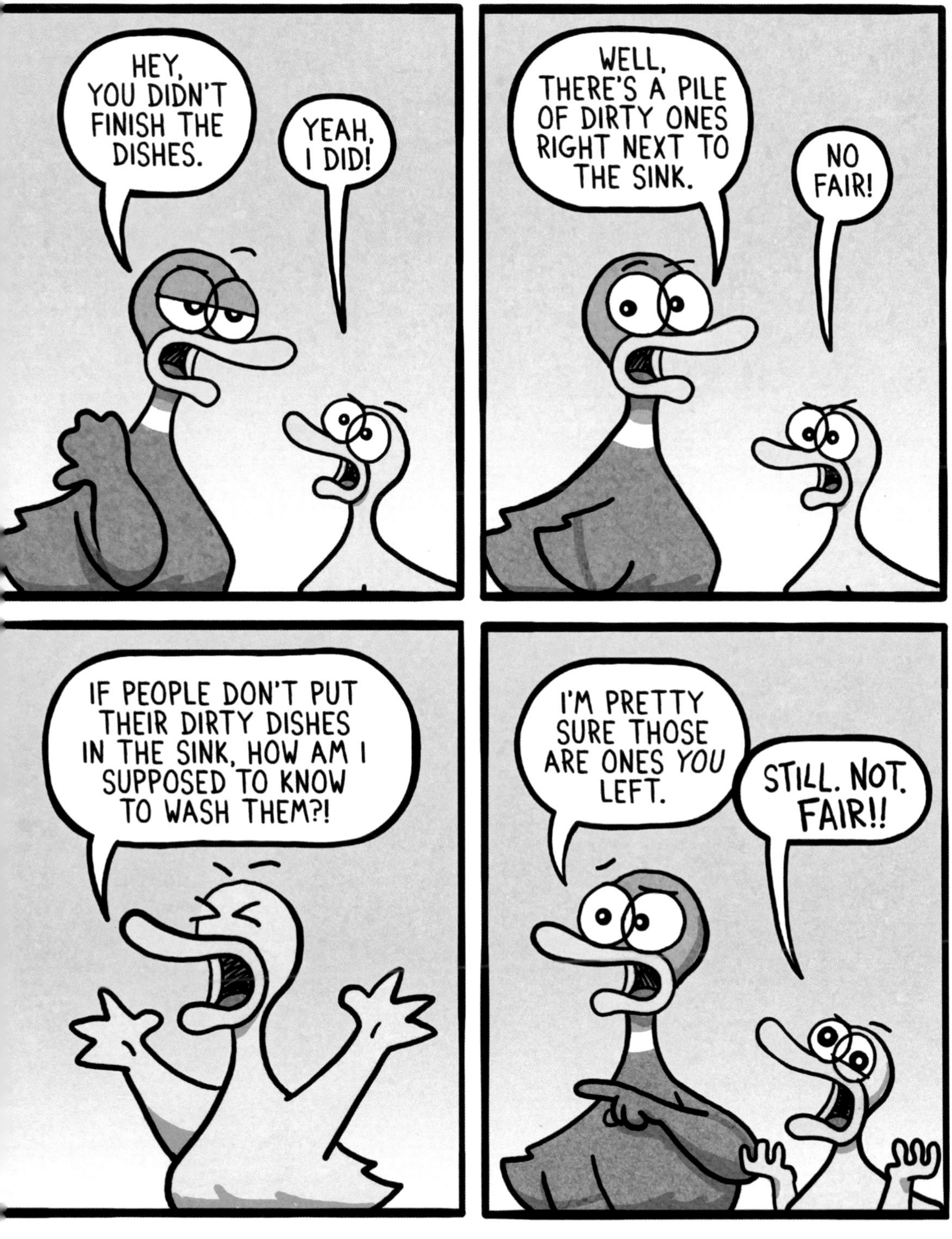
HEY, YOU DIDN'T FINISH THE DISHES.
YEAH, I DID!
WELL, THERE'S A PILE OF DIRTY ONES RIGHT NEXT TO THE SINK.
NO FAIR!
IF PEOPLE DON'T PUT THEIR DIRTY DISHES IN THE SINK, HOW AM I SUPPOSED TO KNOW TO WASH THEM?!
I'M PRETTY SURE THOSE ARE ONES *YOU* LEFT.
STILL. NOT. FAIR!!

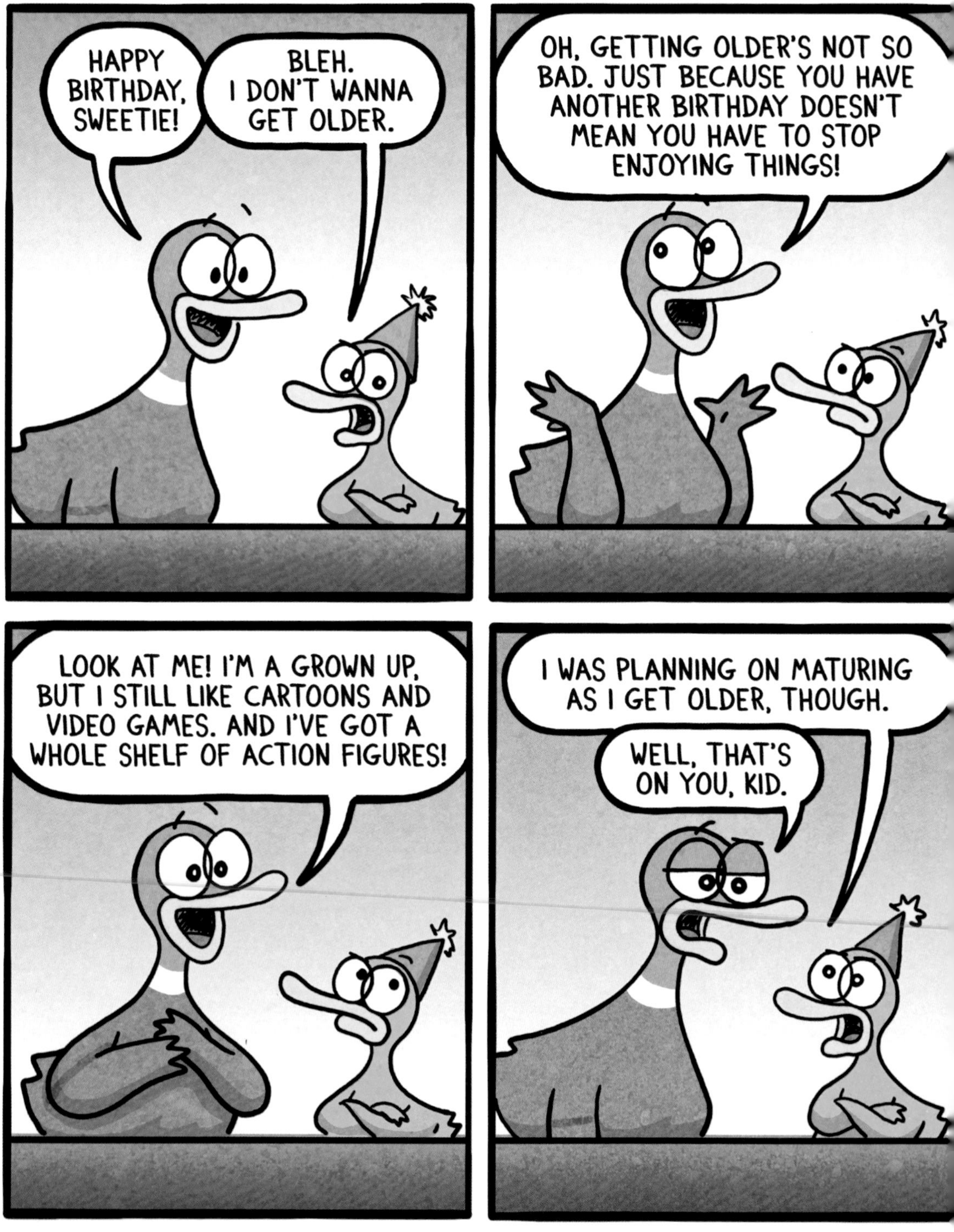
HAPPY BIRTHDAY, SWEETIE!
BLEH. I DON'T WANNA GET OLDER.
OH, GETTING OLDER'S NOT SO BAD. JUST BECAUSE YOU HAVE ANOTHER BIRTHDAY DOESN'T MEAN YOU HAVE TO STOP ENJOYING THINGS!
LOOK AT ME! I'M A GROWN UP, BUT I STILL LIKE CARTOONS AND VIDEO GAMES. AND I'VE GOT A WHOLE SHELF OF ACTION FIGURES!
I WAS PLANNING ON MATURING AS I GET OLDER, THOUGH.
WELL, THAT'S ON YOU, KID.

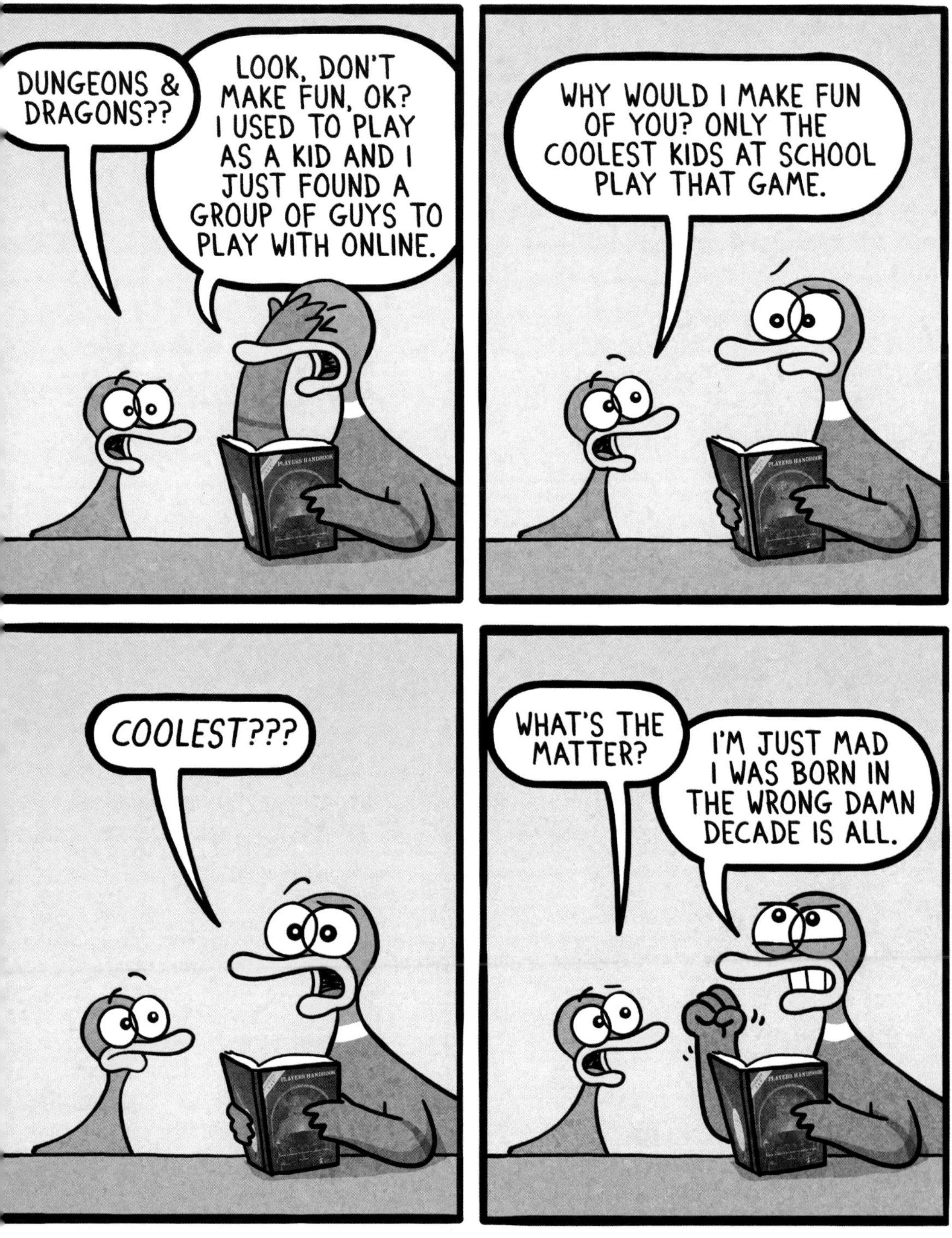
DUNGEONS & DRAGONS??
LOOK, DON'T MAKE FUN, OK? I USED TO PLAY AS A KID AND I JUST FOUND A GROUP OF GUYS TO PLAY WITH ONLINE.
WHY WOULD I MAKE FUN OF YOU? ONLY THE COOLEST KIDS AT SCHOOL PLAY THAT GAME.
PLAYERS HANDBOOK
COOLEST???
WHAT'S THE MATTER?
I'M JUST MAD I WAS BORN IN THE WRONG DAMN DECADE IS ALL.

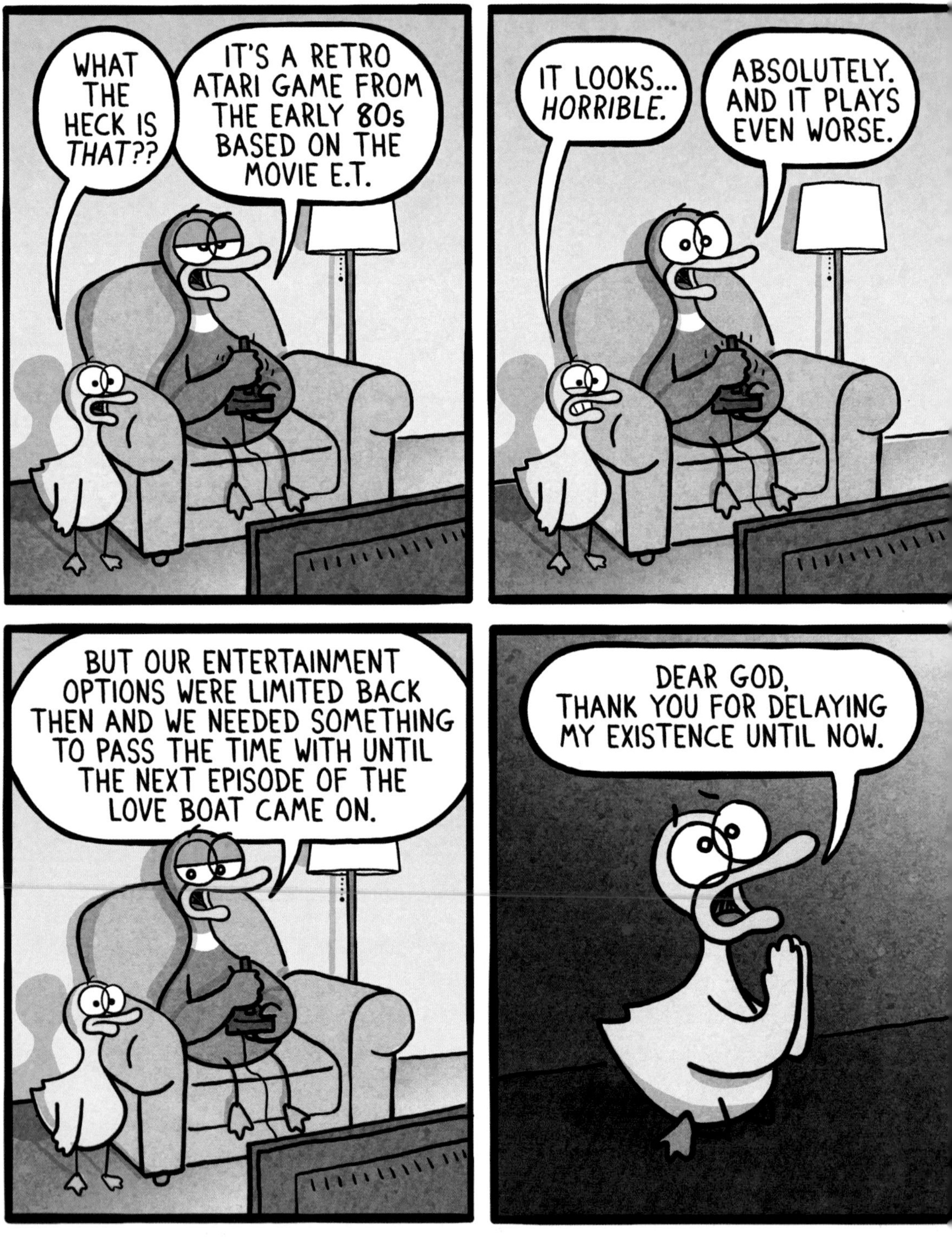
WHAT THE HECK IS *THAT??*
IT'S A RETRO ATARI GAME FROM THE EARLY 80s BASED ON THE MOVIE E.T.
IT LOOKS... *HORRIBLE.*
ABSOLUTELY. AND IT PLAYS EVEN WORSE.
BUT OUR ENTERTAINMENT OPTIONS WERE LIMITED BACK THEN AND WE NEEDED SOMETHING TO PASS THE TIME WITH UNTIL THE NEXT EPISODE OF THE LOVE BOAT CAME ON.
DEAR GOD, THANK YOU FOR DELAYING MY EXISTENCE UNTIL NOW.

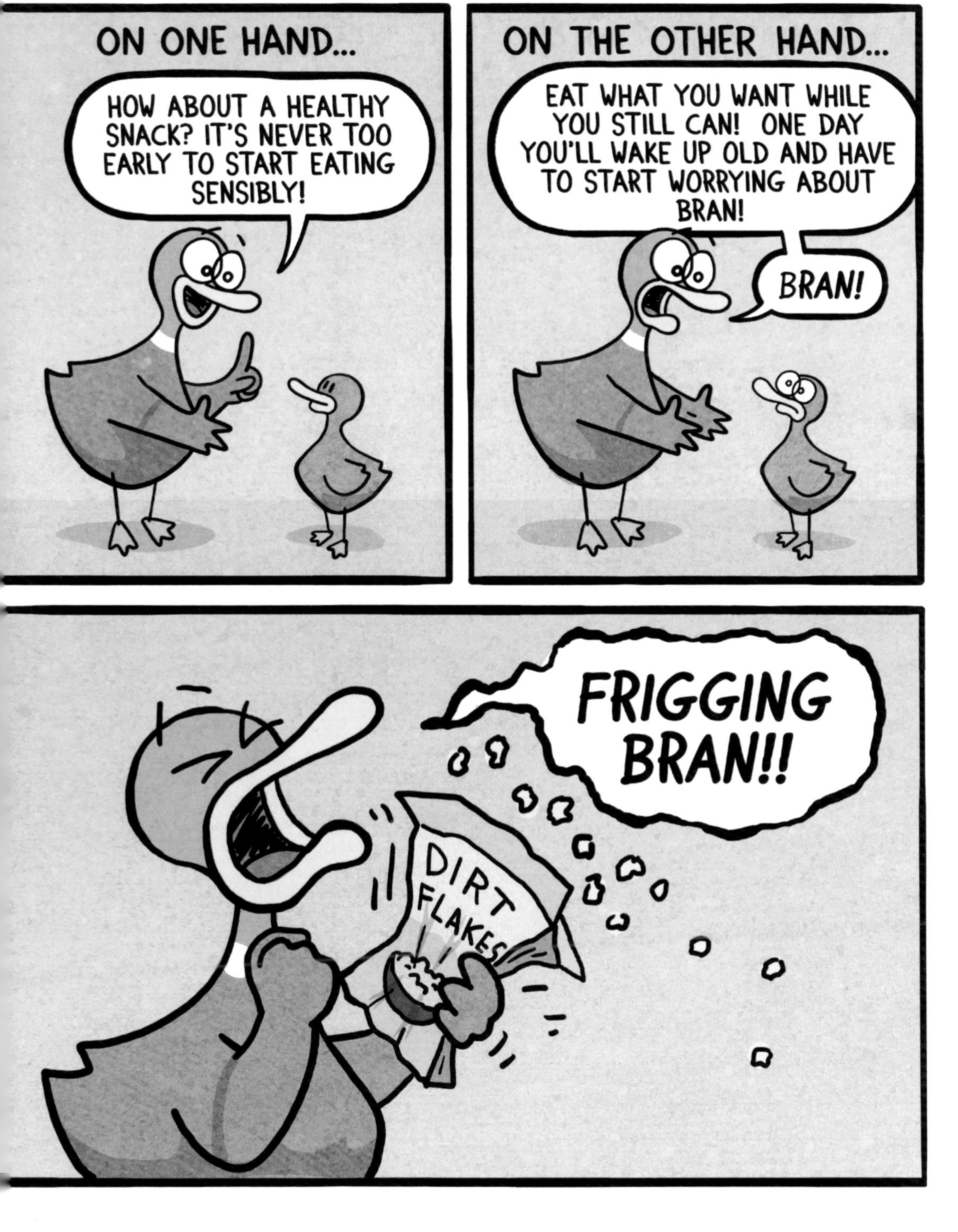
ON ONE HAND...
HOW ABOUT A HEALTHY SNACK? IT'S NEVER TOO EARLY TO START EATING SENSIBLY!
ON THE OTHER HAND...
EAT WHAT YOU WANT WHILE YOU STILL CAN! ONE DAY YOU'LL WAKE UP OLD AND HAVE TO START WORRYING ABOUT BRAN!
BRAN!
FRIGGING BRAN!!
DIRT FLAKES

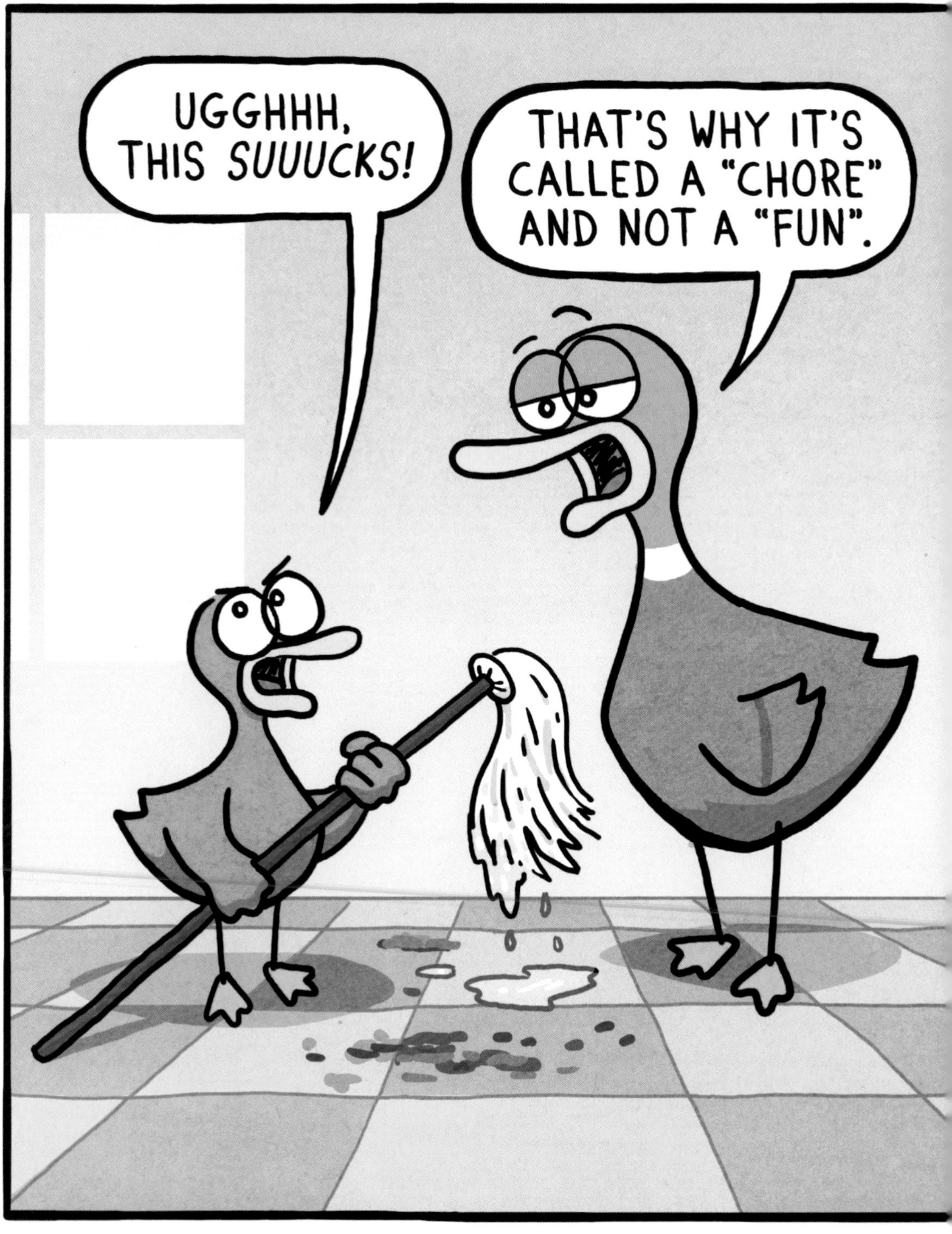
UGGHHH, THIS *SUUUCKS!*
THAT'S WHY IT'S CALLED A "CHORE" AND NOT A "FUN".

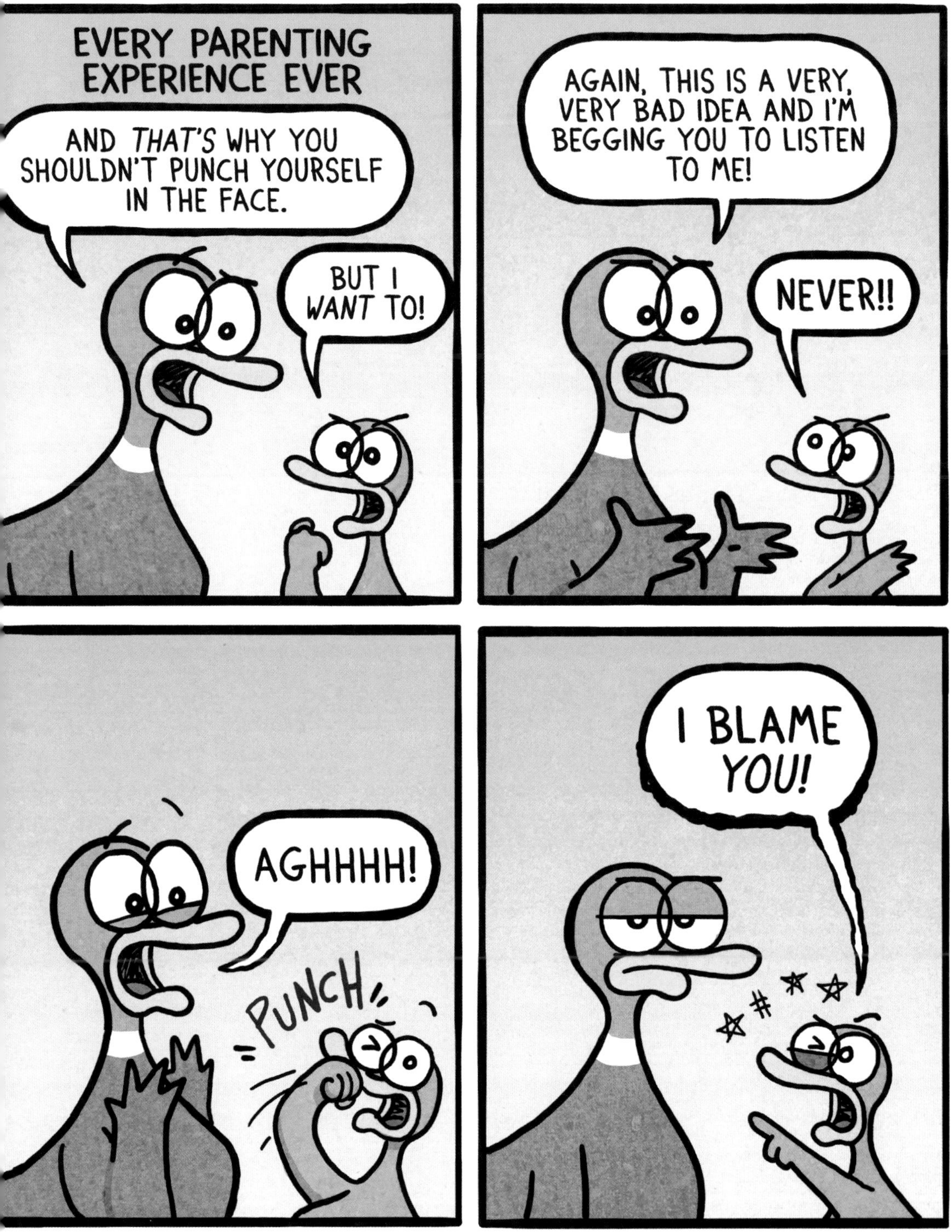
EVERY PARENTING EXPERIENCE EVER
AND *THAT'S* WHY YOU SHOULDN'T PUNCH YOURSELF IN THE FACE.
BUT I *WANT* TO!
AGAIN, THIS IS A VERY, VERY BAD IDEA AND I'M BEGGING YOU TO LISTEN TO ME!
NEVER!!
AGHHHH!
PUNCH
I BLAME *YOU!*

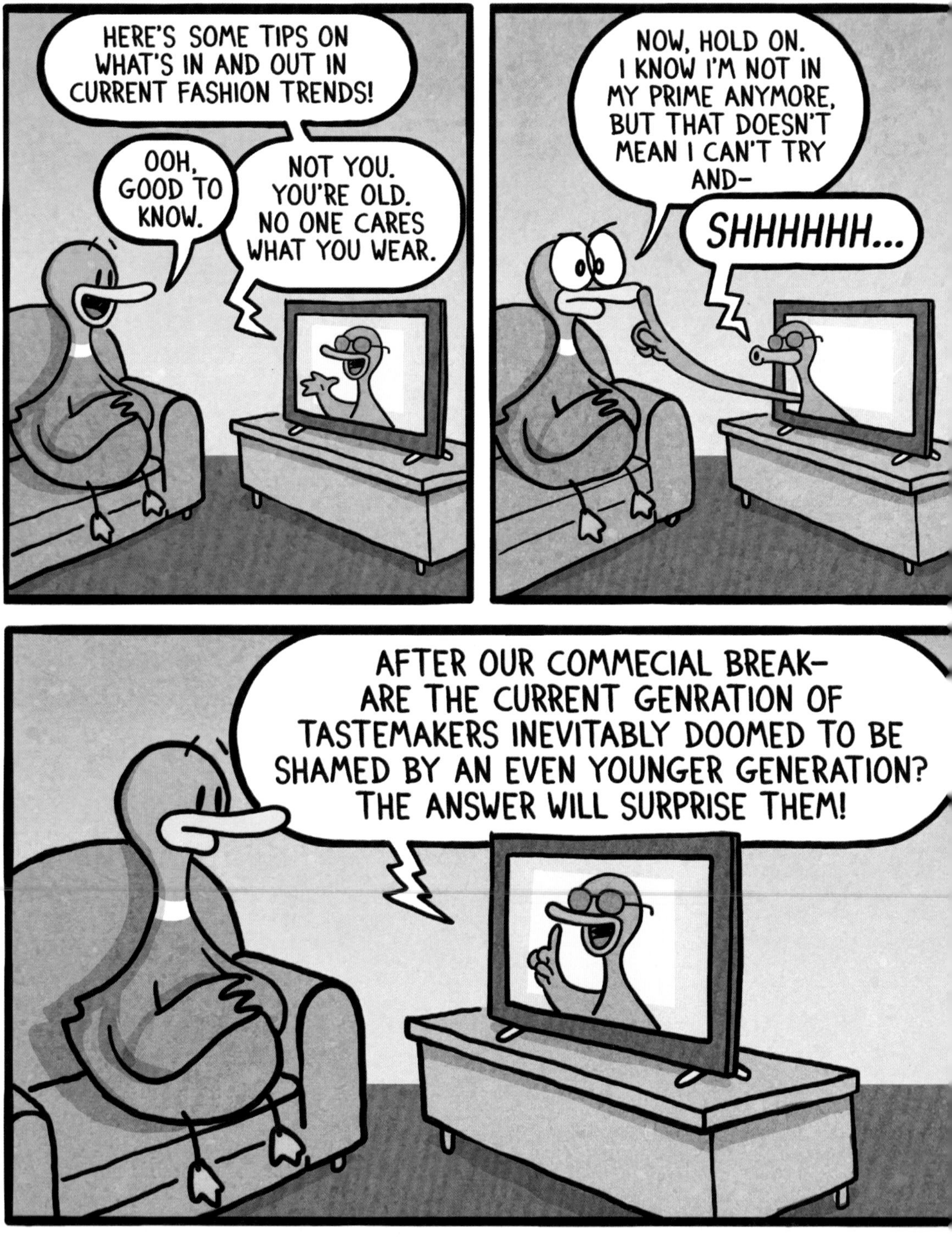
HERE'S SOME TIPS ON WHAT'S IN AND OUT IN CURRENT FASHION TRENDS!
OOH, GOOD TO KNOW.
NOT YOU. YOU'RE OLD. NO ONE CARES WHAT YOU WEAR.
NOW, HOLD ON. I KNOW I'M NOT IN MY PRIME ANYMORE, BUT THAT DOESN'T MEAN I CAN'T TRY AND–
SHHHHHH...
AFTER OUR COMMECIAL BREAK– ARE THE CURRENT GENRATION OF TASTEMAKERS INEVITABLY DOOMED TO BE SHAMED BY AN EVEN YOUNGER GENERATION? THE ANSWER WILL SURPRISE THEM!

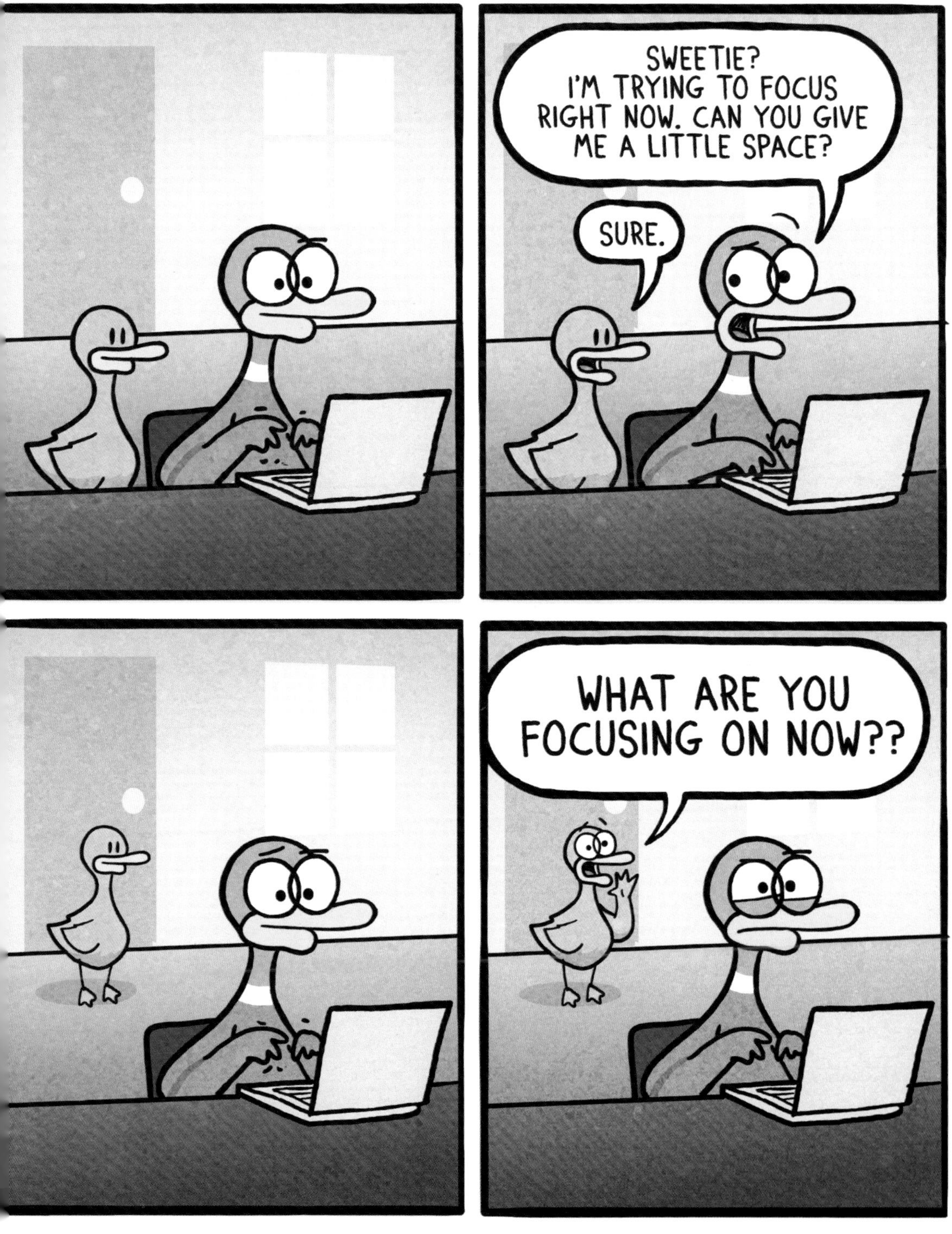
SWEETIE? I'M TRYING TO FOCUS RIGHT NOW. CAN YOU GIVE ME A LITTLE SPACE?
SURE.
WHAT ARE YOU FOCUSING ON NOW??

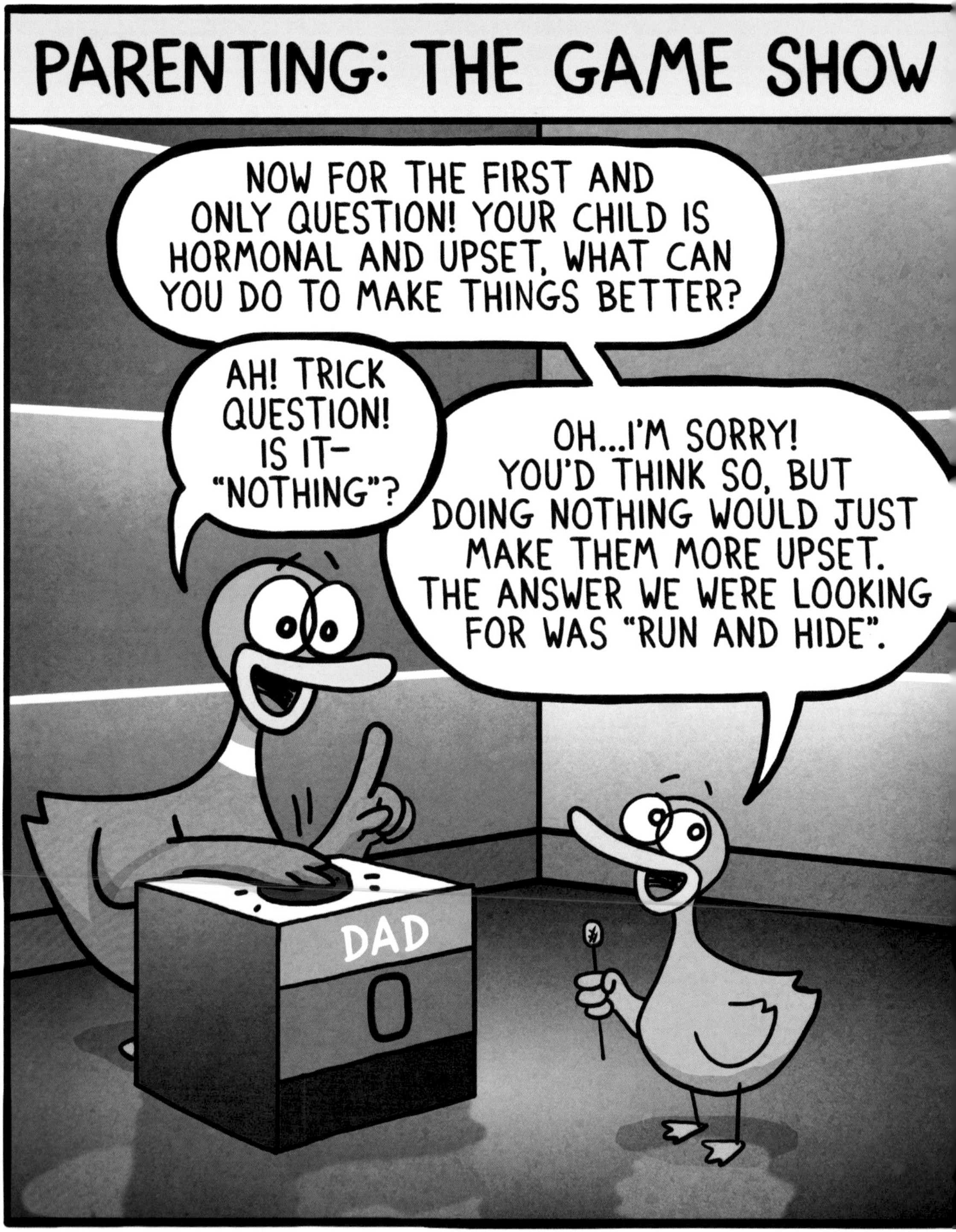
PARENTING: THE GAME SHOW
NOW FOR THE FIRST AND ONLY QUESTION! YOUR CHILD IS HORMONAL AND UPSET, WHAT CAN YOU DO TO MAKE THINGS BETTER?
AH! TRICK QUESTION! IS IT– "NOTHING"?
OH...I'M SORRY! YOU'D THINK SO, BUT DOING NOTHING WOULD JUST MAKE THEM MORE UPSET. THE ANSWER WE WERE LOOKING FOR WAS "RUN AND HIDE".
DAD
0

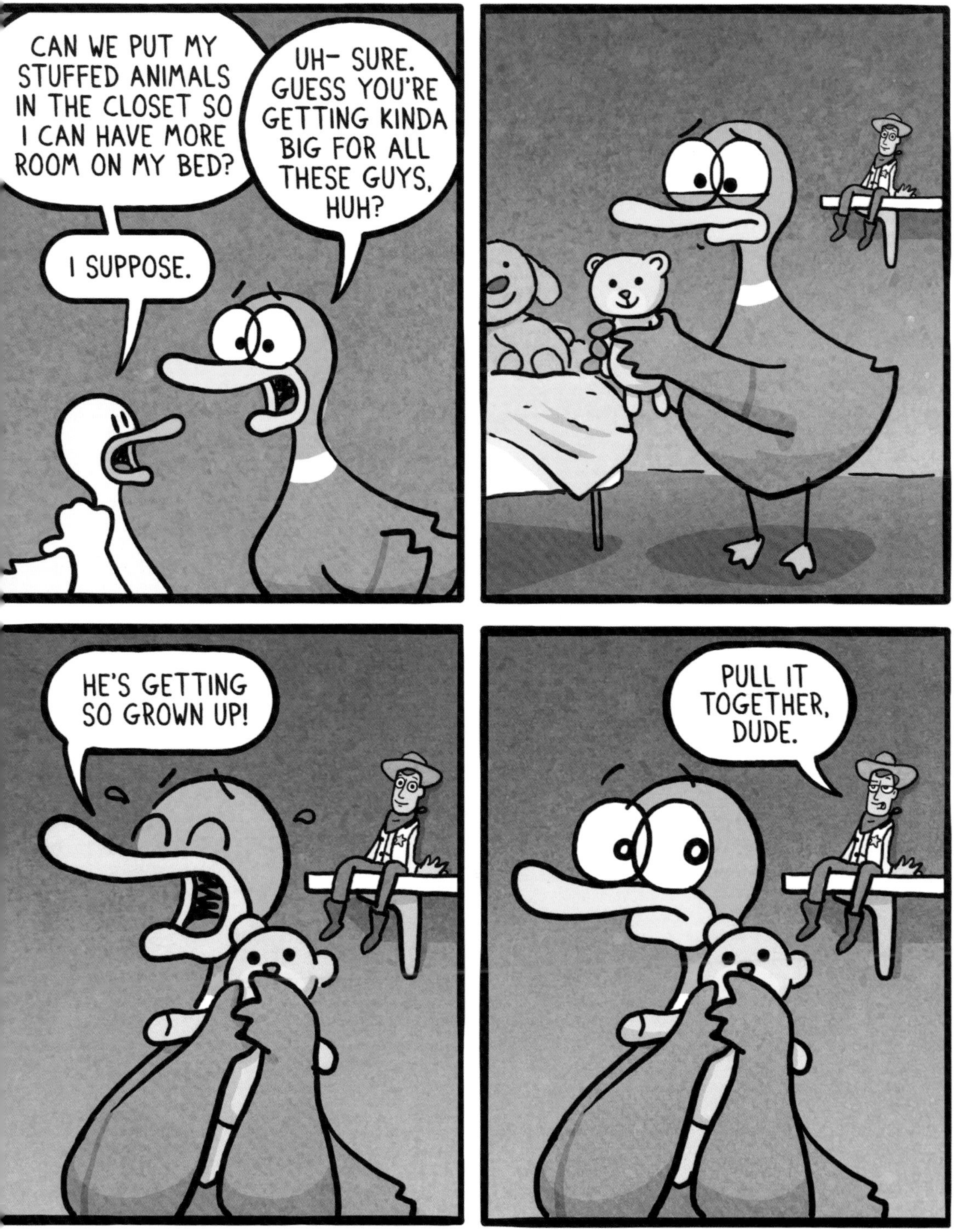
CAN WE PUT MY STUFFED ANIMALS IN THE CLOSET SO I CAN HAVE MORE ROOM ON MY BED?
UH– SURE. GUESS YOU'RE GETTING KINDA BIG FOR ALL THESE GUYS, HUH?
I SUPPOSE.
HE'S GETTING SO GROWN UP!
PULL IT TOGETHER, DUDE.

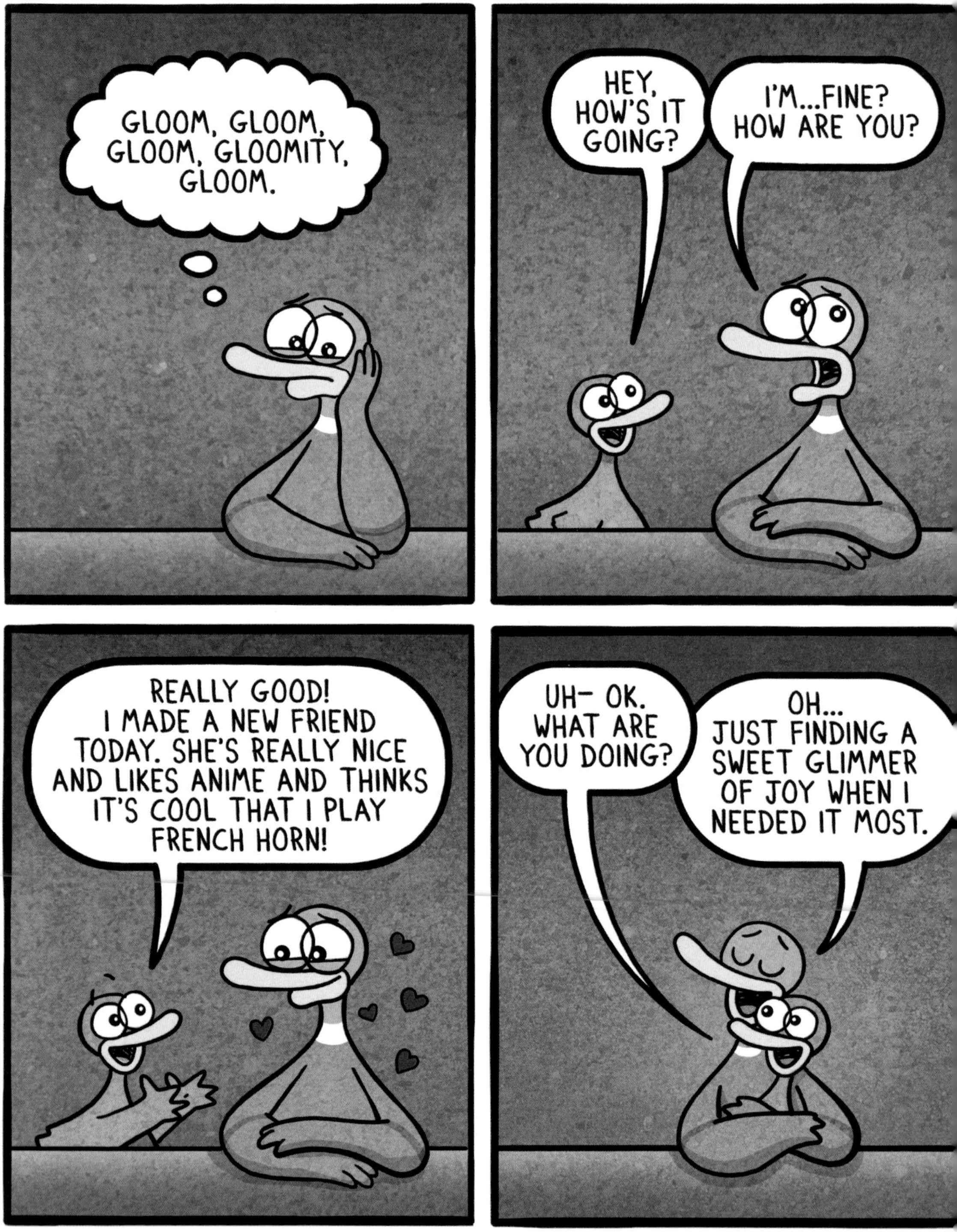
GLOOM, GLOOM, GLOOM, GLOOMITY, GLOOM.
HEY, HOW'S IT GOING?
I'M...FINE? HOW ARE YOU?
REALLY GOOD! I MADE A NEW FRIEND TODAY. SHE'S REALLY NICE AND LIKES ANIME AND THINKS IT'S COOL THAT I PLAY FRENCH HORN!
UH– OK. WHAT ARE YOU DOING?
OH... JUST FINDING A SWEET GLIMMER OF JOY WHEN I NEEDED IT MOST.

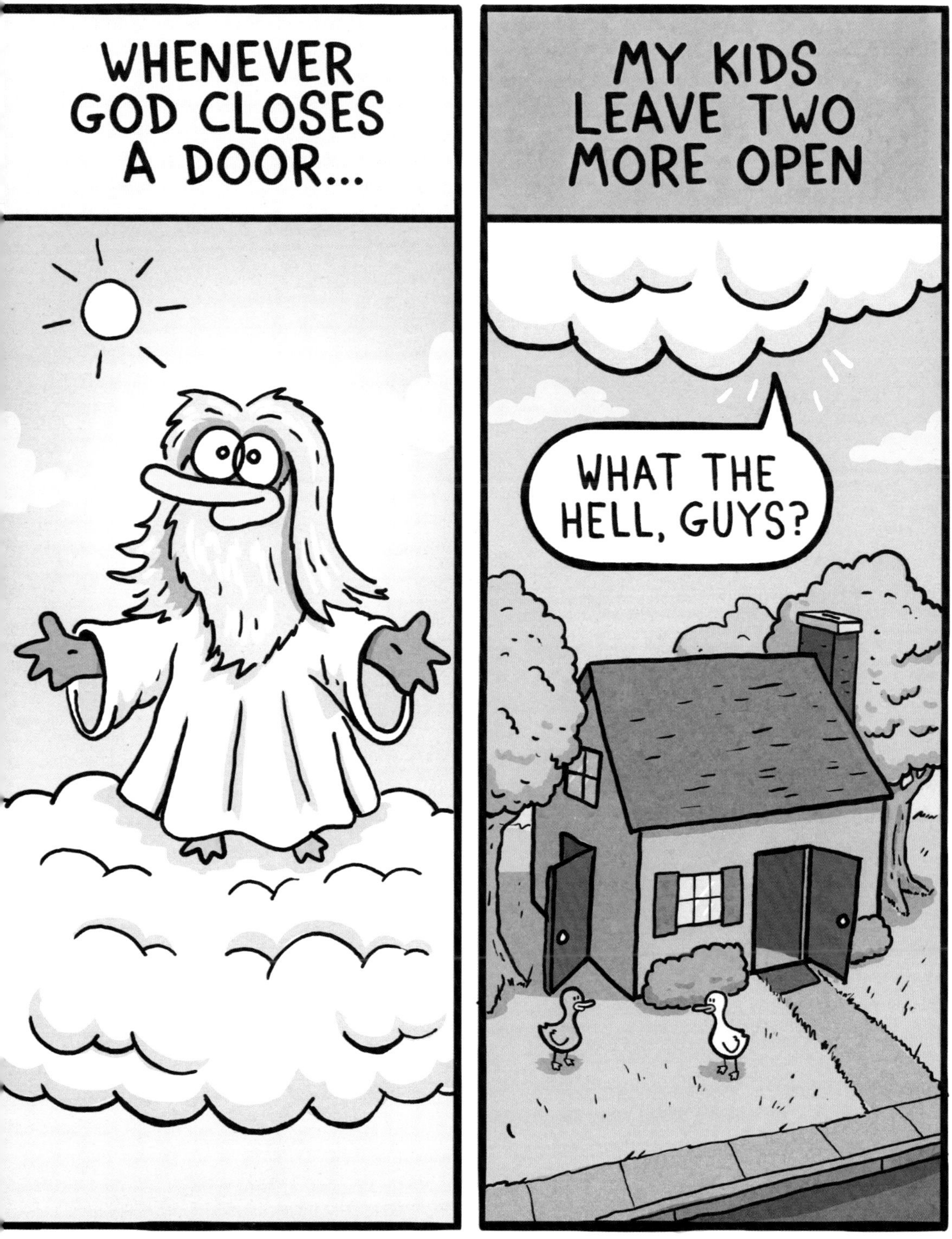
WHENEVER GOD CLOSES A DOOR...
MY KIDS LEAVE TWO MORE OPEN
WHAT THE HELL, GUYS?

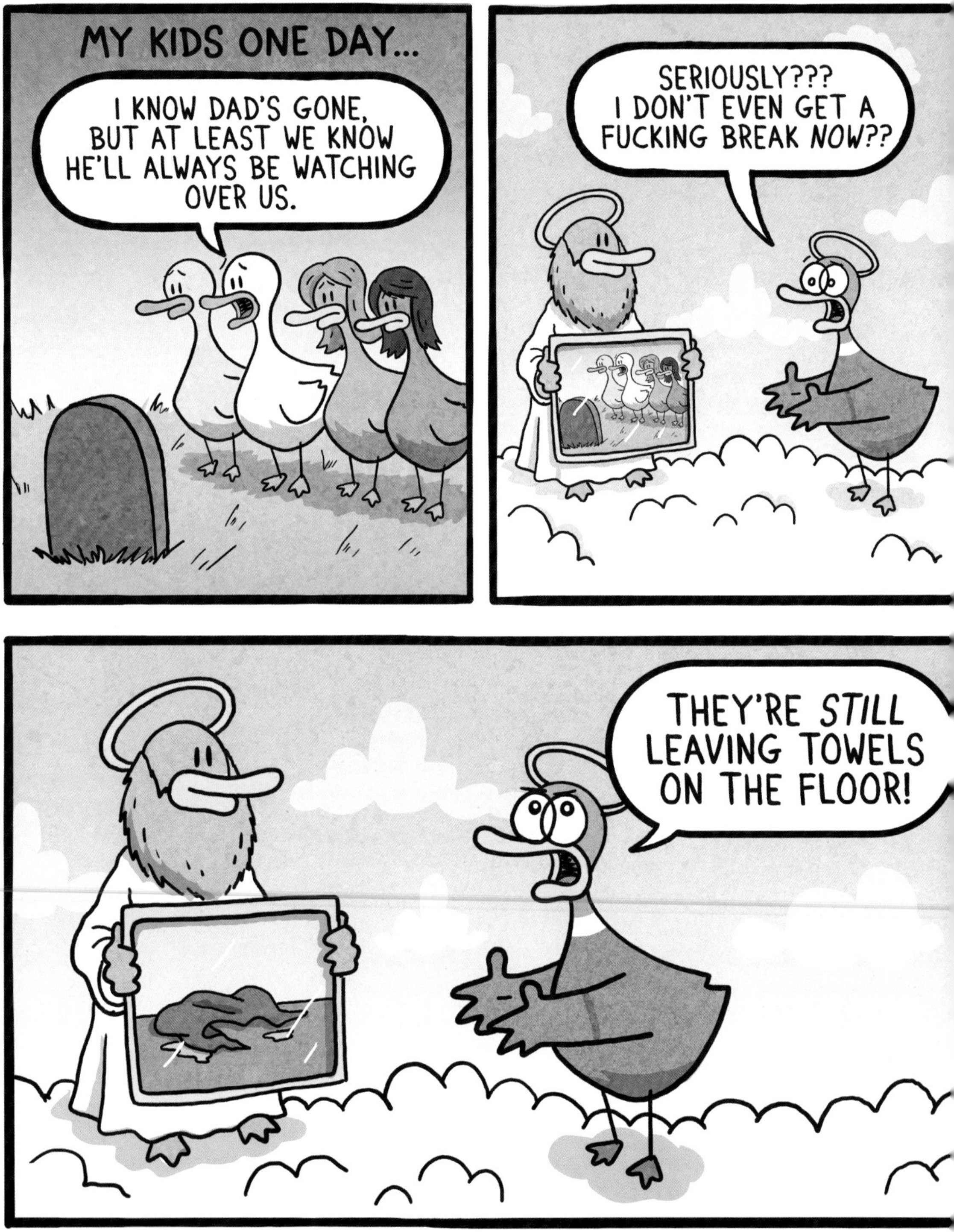

MY KIDS ONE DAY...
I KNOW DAD'S GONE, BUT AT LEAST WE KNOW HE'LL ALWAYS BE WATCHING OVER US.
SERIOUSLY??? I DON'T EVEN GET A FUCKING BREAK NOW??
THEY'RE STILL LEAVING TOWELS ON THE FLOOR!

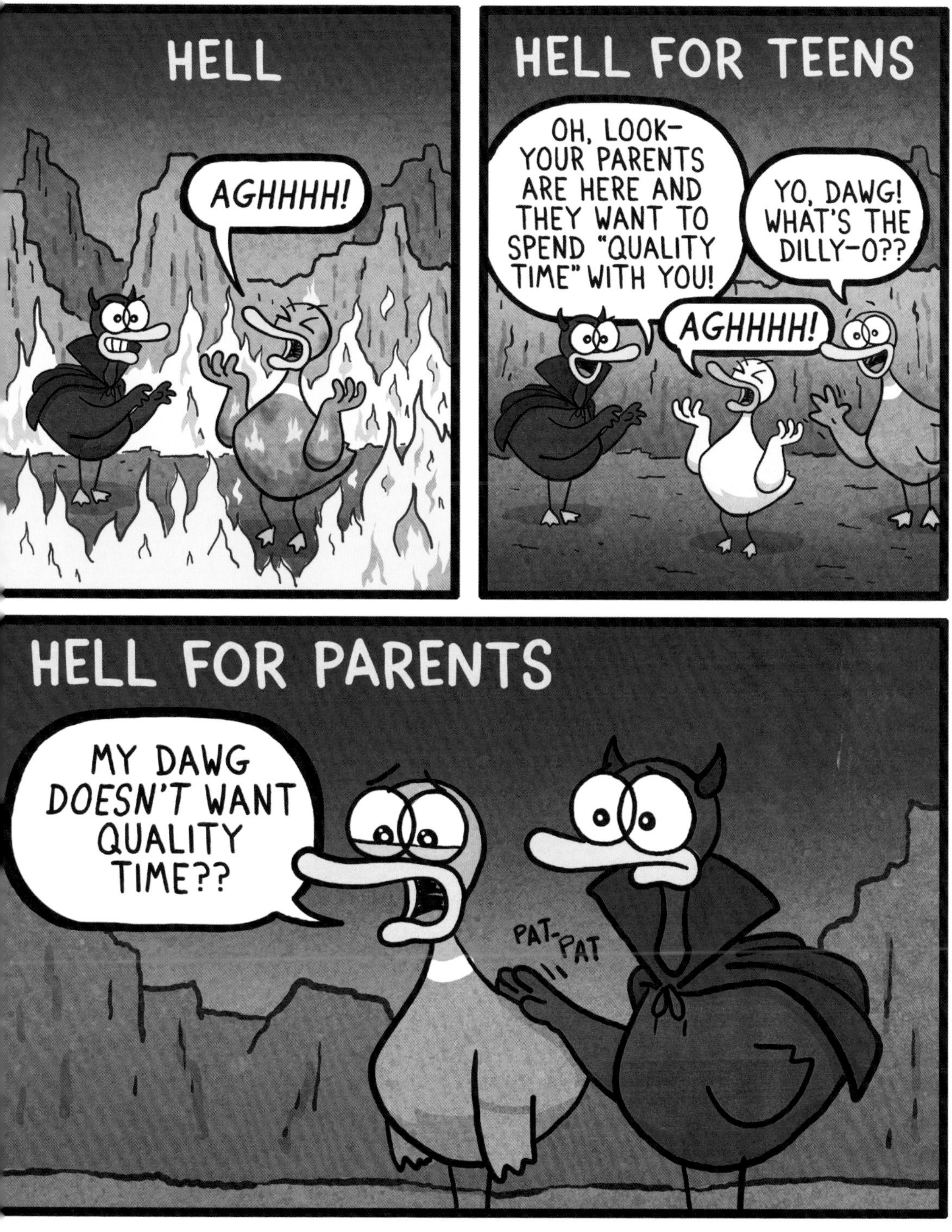
HELL
AGHHHH!
HELL FOR TEENS
OH, LOOK- YOUR PARENTS ARE HERE AND THEY WANT TO SPEND "QUALITY TIME" WITH YOU!
YO, DAWG! WHAT'S THE DILLY-O??
AGHHHH!
HELL FOR PARENTS
MY DAWG DOESN'T WANT QUALITY TIME??
PAT-PAT

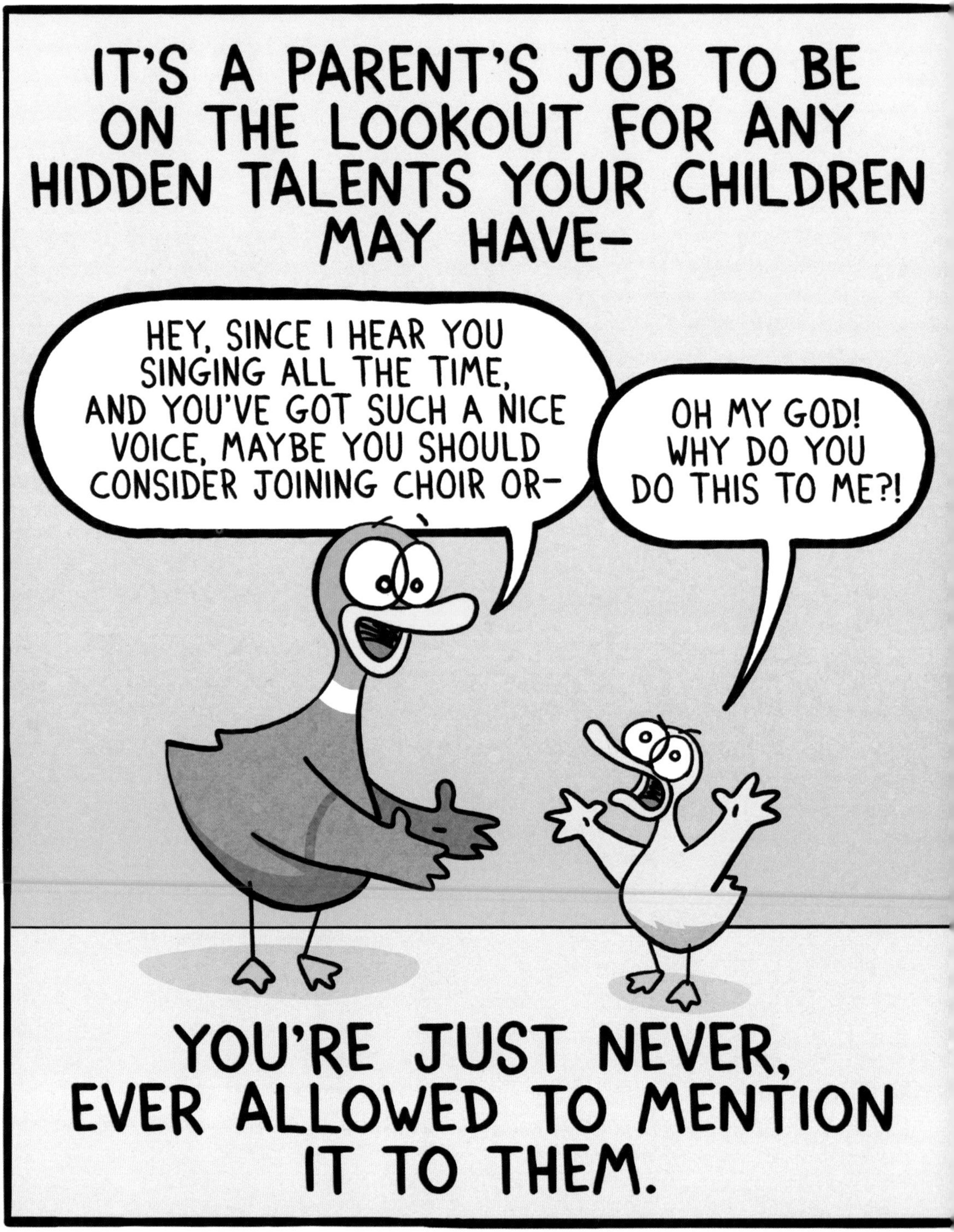
IT'S A PARENT'S JOB TO BE ON THE LOOKOUT FOR ANY HIDDEN TALENTS YOUR CHILDREN MAY HAVE–
HEY, SINCE I HEAR YOU SINGING ALL THE TIME, AND YOU'VE GOT SUCH A NICE VOICE, MAYBE YOU SHOULD CONSIDER JOINING CHOIR OR–
OH MY GOD! WHY DO YOU DO THIS TO ME?!
YOU'RE JUST NEVER, EVER ALLOWED TO MENTION IT TO THEM.

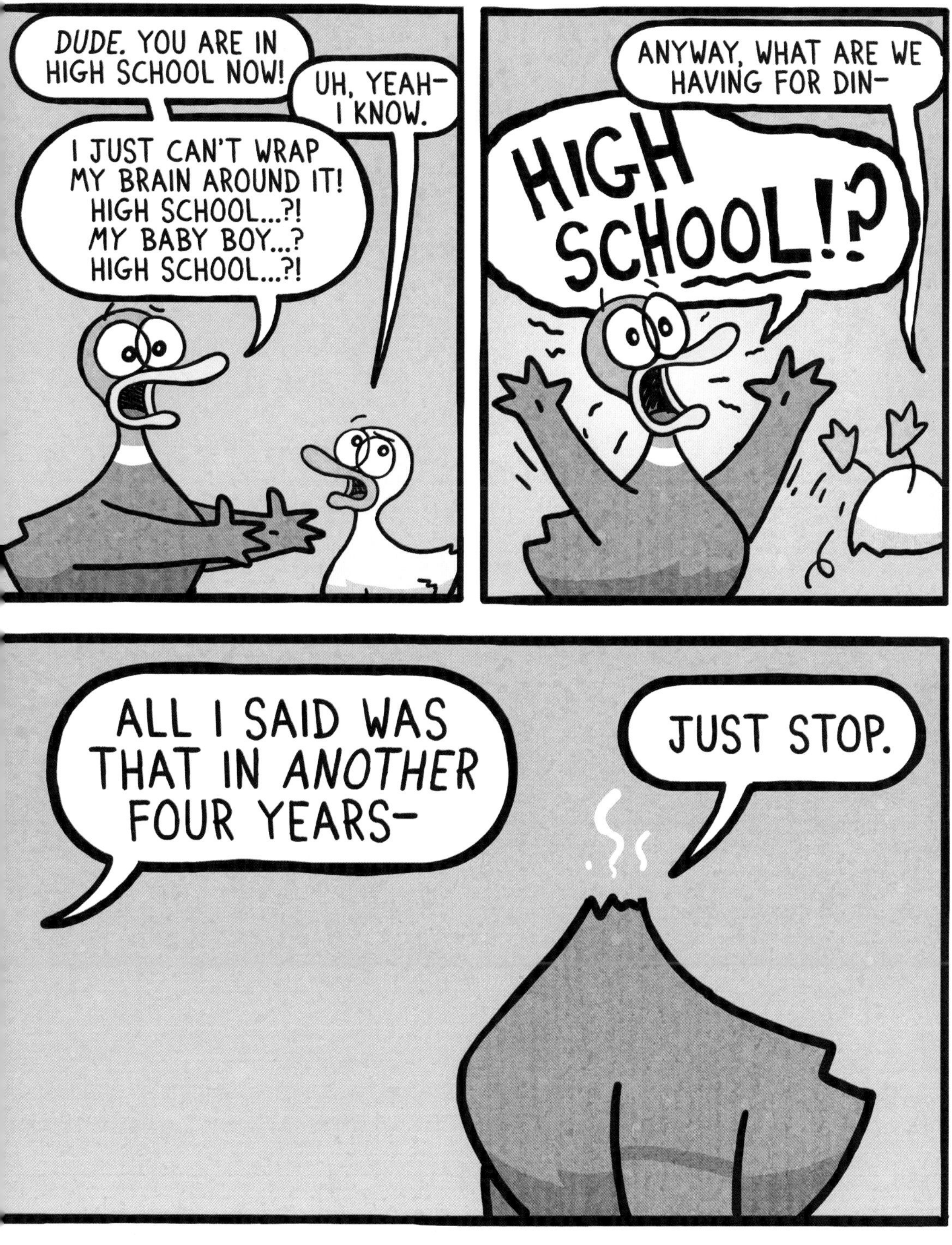
DUDE. YOU ARE IN HIGH SCHOOL NOW!
UH, YEAH– I KNOW.
I JUST CAN'T WRAP MY BRAIN AROUND IT! HIGH SCHOOL...?! MY BABY BOY...? HIGH SCHOOL...?!
ANYWAY, WHAT ARE WE HAVING FOR DIN–
HIGH SCHOOL!?
ALL I SAID WAS THAT IN ANOTHER FOUR YEARS–
JUST STOP.

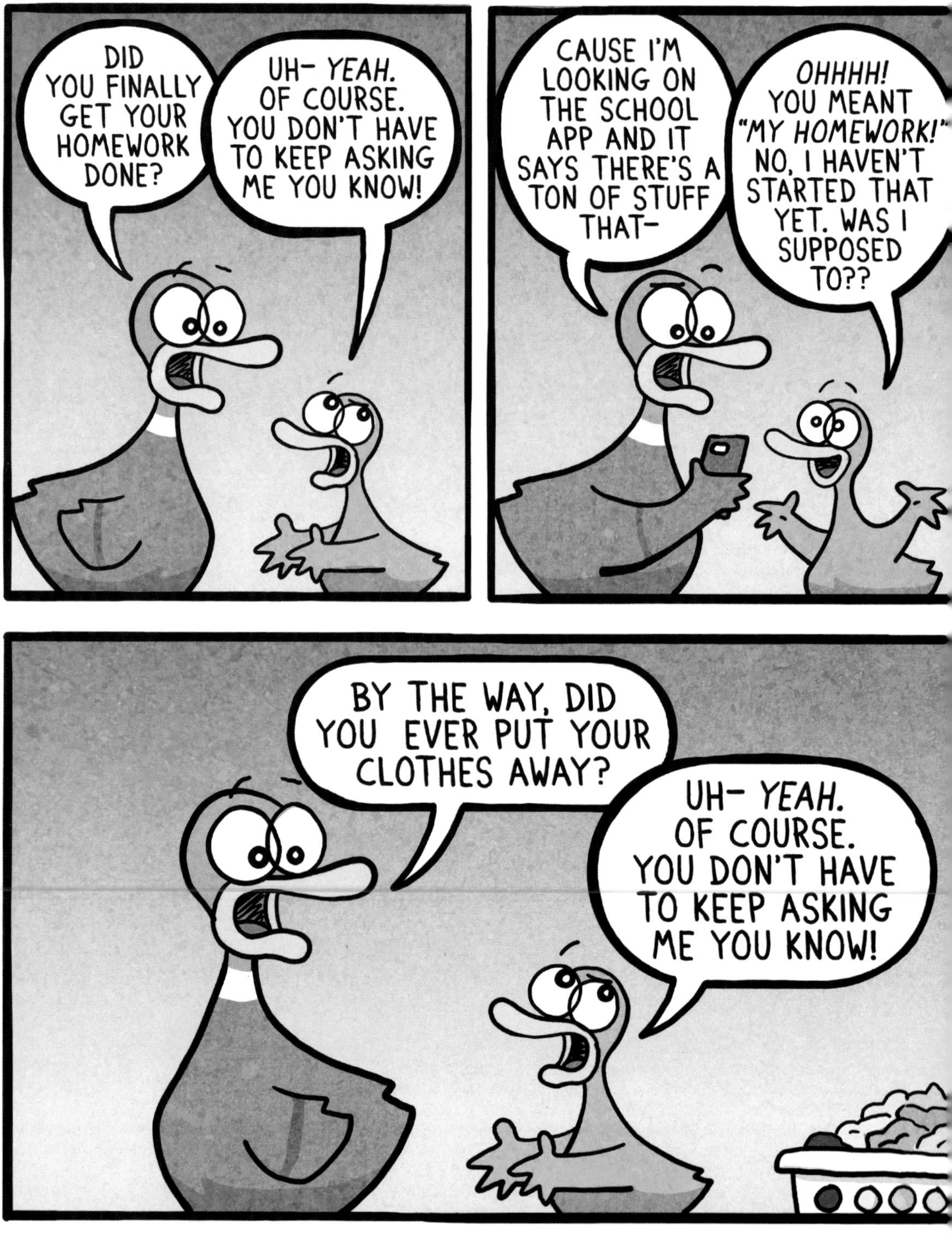
DID YOU FINALLY GET YOUR HOMEWORK DONE?
UH– *YEAH.* OF COURSE. YOU DON'T HAVE TO KEEP ASKING ME YOU KNOW!
CAUSE I'M LOOKING ON THE SCHOOL APP AND IT SAYS THERE'S A TON OF STUFF THAT–
OHHHH! YOU MEANT "*MY HOMEWORK!*" NO, I HAVEN'T STARTED THAT YET. WAS I SUPPOSED TO??
BY THE WAY, DID YOU EVER PUT YOUR CLOTHES AWAY?
UH– *YEAH.* OF COURSE. YOU DON'T HAVE TO KEEP ASKING ME YOU KNOW!

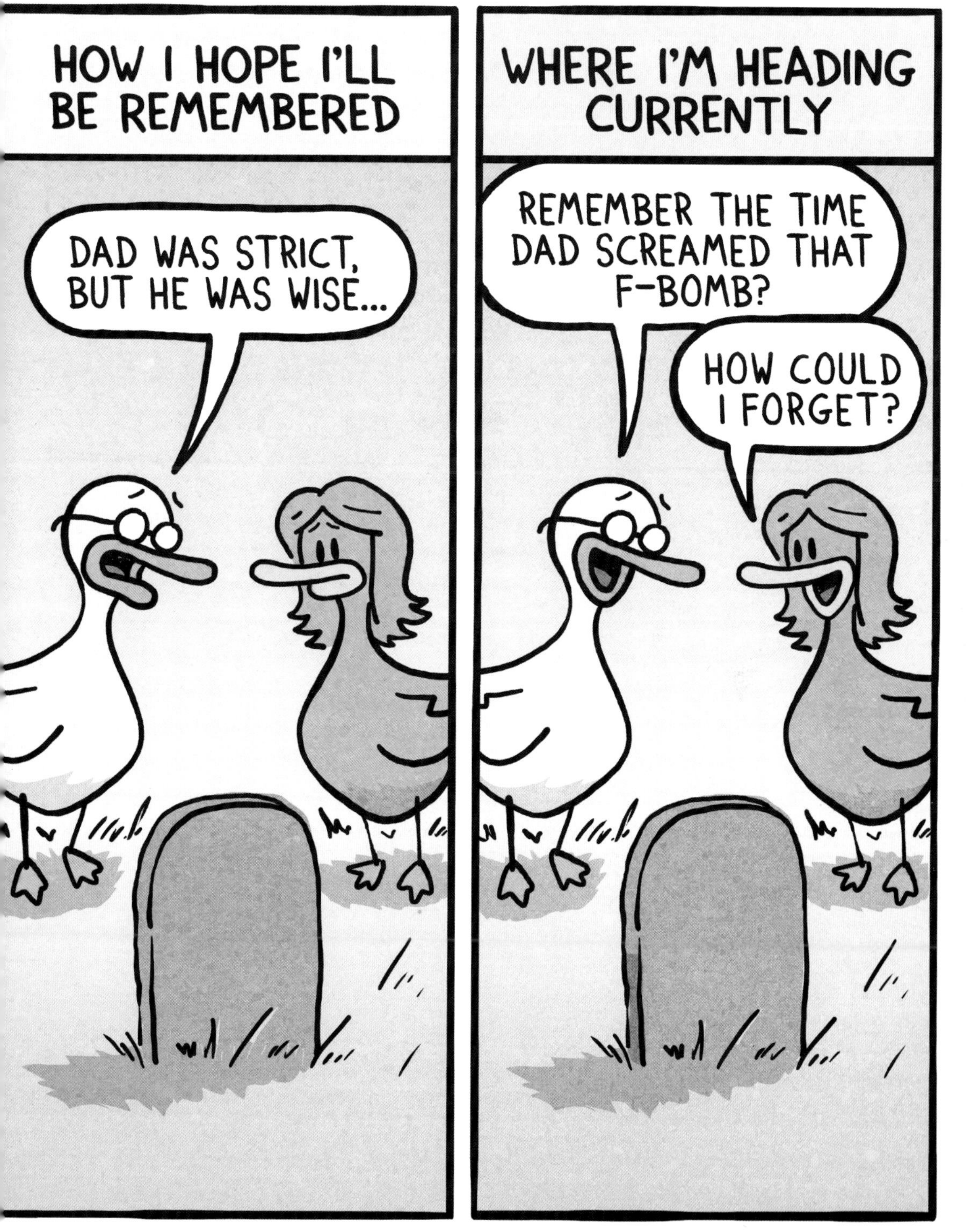
HOW I HOPE I'LL BE REMEMBERED
DAD WAS STRICT, BUT HE WAS WISE...
WHERE I'M HEADING CURRENTLY
REMEMBER THE TIME DAD SCREAMED THAT F-BOMB?
HOW COULD I FORGET?

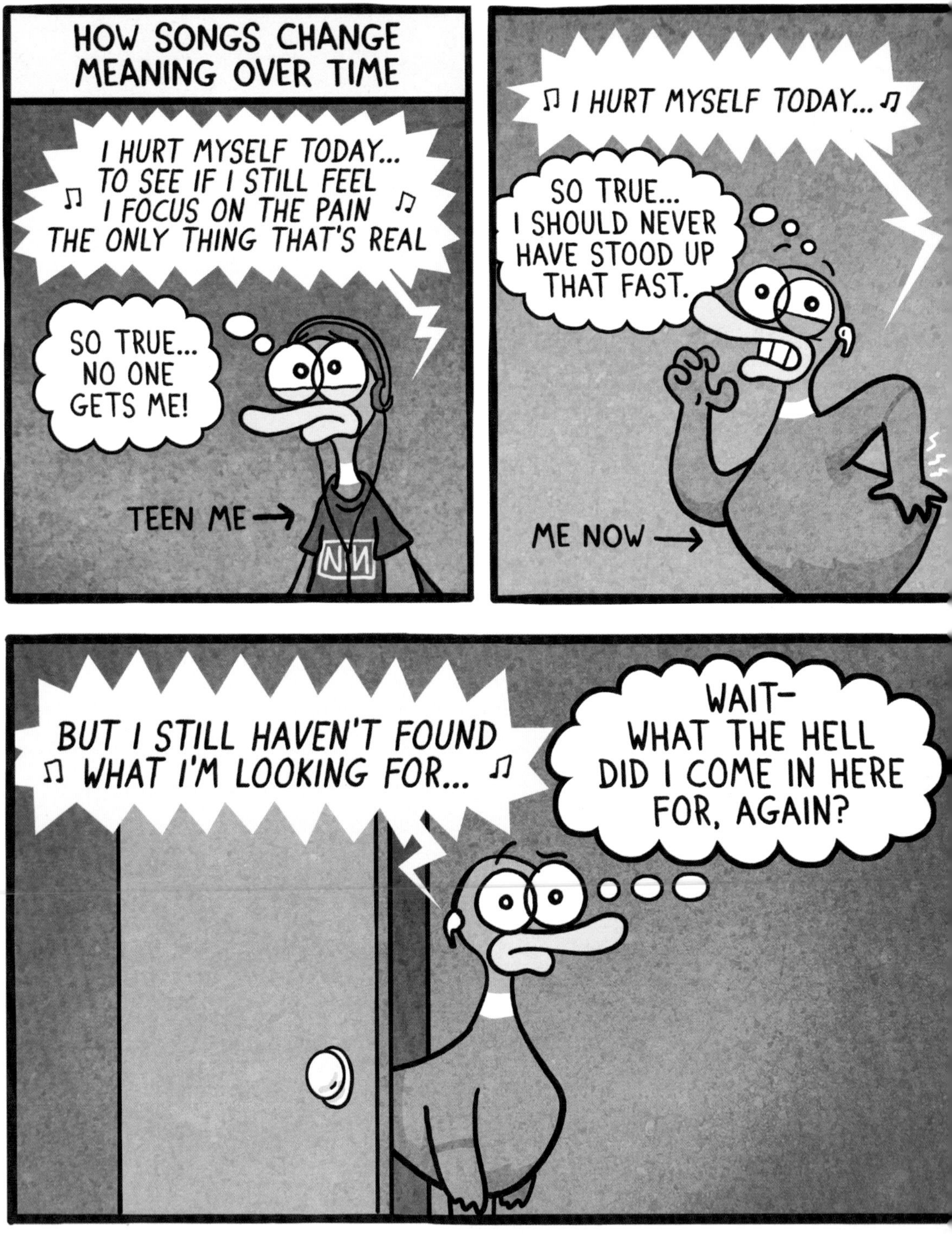
HOW SONGS CHANGE MEANING OVER TIME
♫ I HURT MYSELF TODAY... TO SEE IF I STILL FEEL I FOCUS ON THE PAIN THE ONLY THING THAT'S REAL ♫
SO TRUE... NO ONE GETS ME!
TEEN ME →
NIN
♫ I HURT MYSELF TODAY... ♫
SO TRUE... I SHOULD NEVER HAVE STOOD UP THAT FAST.
ME NOW →
BUT I STILL HAVEN'T FOUND ♫ WHAT I'M LOOKING FOR... ♫
WAIT- WHAT THE HELL DID I COME IN HERE FOR, AGAIN?

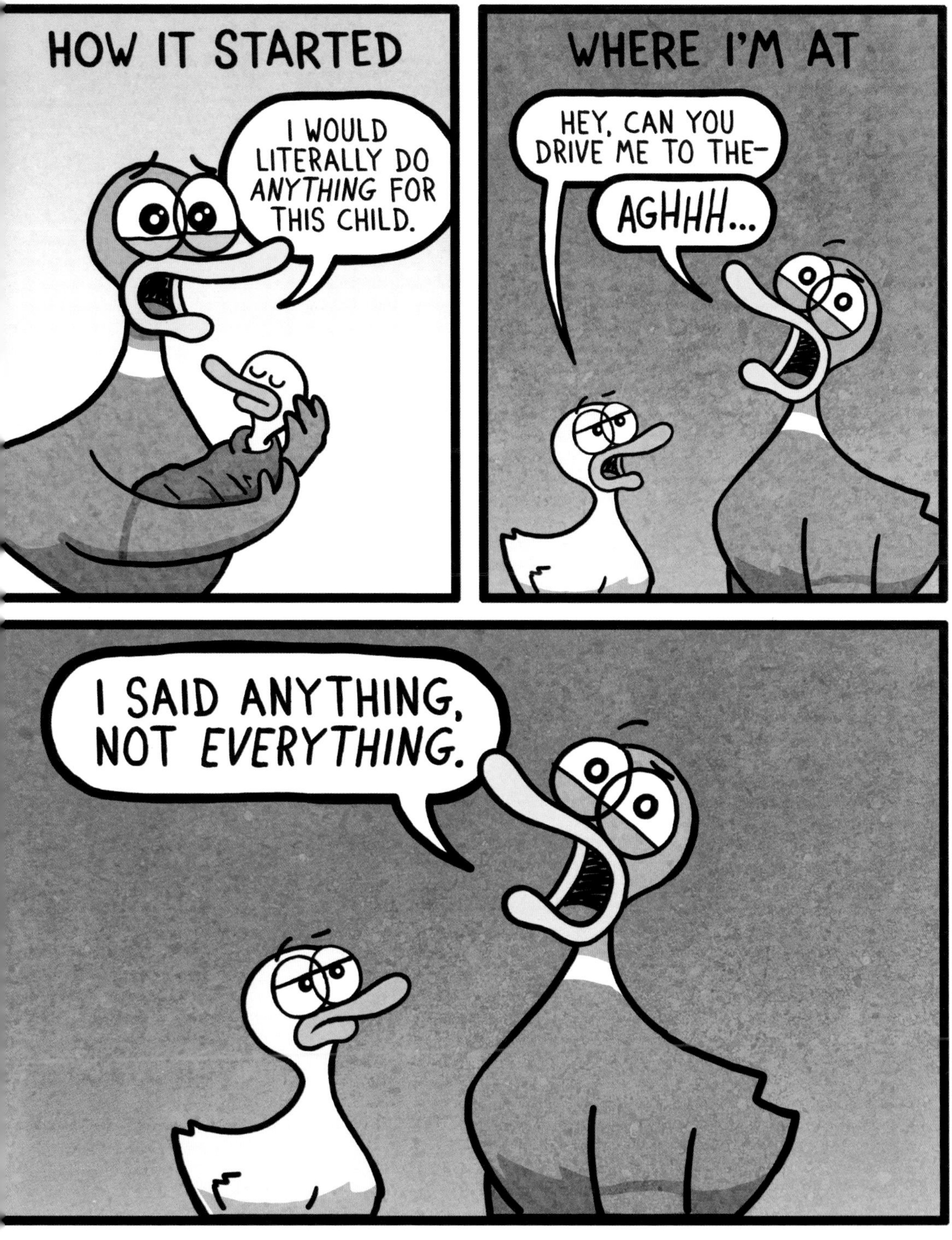
HOW IT STARTED
I WOULD LITERALLY DO ANYTHING FOR THIS CHILD.
WHERE I'M AT
HEY, CAN YOU DRIVE ME TO THE-
AGHHH...
I SAID ANYTHING, NOT EVERYTHING.

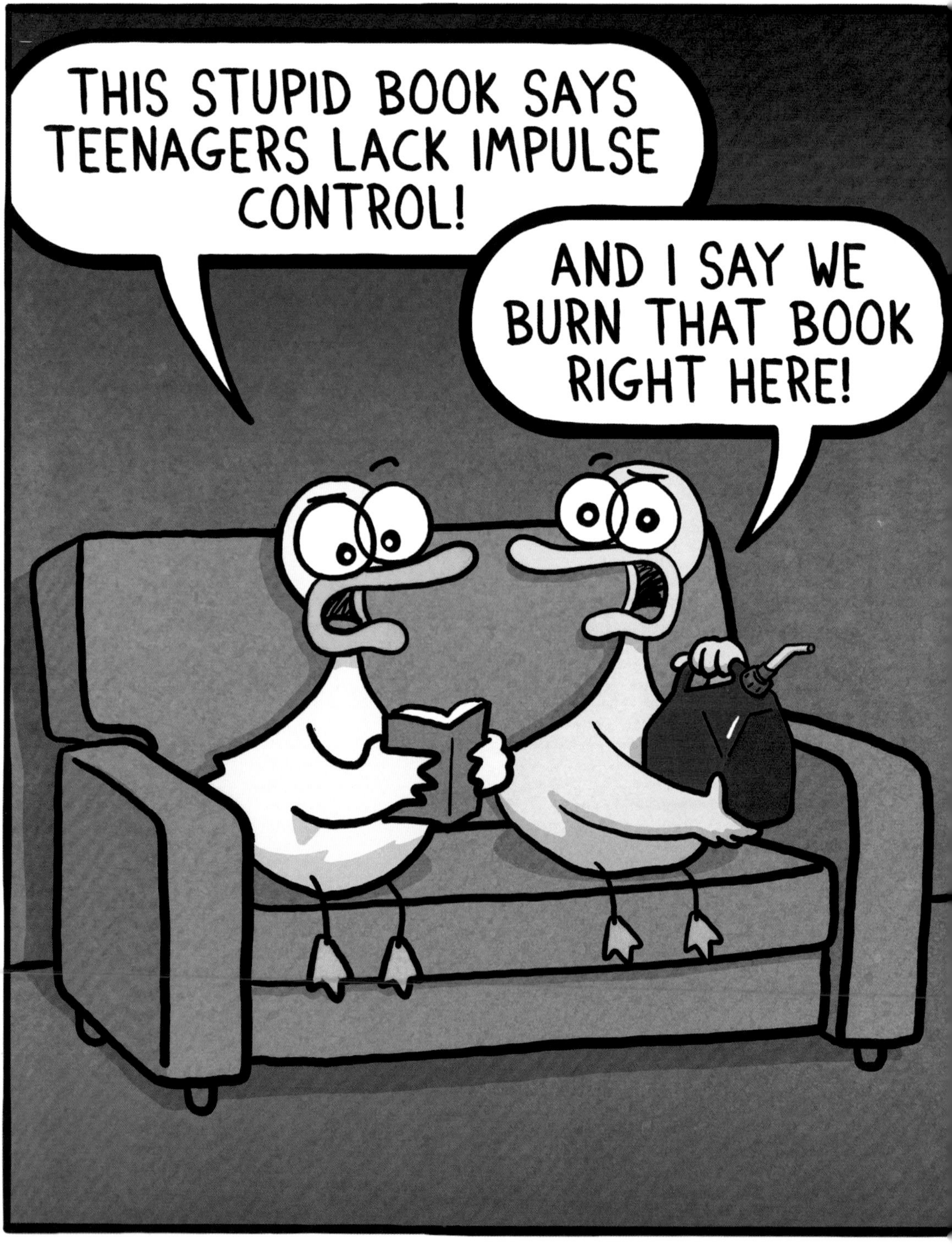
THIS STUPID BOOK SAYS TEENAGERS LACK IMPULSE CONTROL!
AND I SAY WE BURN THAT BOOK RIGHT HERE!

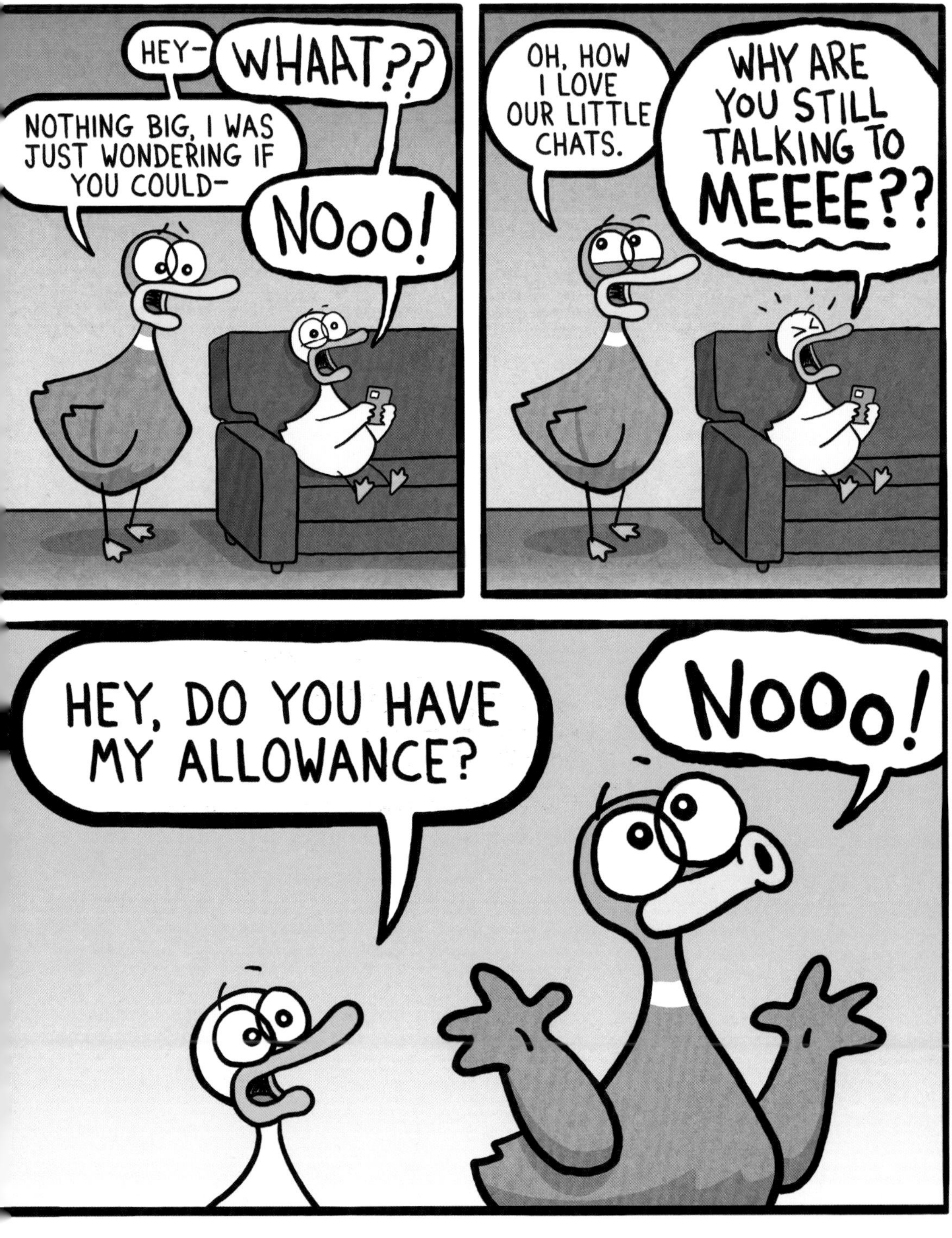
HEY-
WHAAT??
NOTHING BIG, I WAS JUST WONDERING IF YOU COULD-
NOoo!
OH, HOW I LOVE OUR LITTLE CHATS.
WHY ARE YOU STILL TALKING TO MEEEE??
HEY, DO YOU HAVE MY ALLOWANCE?
NOOo!

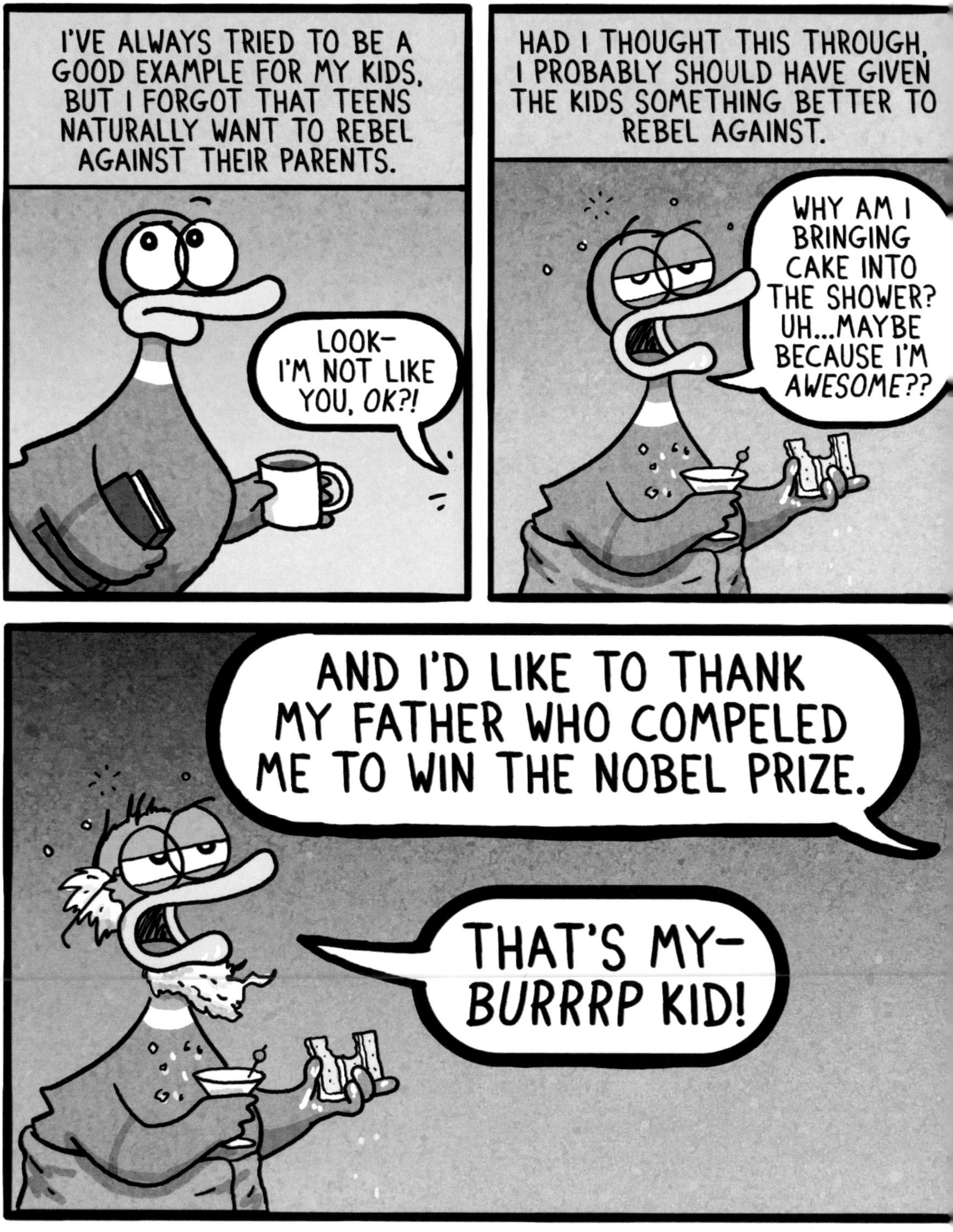
I'VE ALWAYS TRIED TO BE A GOOD EXAMPLE FOR MY KIDS, BUT I FORGOT THAT TEENS NATURALLY WANT TO REBEL AGAINST THEIR PARENTS.
LOOK— I'M NOT LIKE YOU, *OK?!*
HAD I THOUGHT THIS THROUGH, I PROBABLY SHOULD HAVE GIVEN THE KIDS SOMETHING BETTER TO REBEL AGAINST.
WHY AM I BRINGING CAKE INTO THE SHOWER? UH...MAYBE BECAUSE I'M *AWESOME??*
AND I'D LIKE TO THANK MY FATHER WHO COMPELED ME TO WIN THE NOBEL PRIZE.
THAT'S MY— *BURRRP* KID!

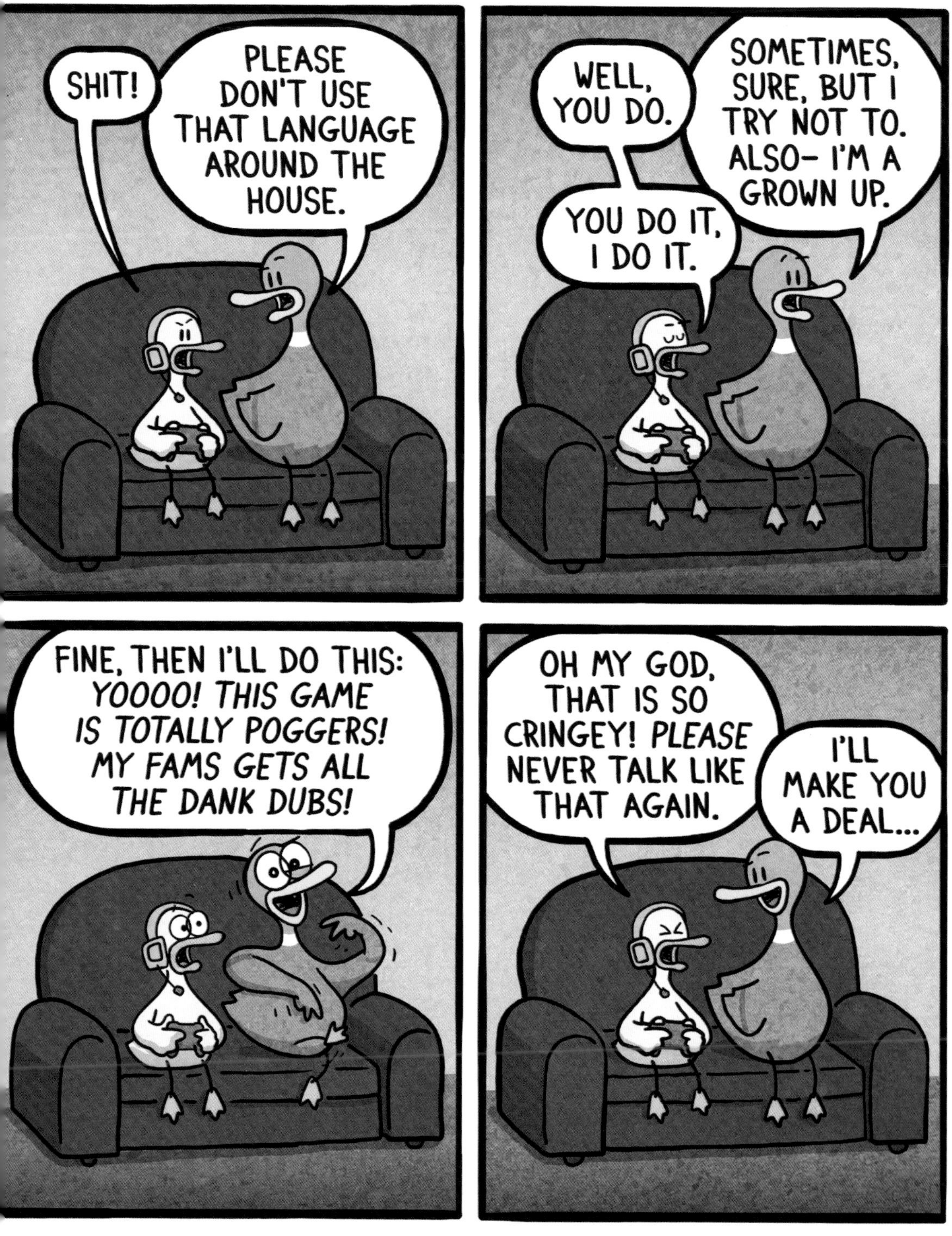
SHIT!
PLEASE DON'T USE THAT LANGUAGE AROUND THE HOUSE.
WELL, YOU DO.
YOU DO IT, I DO IT.
SOMETIMES, SURE, BUT I TRY NOT TO. ALSO– I'M A GROWN UP.
FINE, THEN I'LL DO THIS: *YOOOO! THIS GAME IS TOTALLY POGGERS! MY FAMS GETS ALL THE DANK DUBS!*
OH MY GOD, THAT IS SO CRINGEY! *PLEASE* NEVER TALK LIKE THAT AGAIN.
I'LL MAKE YOU A DEAL...

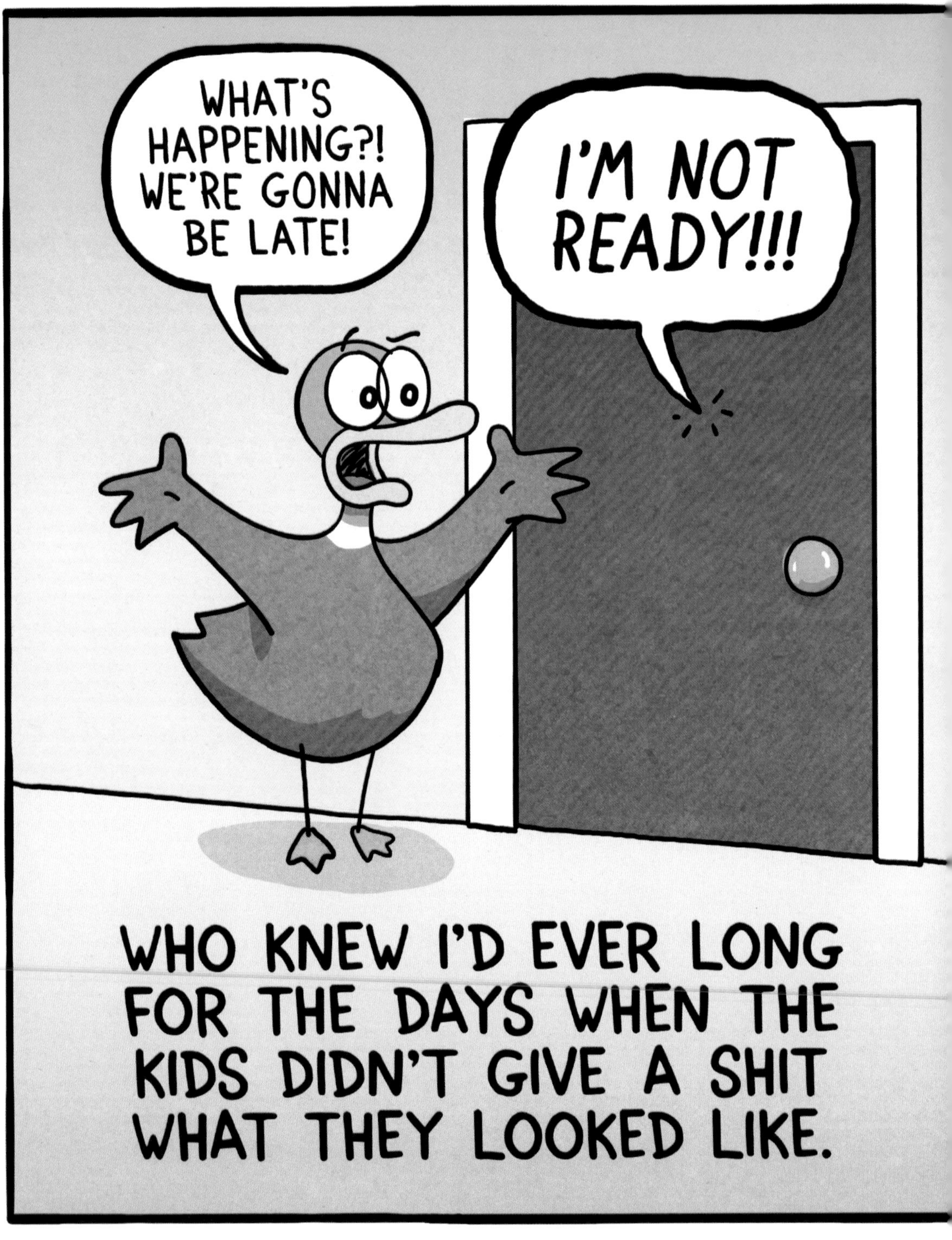
WHAT'S HAPPENING?! WE'RE GONNA BE LATE!
I'M NOT READY!!!
WHO KNEW I'D EVER LONG FOR THE DAYS WHEN THE KIDS DIDN'T GIVE A SHIT WHAT THEY LOOKED LIKE.

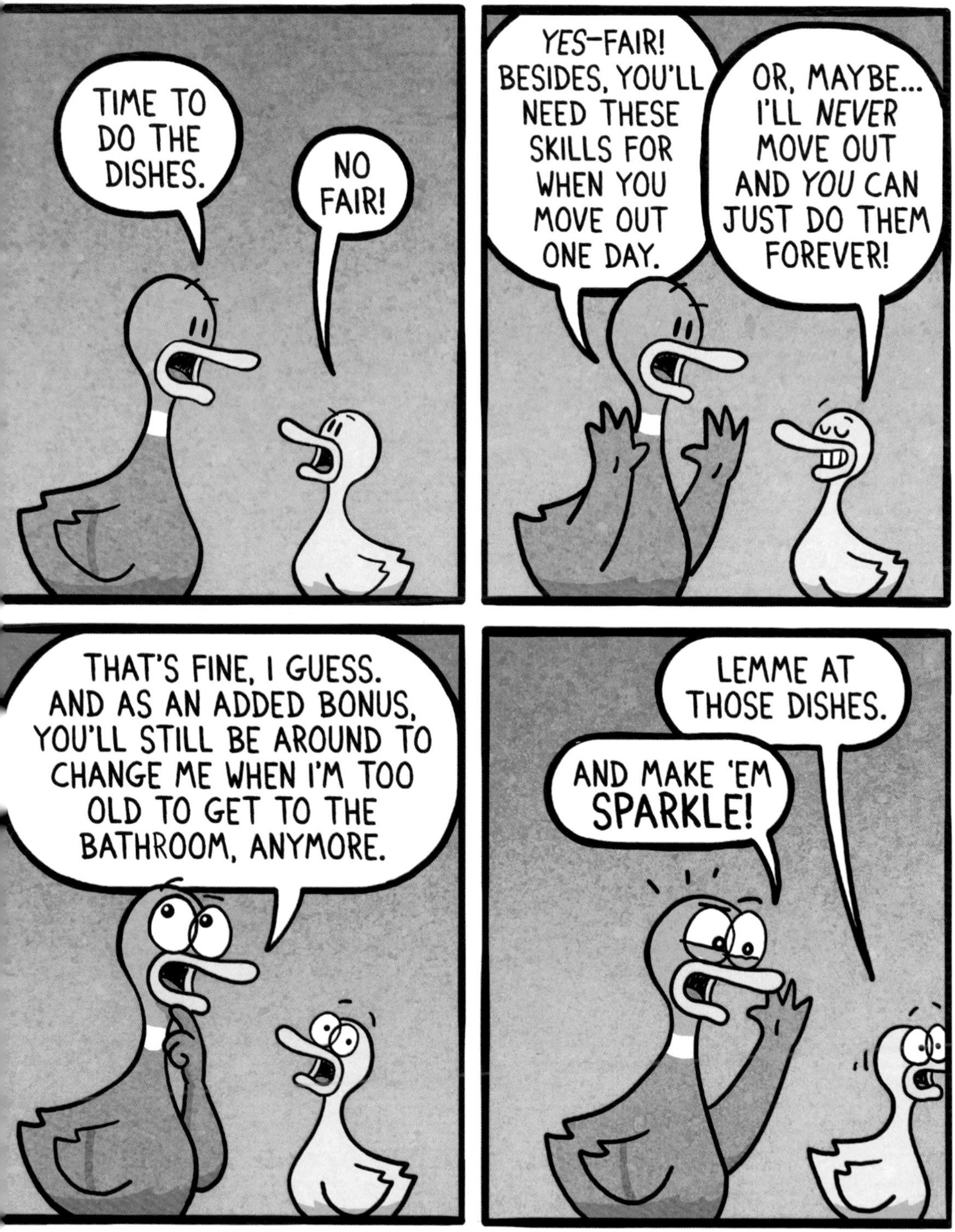
TIME TO DO THE DISHES.
NO FAIR!
YES—FAIR! BESIDES, YOU'LL NEED THESE SKILLS FOR WHEN YOU MOVE OUT ONE DAY.
OR, MAYBE... I'LL NEVER MOVE OUT AND YOU CAN JUST DO THEM FOREVER!
THAT'S FINE, I GUESS. AND AS AN ADDED BONUS, YOU'LL STILL BE AROUND TO CHANGE ME WHEN I'M TOO OLD TO GET TO THE BATHROOM, ANYMORE.
LEMME AT THOSE DISHES.
AND MAKE 'EM SPARKLE!

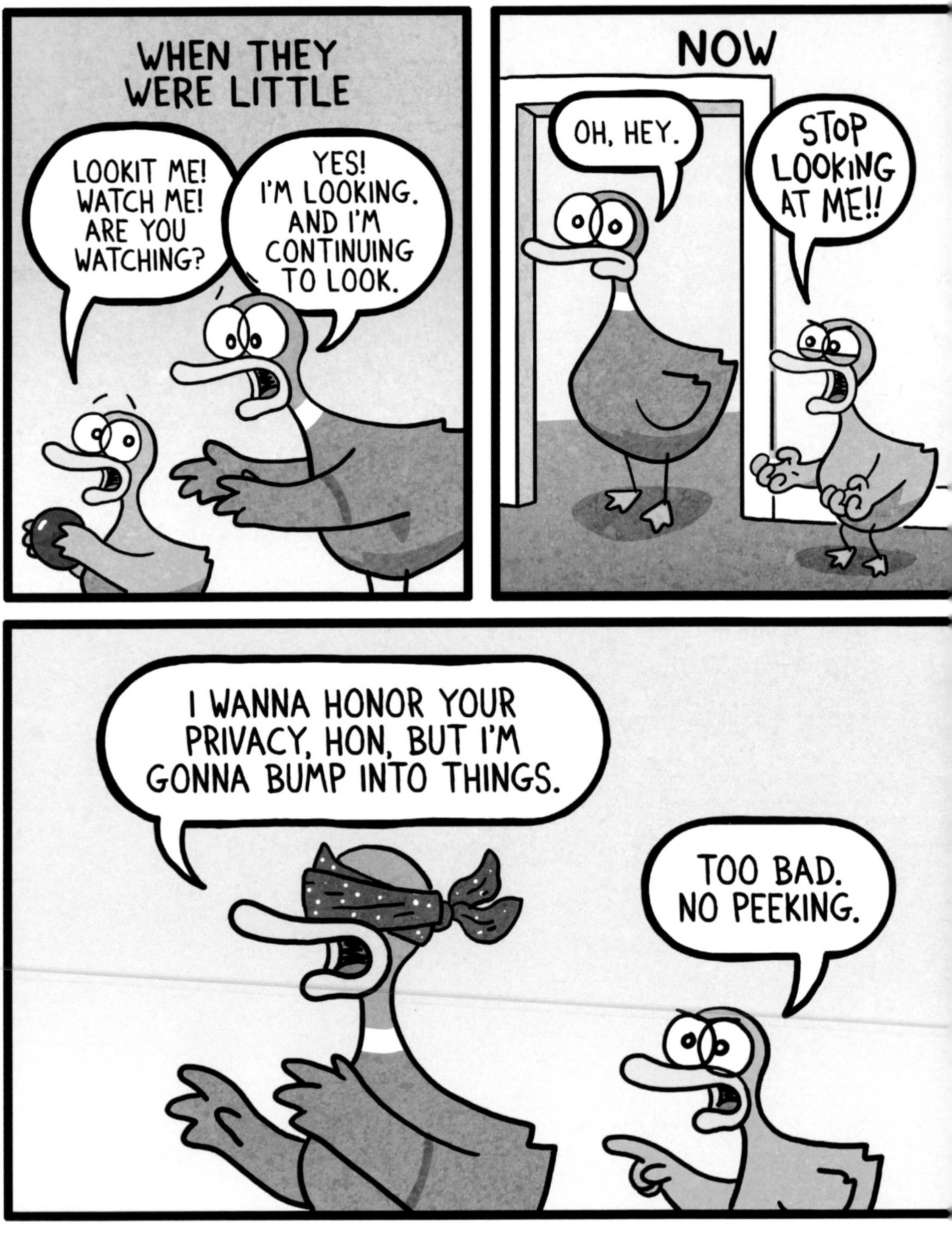
WHEN THEY WERE LITTLE
LOOKIT ME! WATCH ME! ARE YOU WATCHING?
YES! I'M LOOKING. AND I'M CONTINUING TO LOOK.
NOW
OH, HEY.
STOP LOOKING AT ME!!
I WANNA HONOR YOUR PRIVACY, HON, BUT I'M GONNA BUMP INTO THINGS.
TOO BAD. NO PEEKING.

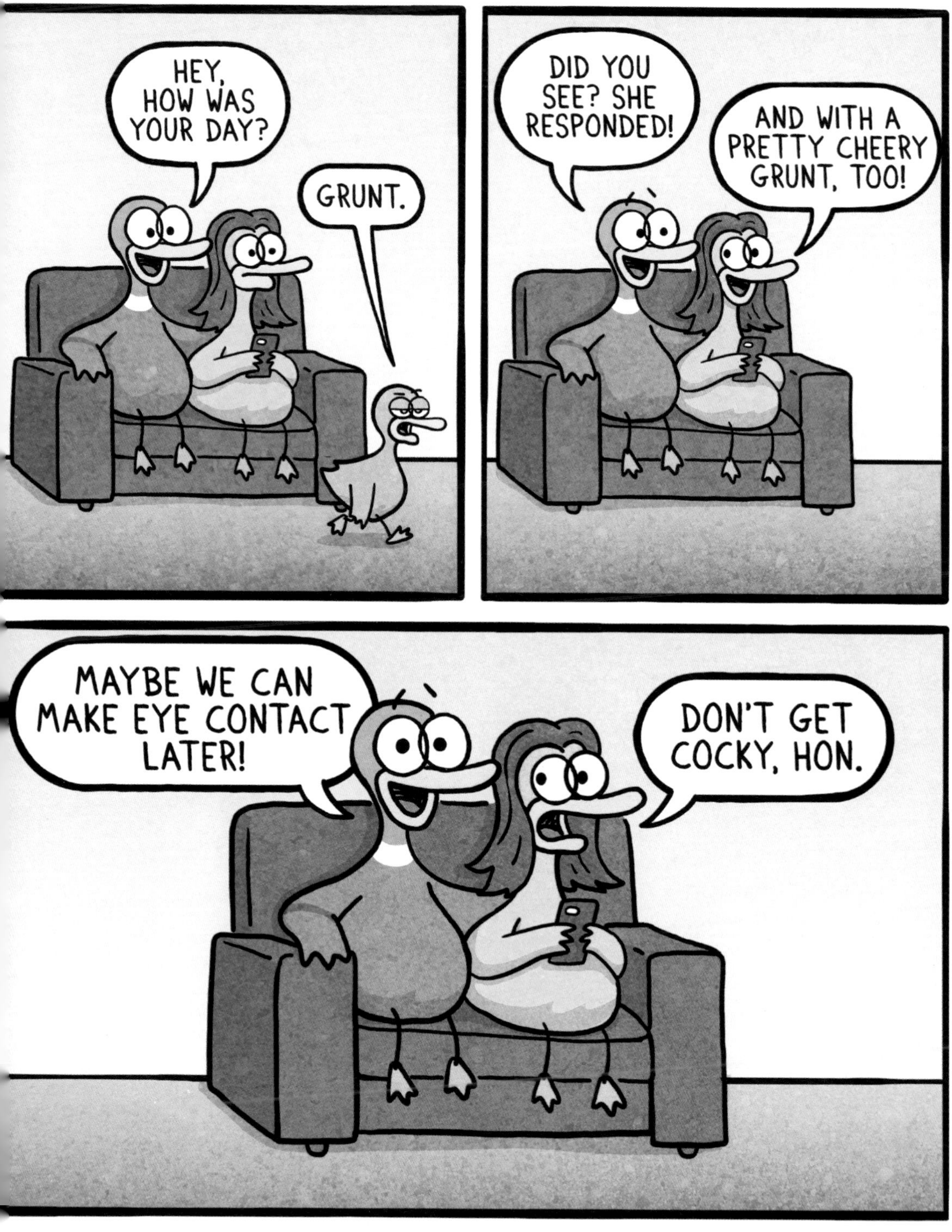
HEY, HOW WAS YOUR DAY?
GRUNT.
DID YOU SEE? SHE RESPONDED!
AND WITH A PRETTY CHEERY GRUNT, TOO!
MAYBE WE CAN MAKE EYE CONTACT LATER!
DON'T GET COCKY, HON.

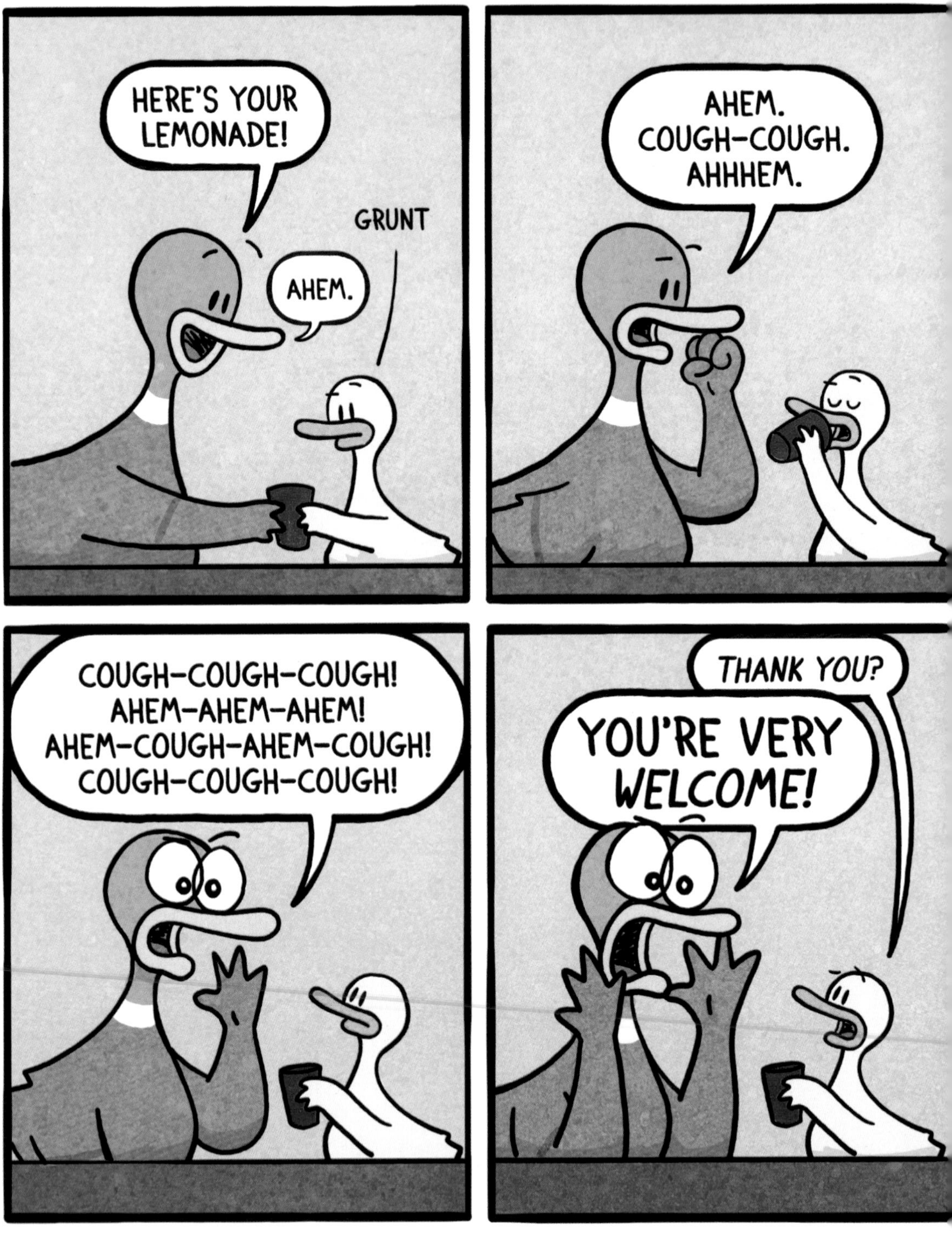
HERE'S YOUR LEMONADE!
AHEM.
GRUNT
AHEM. COUGH-COUGH. AHHHEM.
COUGH-COUGH-COUGH! AHEM-AHEM-AHEM! AHEM-COUGH-AHEM-COUGH! COUGH-COUGH-COUGH!
THANK YOU?
YOU'RE VERY WELCOME!

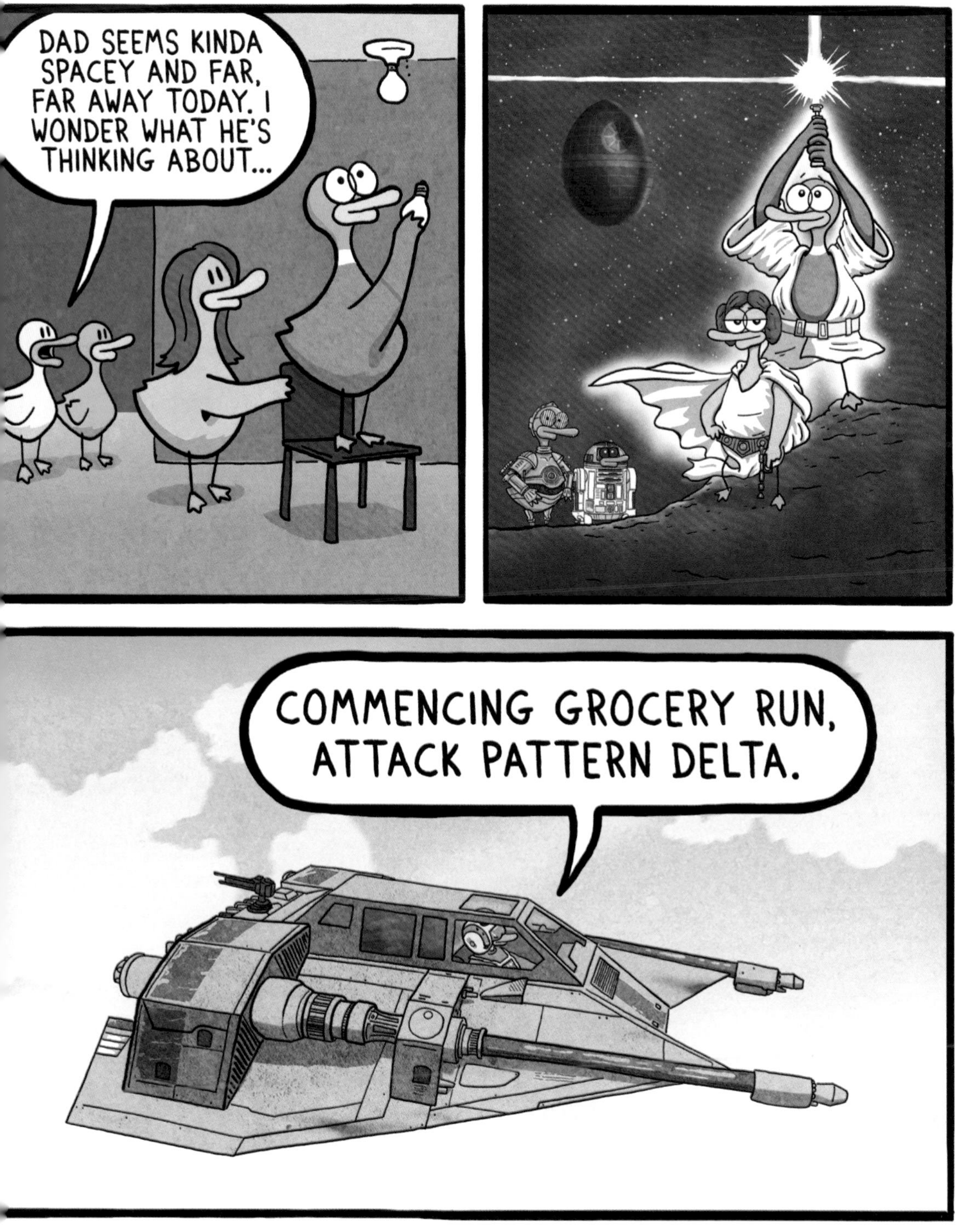
DAD SEEMS KINDA SPACEY AND FAR, FAR AWAY TODAY. I WONDER WHAT HE'S THINKING ABOUT...
COMMENCING GROCERY RUN, ATTACK PATTERN DELTA.

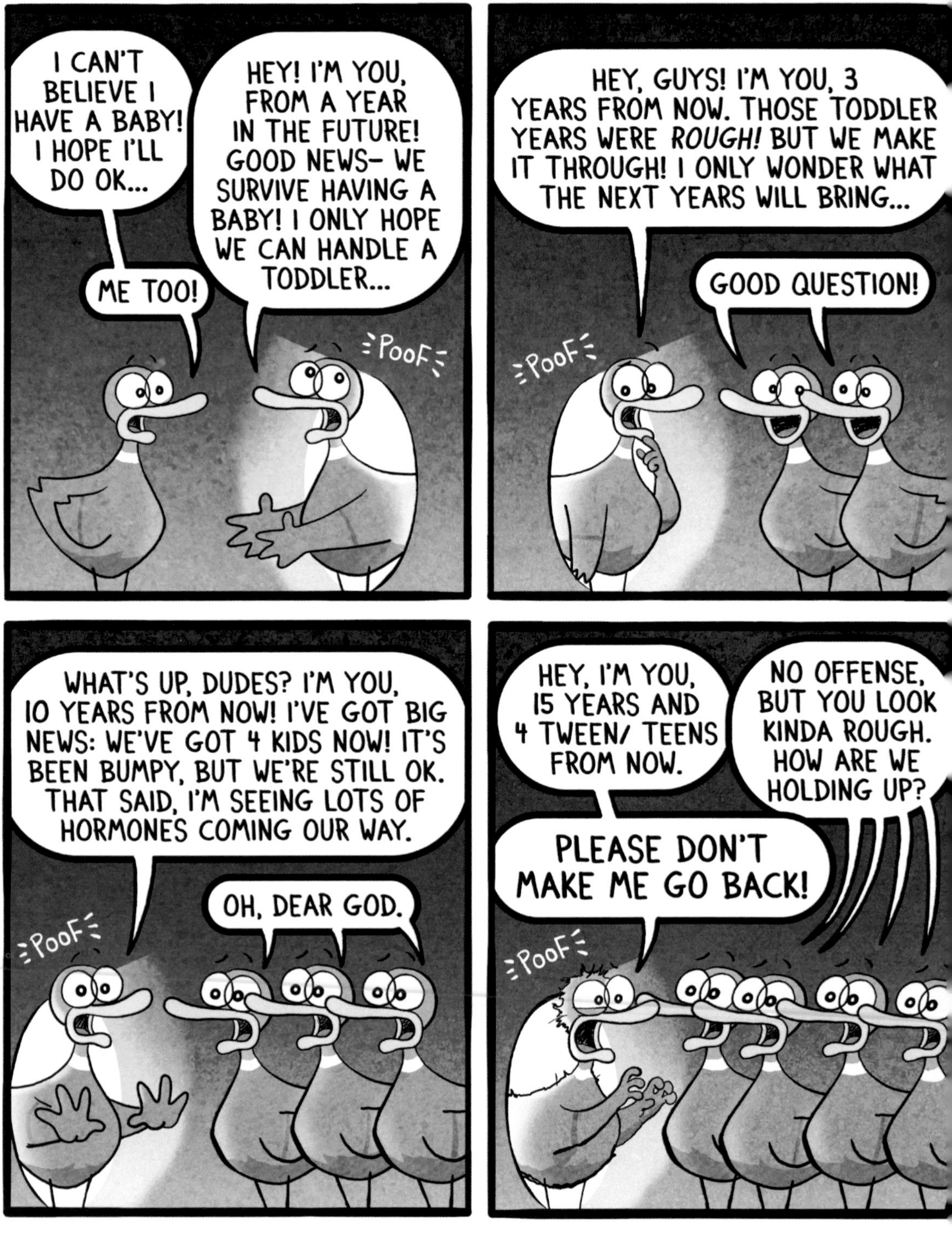
I CAN'T BELIEVE I HAVE A BABY! I HOPE I'LL DO OK...
ME TOO!
HEY! I'M YOU, FROM A YEAR IN THE FUTURE! GOOD NEWS- WE SURVIVE HAVING A BABY! I ONLY HOPE WE CAN HANDLE A TODDLER...
POOF
HEY, GUYS! I'M YOU, 3 YEARS FROM NOW. THOSE TODDLER YEARS WERE *ROUGH!* BUT WE MAKE IT THROUGH! I ONLY WONDER WHAT THE NEXT YEARS WILL BRING...
POOF
GOOD QUESTION!
WHAT'S UP, DUDES? I'M YOU, 10 YEARS FROM NOW! I'VE GOT BIG NEWS: WE'VE GOT 4 KIDS NOW! IT'S BEEN BUMPY, BUT WE'RE STILL OK. THAT SAID, I'M SEEING LOTS OF HORMONES COMING OUR WAY.
POOF
OH, DEAR GOD.
HEY, I'M YOU, 15 YEARS AND 4 TWEEN/ TEENS FROM NOW.
NO OFFENSE, BUT YOU LOOK KINDA ROUGH. HOW ARE WE HOLDING UP?
PLEASE DON'T MAKE ME GO BACK!
POOF

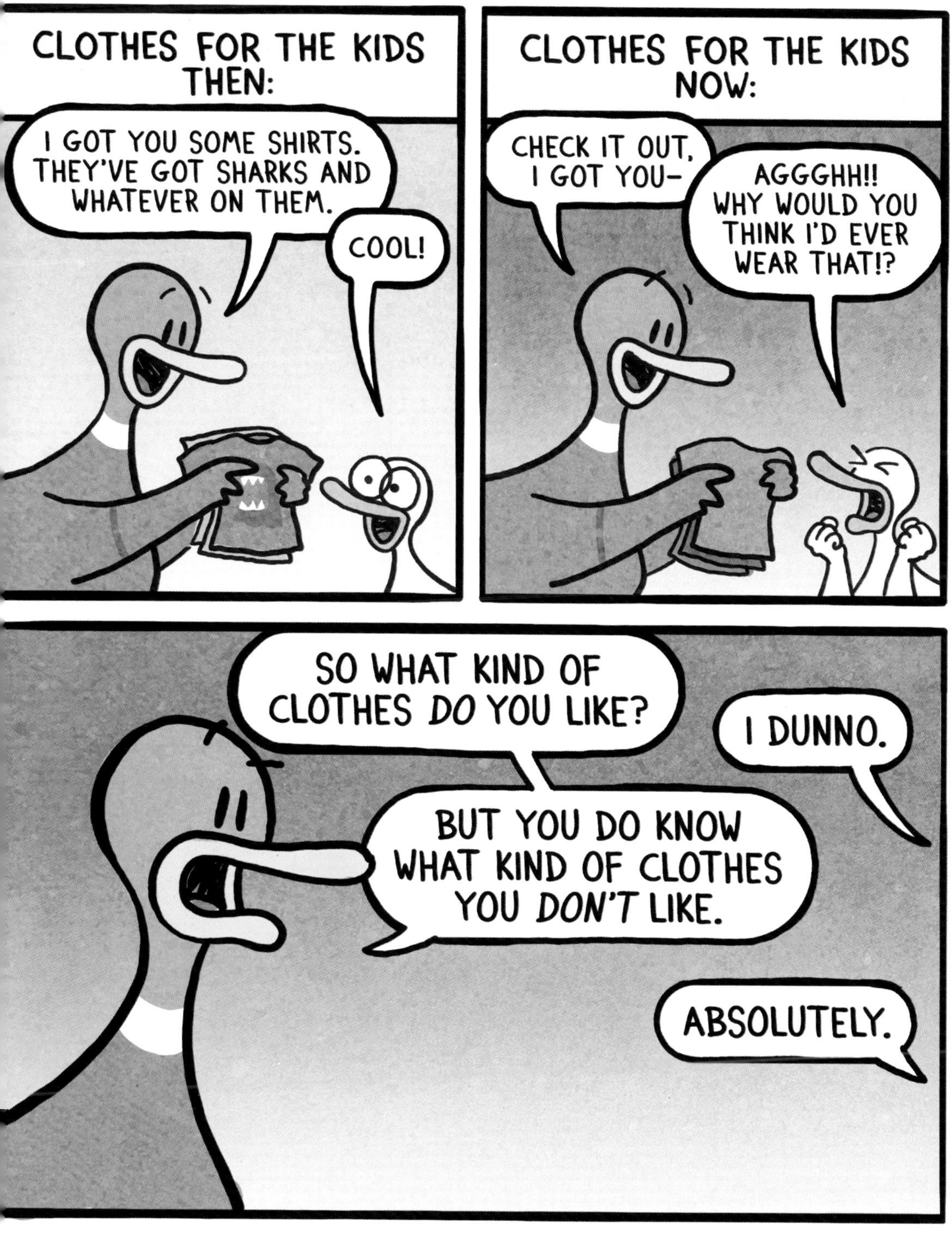

CLOTHES FOR THE KIDS THEN:
I GOT YOU SOME SHIRTS. THEY'VE GOT SHARKS AND WHATEVER ON THEM.
COOL!
CLOTHES FOR THE KIDS NOW:
CHECK IT OUT, I GOT YOU–
AGGGHH!! WHY WOULD YOU THINK I'D EVER WEAR THAT!?
SO WHAT KIND OF CLOTHES *DO* YOU LIKE?
I DUNNO.
BUT YOU DO KNOW WHAT KIND OF CLOTHES YOU *DON'T* LIKE.
ABSOLUTELY.

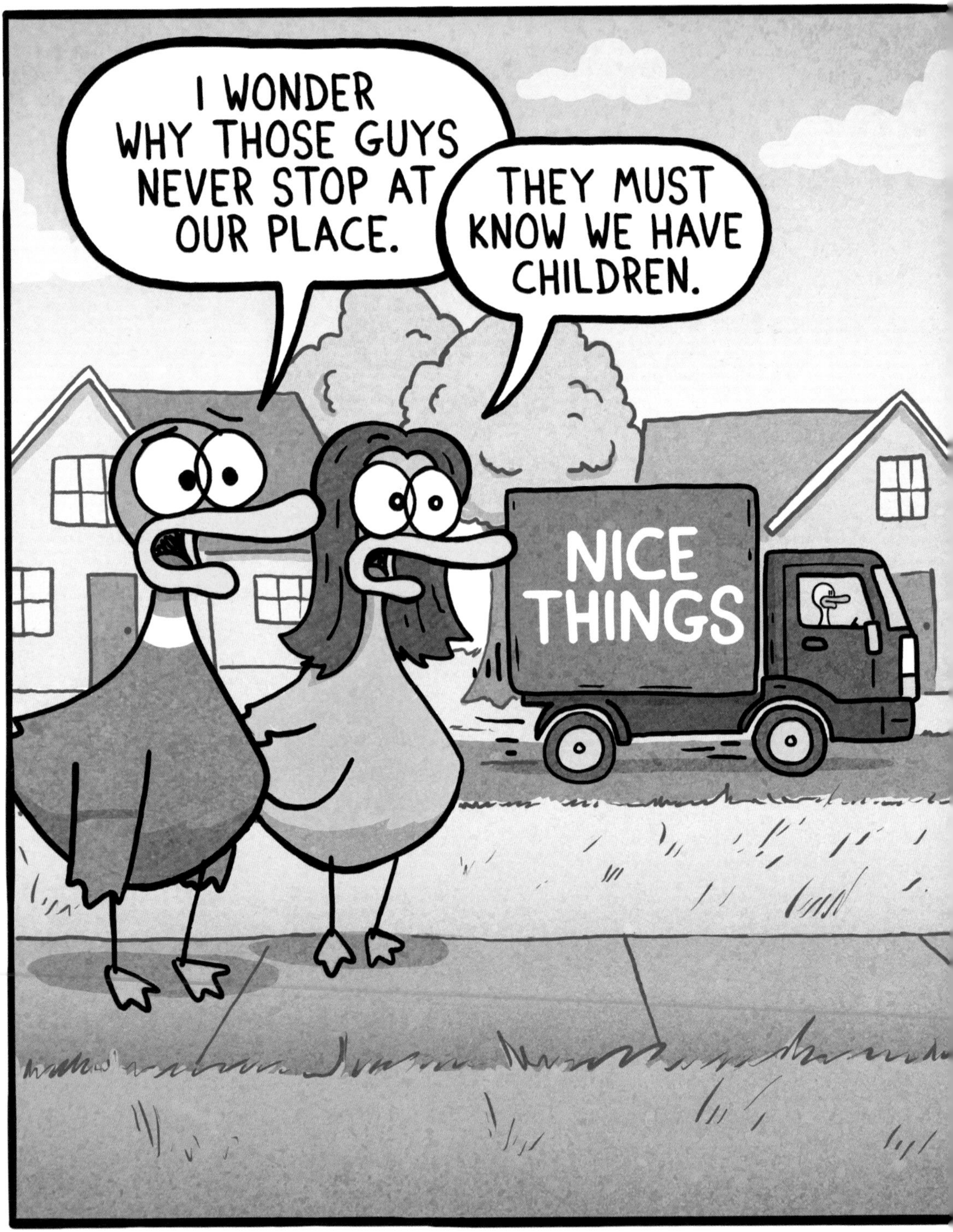
I WONDER WHY THOSE GUYS NEVER STOP AT OUR PLACE.
THEY MUST KNOW WE HAVE CHILDREN.
NICE THINGS

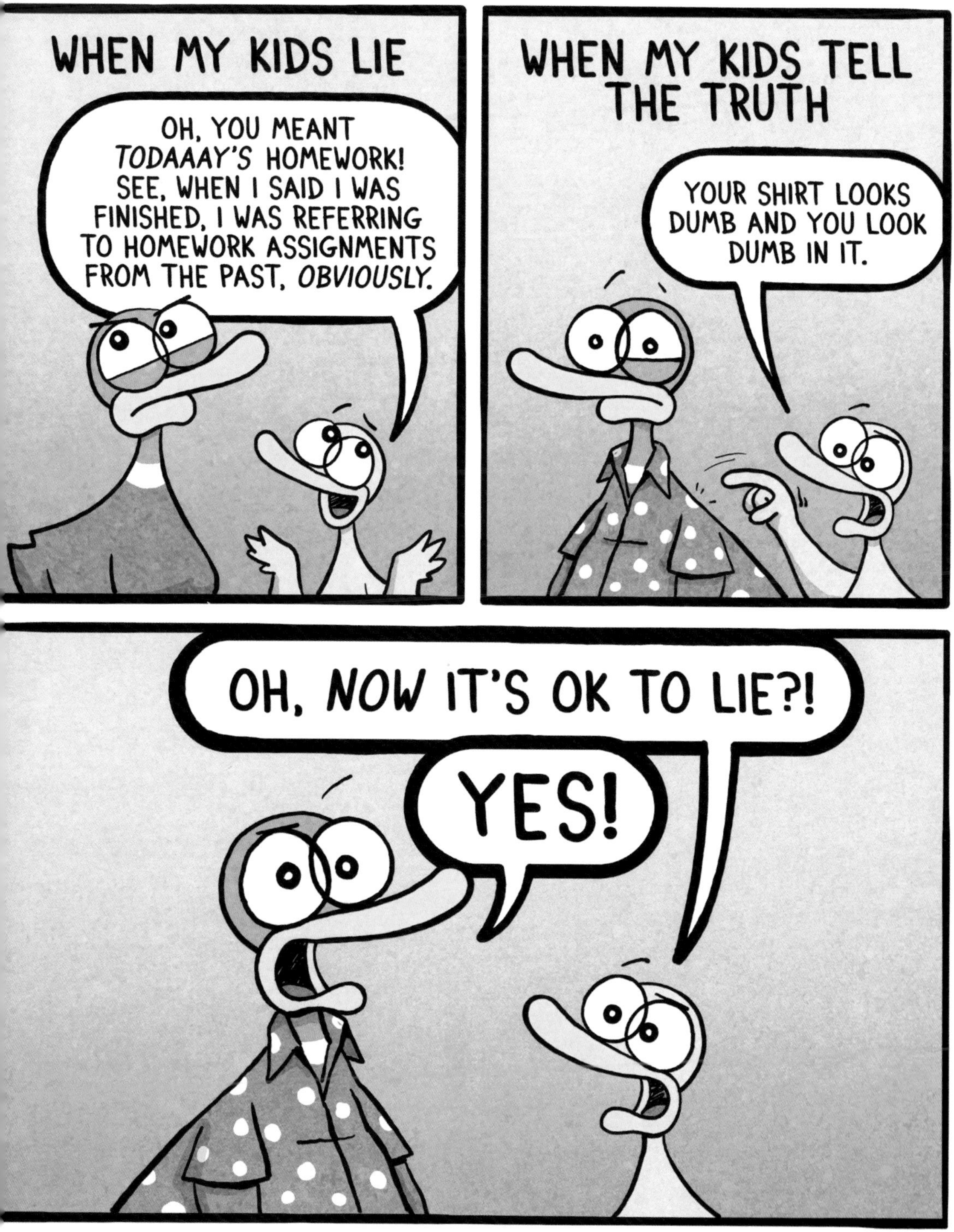
WHEN MY KIDS LIE
OH, YOU MEANT *TODAAAY'S* HOMEWORK! SEE, WHEN I SAID I WAS FINISHED, I WAS REFERRING TO HOMEWORK ASSIGNMENTS FROM THE PAST, *OBVIOUSLY.*
WHEN MY KIDS TELL THE TRUTH
YOUR SHIRT LOOKS DUMB AND YOU LOOK DUMB IN IT.
OH, *NOW* IT'S OK TO LIE?!
YES!

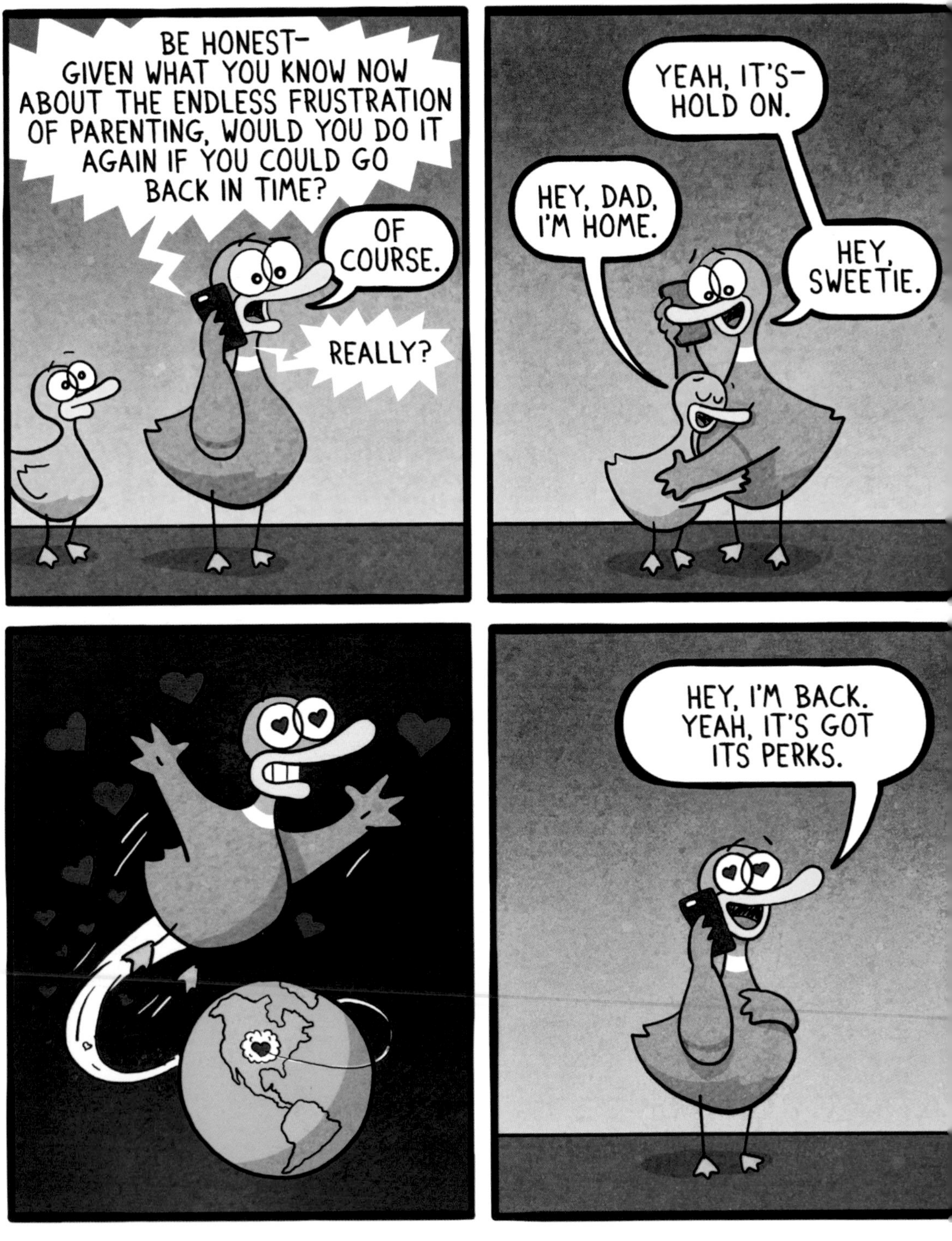
BE HONEST- GIVEN WHAT YOU KNOW NOW ABOUT THE ENDLESS FRUSTRATION OF PARENTING, WOULD YOU DO IT AGAIN IF YOU COULD GO BACK IN TIME?
OF COURSE.
REALLY?
YEAH, IT'S- HOLD ON.
HEY, DAD, I'M HOME.
HEY, SWEETIE.
HEY, I'M BACK. YEAH, IT'S GOT ITS PERKS.

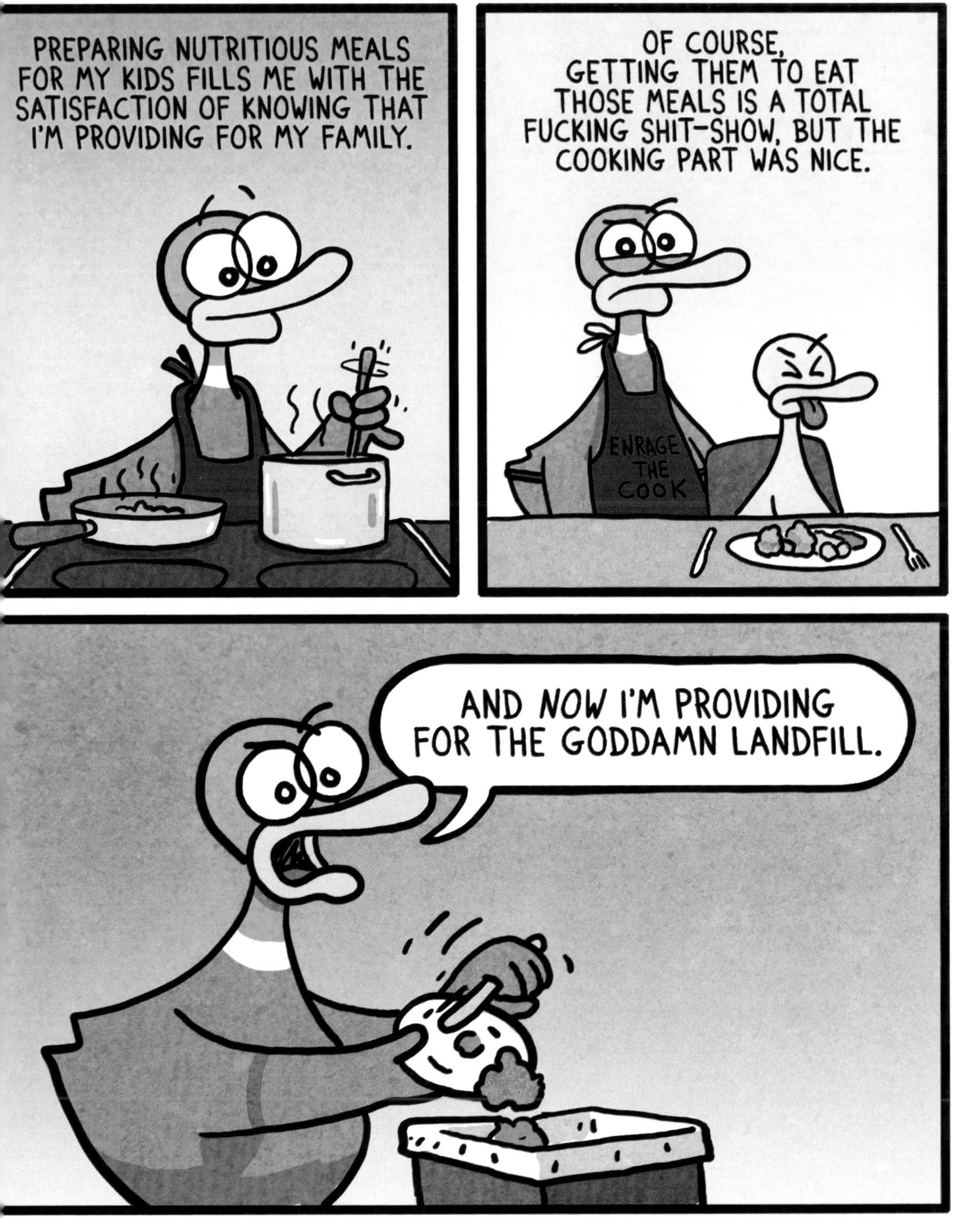
PREPARING NUTRITIOUS MEALS FOR MY KIDS FILLS ME WITH THE SATISFACTION OF KNOWING THAT I'M PROVIDING FOR MY FAMILY.
OF COURSE, GETTING THEM TO EAT THOSE MEALS IS A TOTAL FUCKING SHIT-SHOW, BUT THE COOKING PART WAS NICE.
ENRAGE THE COOK
AND NOW I'M PROVIDING FOR THE GODDAMN LANDFILL.

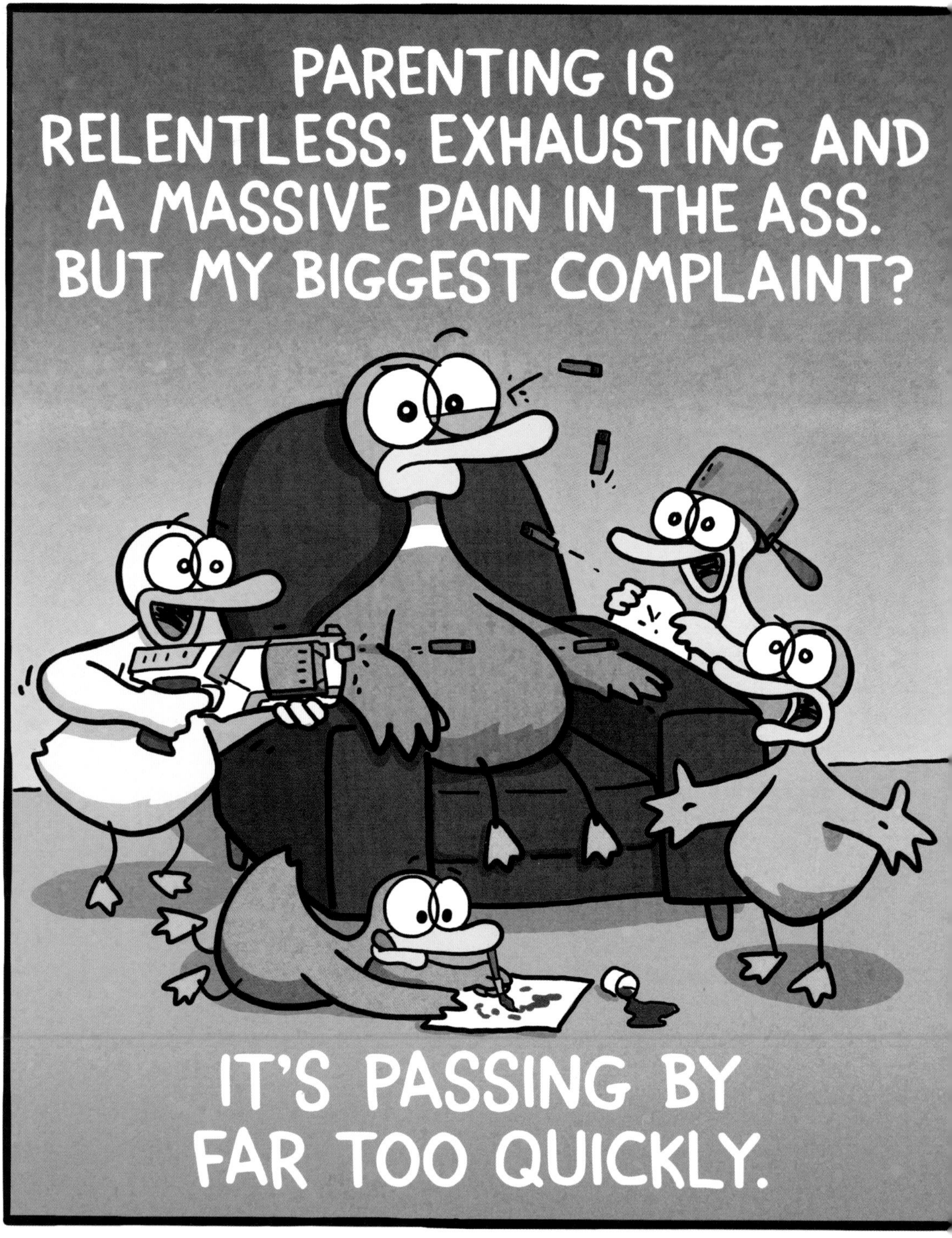
PARENTING IS RELENTLESS, EXHAUSTING AND A MASSIVE PAIN IN THE ASS. BUT MY BIGGEST COMPLAINT?
IT'S PASSING BY FAR TOO QUICKLY.

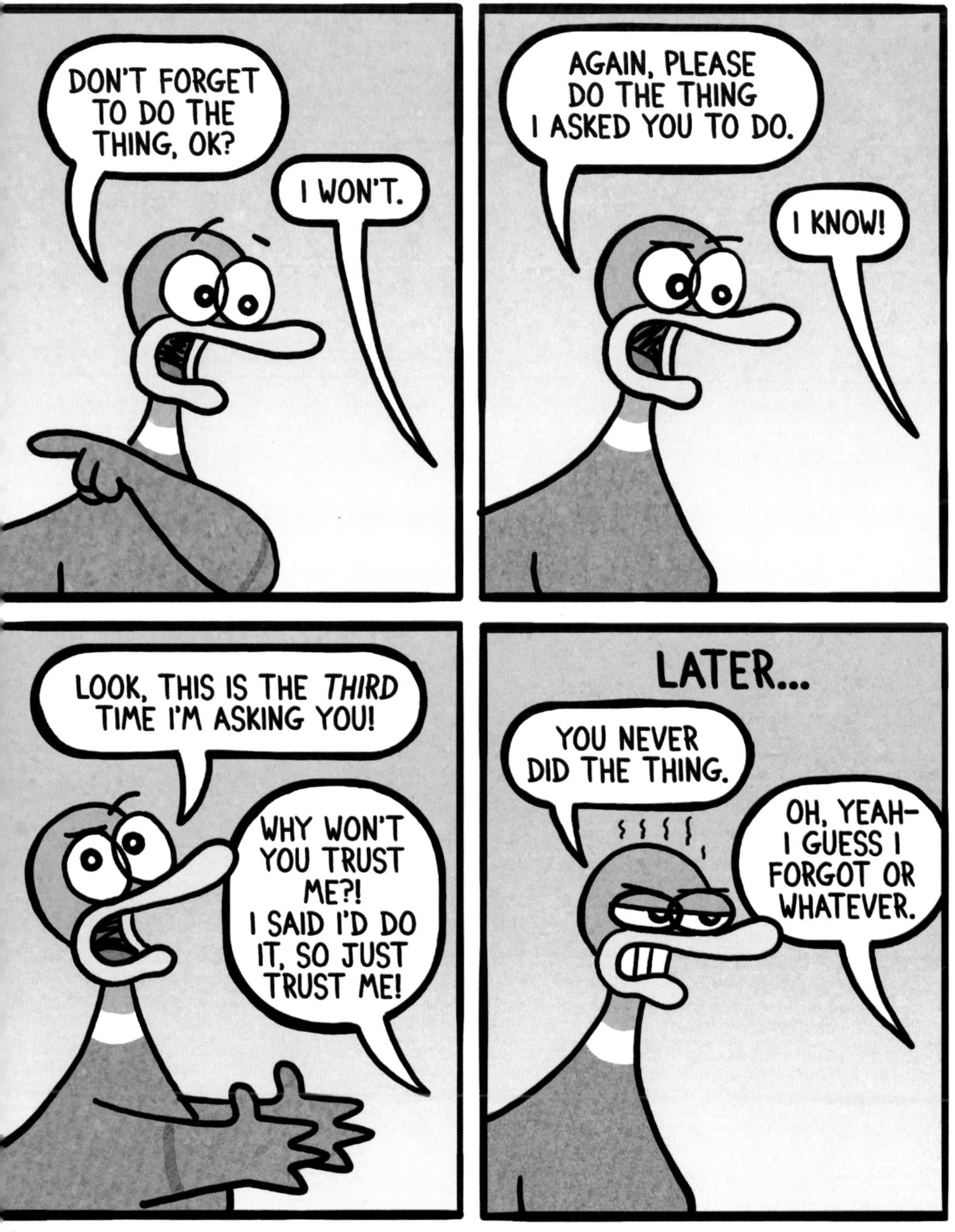
DON'T FORGET TO DO THE THING, OK?
I WON'T.
AGAIN, PLEASE DO THE THING I ASKED YOU TO DO.
I KNOW!
LOOK, THIS IS THE *THIRD* TIME I'M ASKING YOU!
WHY WON'T YOU TRUST ME?! I SAID I'D DO IT, SO JUST TRUST ME!
LATER...
YOU NEVER DID THE THING.
OH, YEAH- I GUESS I FORGOT OR WHATEVER.

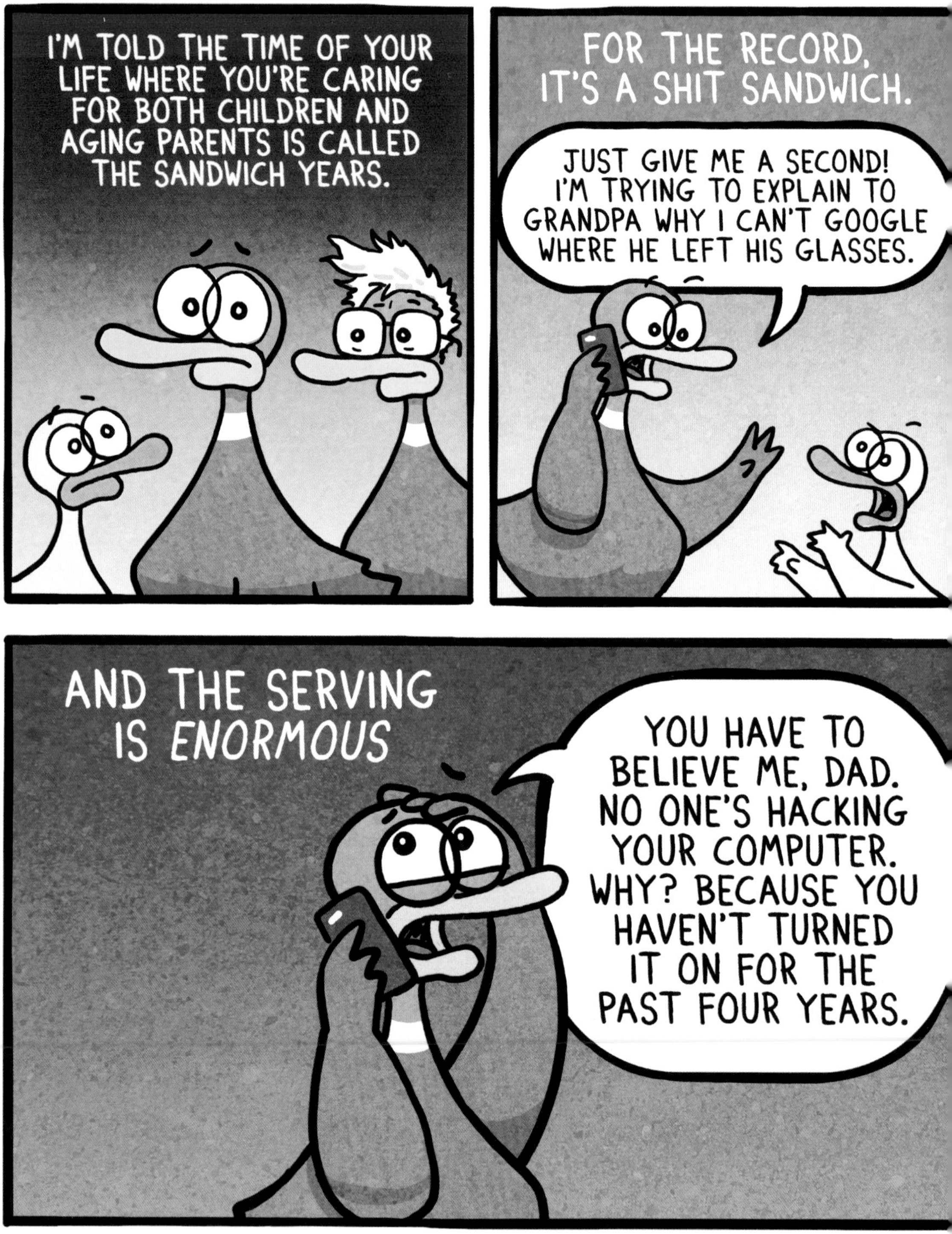
I'M TOLD THE TIME OF YOUR LIFE WHERE YOU'RE CARING FOR BOTH CHILDREN AND AGING PARENTS IS CALLED THE SANDWICH YEARS.
FOR THE RECORD, IT'S A SHIT SANDWICH.
JUST GIVE ME A SECOND! I'M TRYING TO EXPLAIN TO GRANDPA WHY I CAN'T GOOGLE WHERE HE LEFT HIS GLASSES.
AND THE SERVING IS *ENORMOUS*
YOU HAVE TO BELIEVE ME, DAD. NO ONE'S HACKING YOUR COMPUTER. WHY? BECAUSE YOU HAVEN'T TURNED IT ON FOR THE PAST FOUR YEARS.

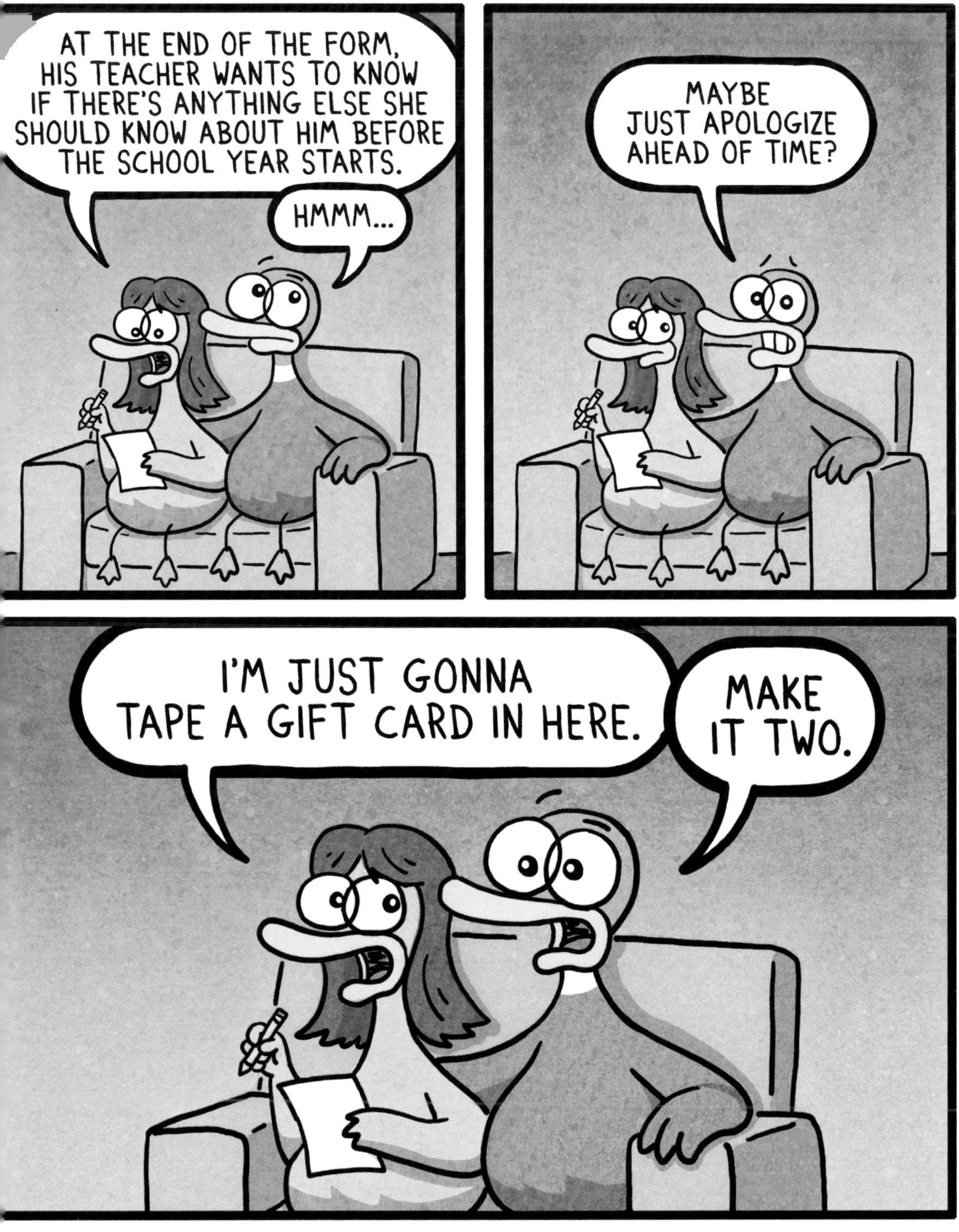
AT THE END OF THE FORM, HIS TEACHER WANTS TO KNOW IF THERE'S ANYTHING ELSE SHE SHOULD KNOW ABOUT HIM BEFORE THE SCHOOL YEAR STARTS.
HMMM...
MAYBE JUST APOLOGIZE AHEAD OF TIME?
I'M JUST GONNA TAPE A GIFT CARD IN HERE.
MAKE IT TWO.

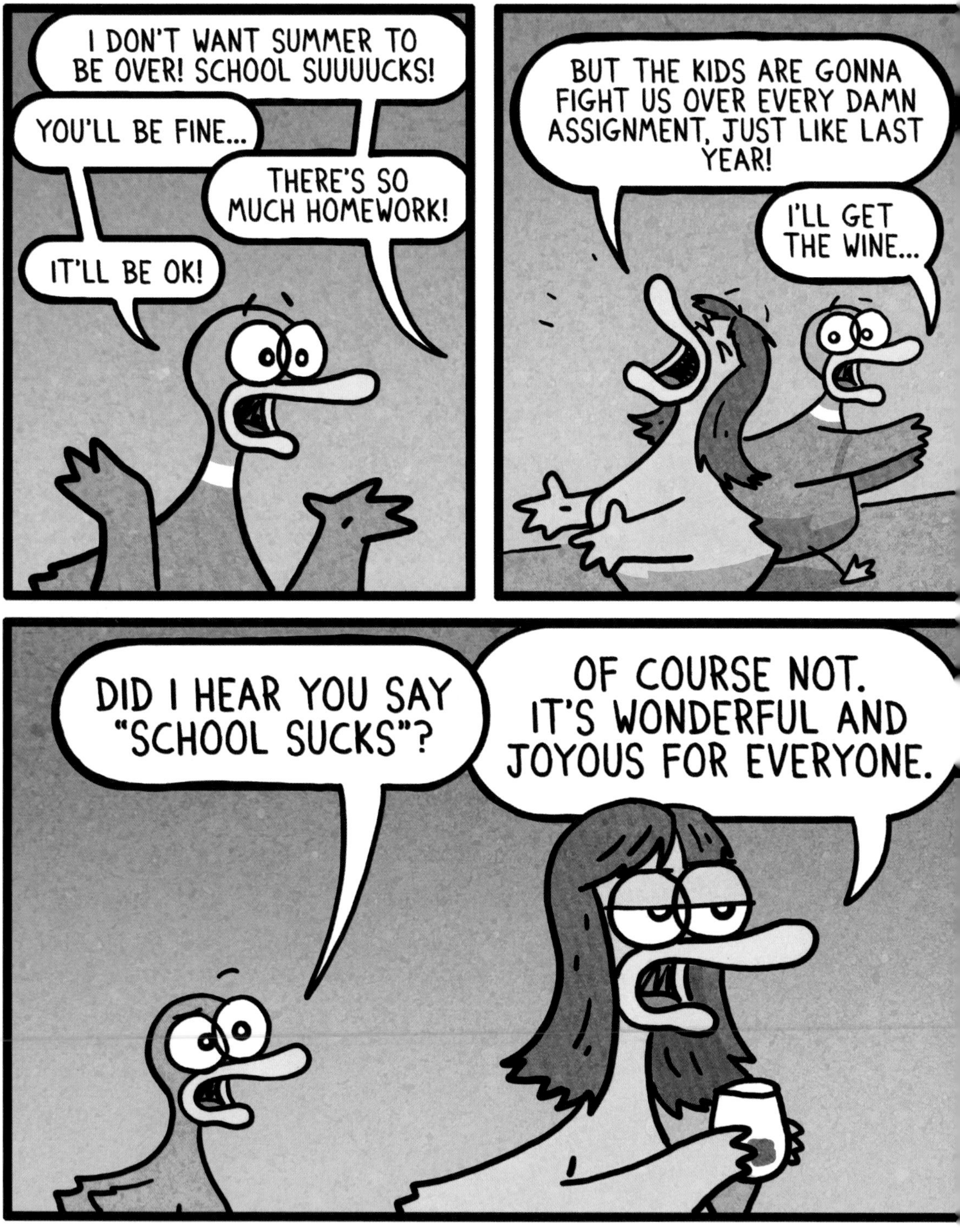
I DON'T WANT SUMMER TO BE OVER! SCHOOL SUUUUCKS!
YOU'LL BE FINE...
THERE'S SO MUCH HOMEWORK!
IT'LL BE OK!
BUT THE KIDS ARE GONNA FIGHT US OVER EVERY DAMN ASSIGNMENT, JUST LIKE LAST YEAR!
I'LL GET THE WINE...
DID I HEAR YOU SAY "SCHOOL SUCKS"?
OF COURSE NOT. IT'S WONDERFUL AND JOYOUS FOR EVERYONE.

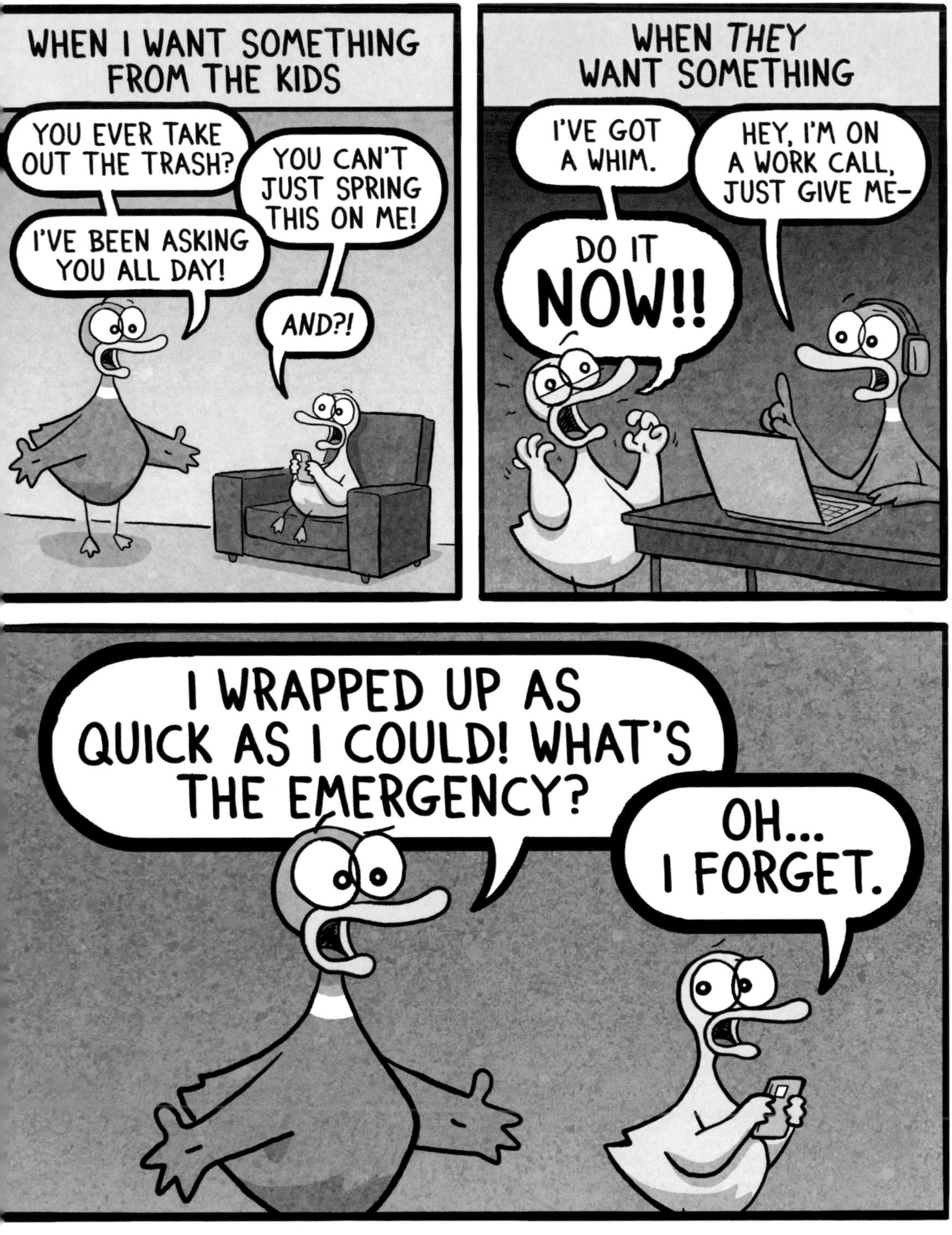
WHEN I WANT SOMETHING FROM THE KIDS
YOU EVER TAKE OUT THE TRASH?
YOU CAN'T JUST SPRING THIS ON ME!
I'VE BEEN ASKING YOU ALL DAY!
AND?!
WHEN *THEY* WANT SOMETHING
I'VE GOT A WHIM.
HEY, I'M ON A WORK CALL, JUST GIVE ME-
DO IT NOW!!
I WRAPPED UP AS QUICK AS I COULD! WHAT'S THE EMERGENCY?
OH... I FORGET.

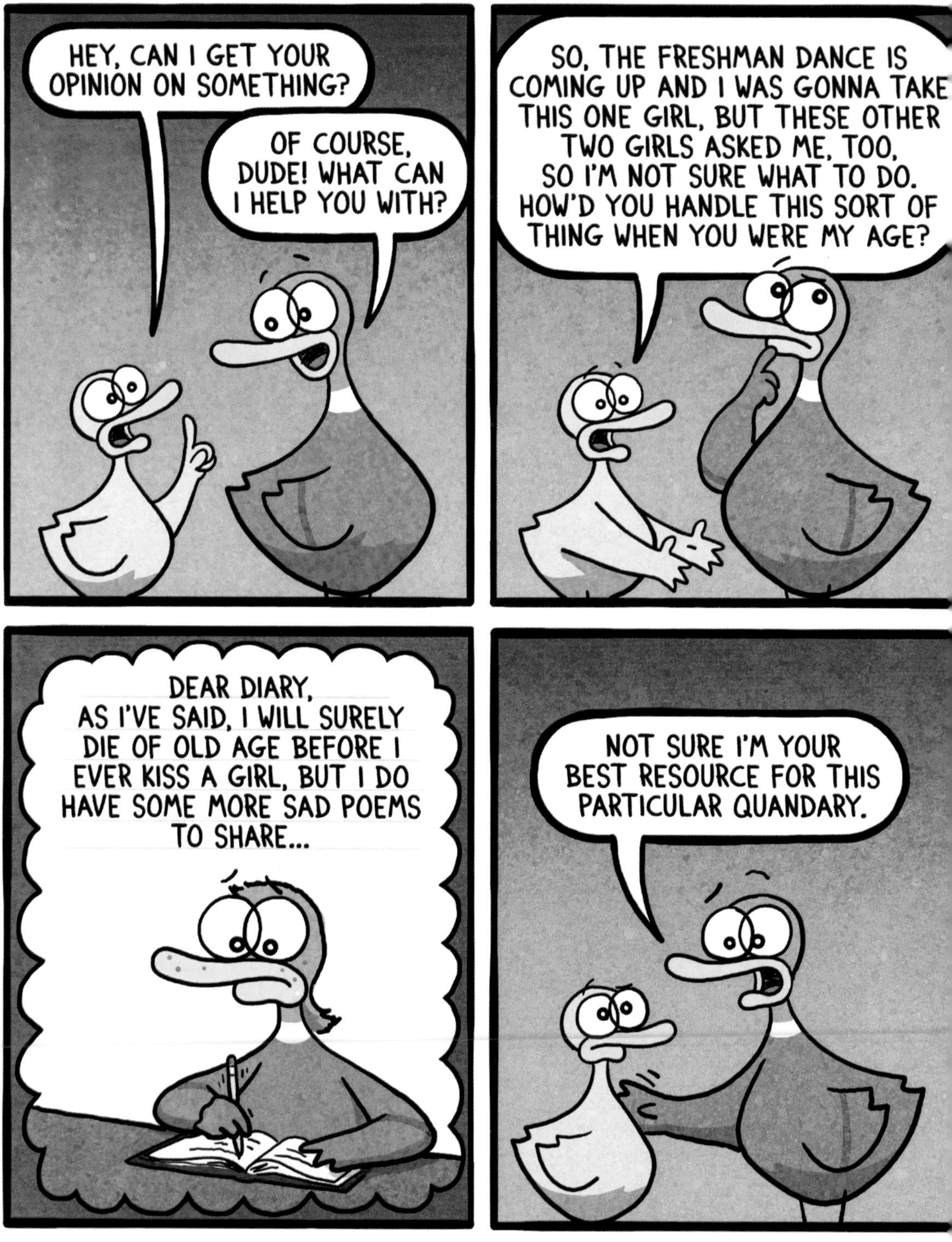

HEY, CAN I GET YOUR OPINION ON SOMETHING?
OF COURSE, DUDE! WHAT CAN I HELP YOU WITH?
SO, THE FRESHMAN DANCE IS COMING UP AND I WAS GONNA TAKE THIS ONE GIRL, BUT THESE OTHER TWO GIRLS ASKED ME, TOO, SO I'M NOT SURE WHAT TO DO. HOW'D YOU HANDLE THIS SORT OF THING WHEN YOU WERE MY AGE?
DEAR DIARY, AS I'VE SAID, I WILL SURELY DIE OF OLD AGE BEFORE I EVER KISS A GIRL, BUT I DO HAVE SOME MORE SAD POEMS TO SHARE...
NOT SURE I'M YOUR BEST RESOURCE FOR THIS PARTICULAR QUANDARY.

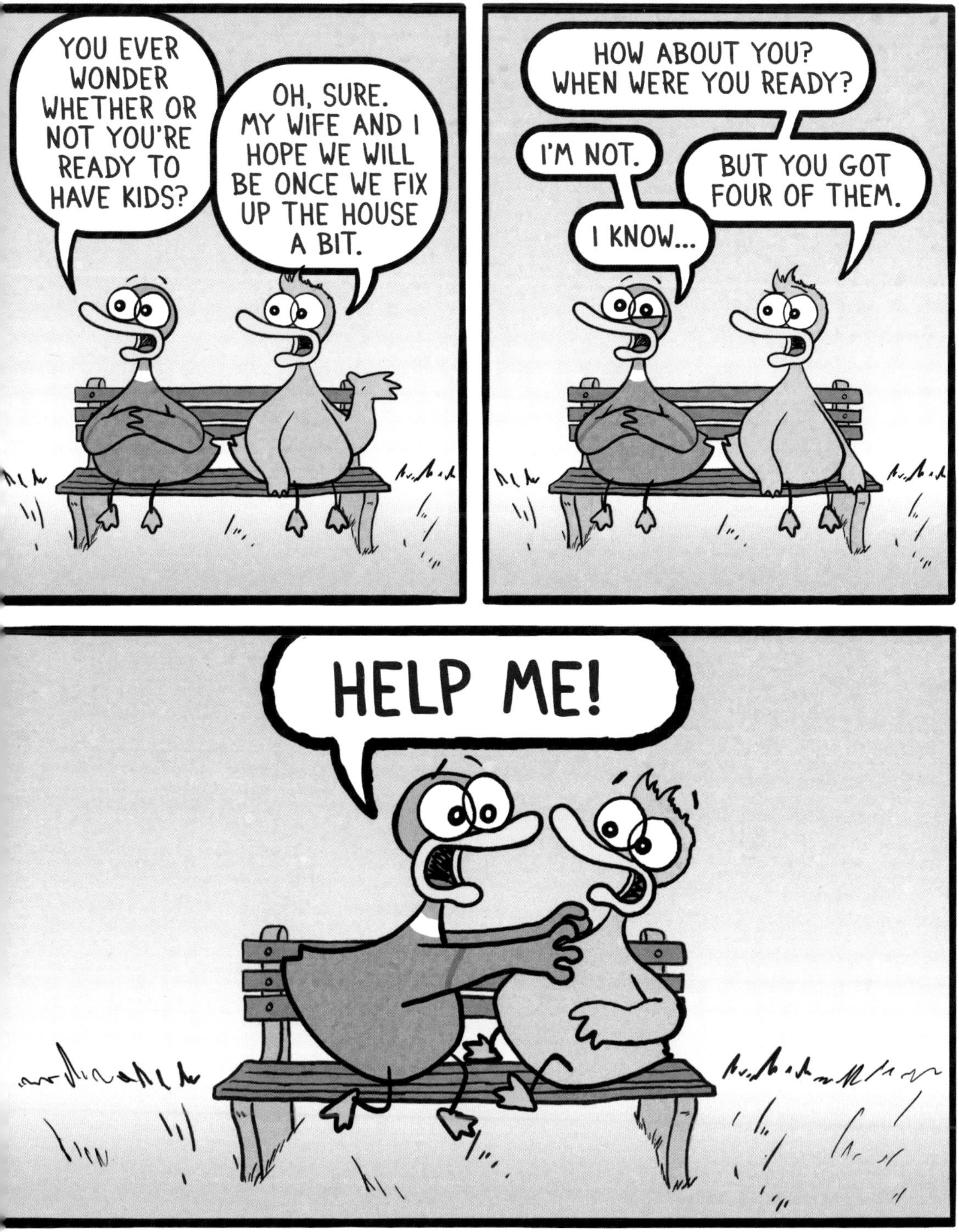
YOU EVER WONDER WHETHER OR NOT YOU'RE READY TO HAVE KIDS?
OH, SURE. MY WIFE AND I HOPE WE WILL BE ONCE WE FIX UP THE HOUSE A BIT.
HOW ABOUT YOU? WHEN WERE YOU READY?
I'M NOT.
BUT YOU GOT FOUR OF THEM.
I KNOW...
HELP ME!

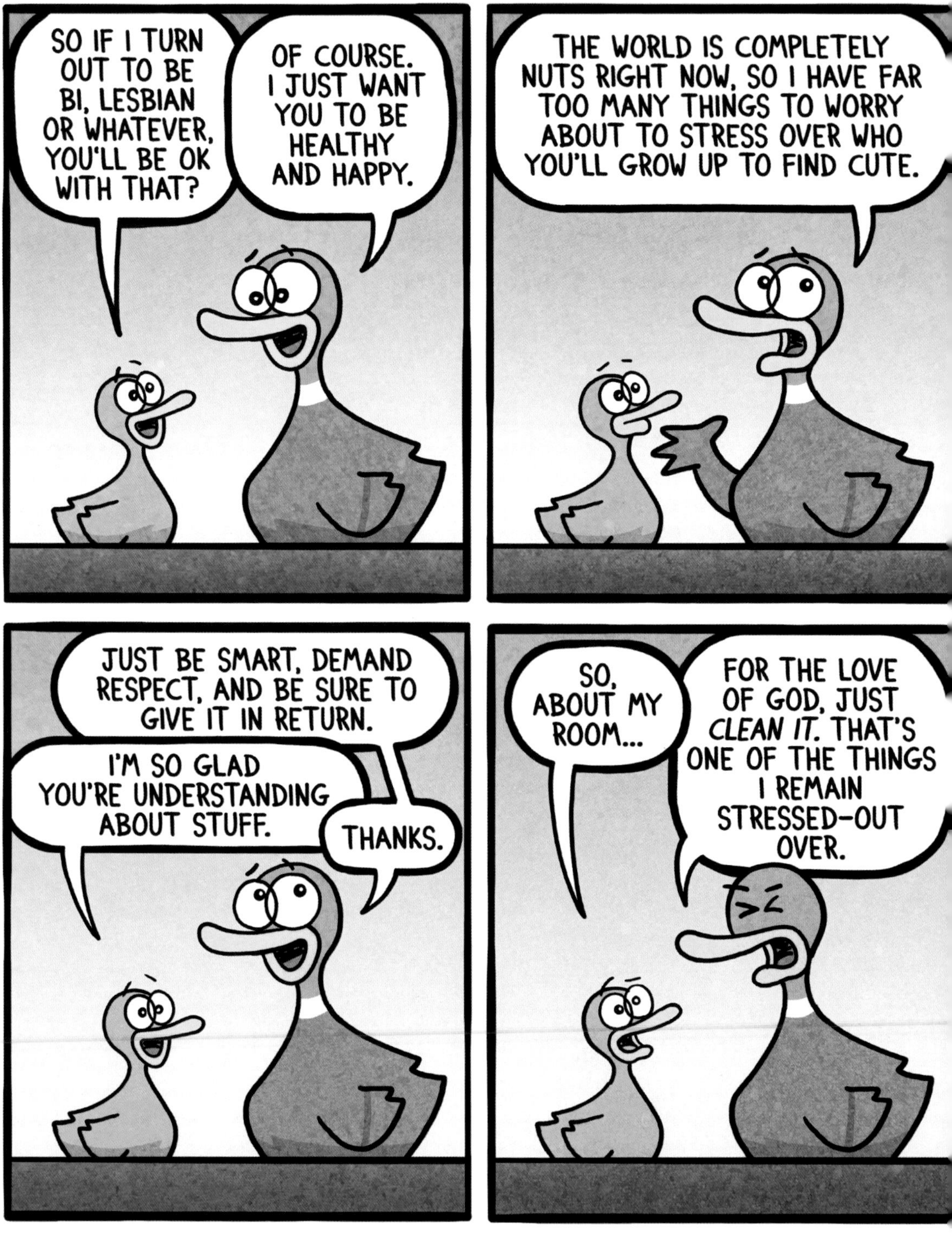
SO IF I TURN OUT TO BE BI, LESBIAN OR WHATEVER, YOU'LL BE OK WITH THAT?
OF COURSE. I JUST WANT YOU TO BE HEALTHY AND HAPPY.
THE WORLD IS COMPLETELY NUTS RIGHT NOW, SO I HAVE FAR TOO MANY THINGS TO WORRY ABOUT TO STRESS OVER WHO YOU'LL GROW UP TO FIND CUTE.
JUST BE SMART, DEMAND RESPECT, AND BE SURE TO GIVE IT IN RETURN.
I'M SO GLAD YOU'RE UNDERSTANDING ABOUT STUFF.
THANKS.
SO, ABOUT MY ROOM...
FOR THE LOVE OF GOD, JUST *CLEAN IT*. THAT'S ONE OF THE THINGS I REMAIN STRESSED-OUT OVER.

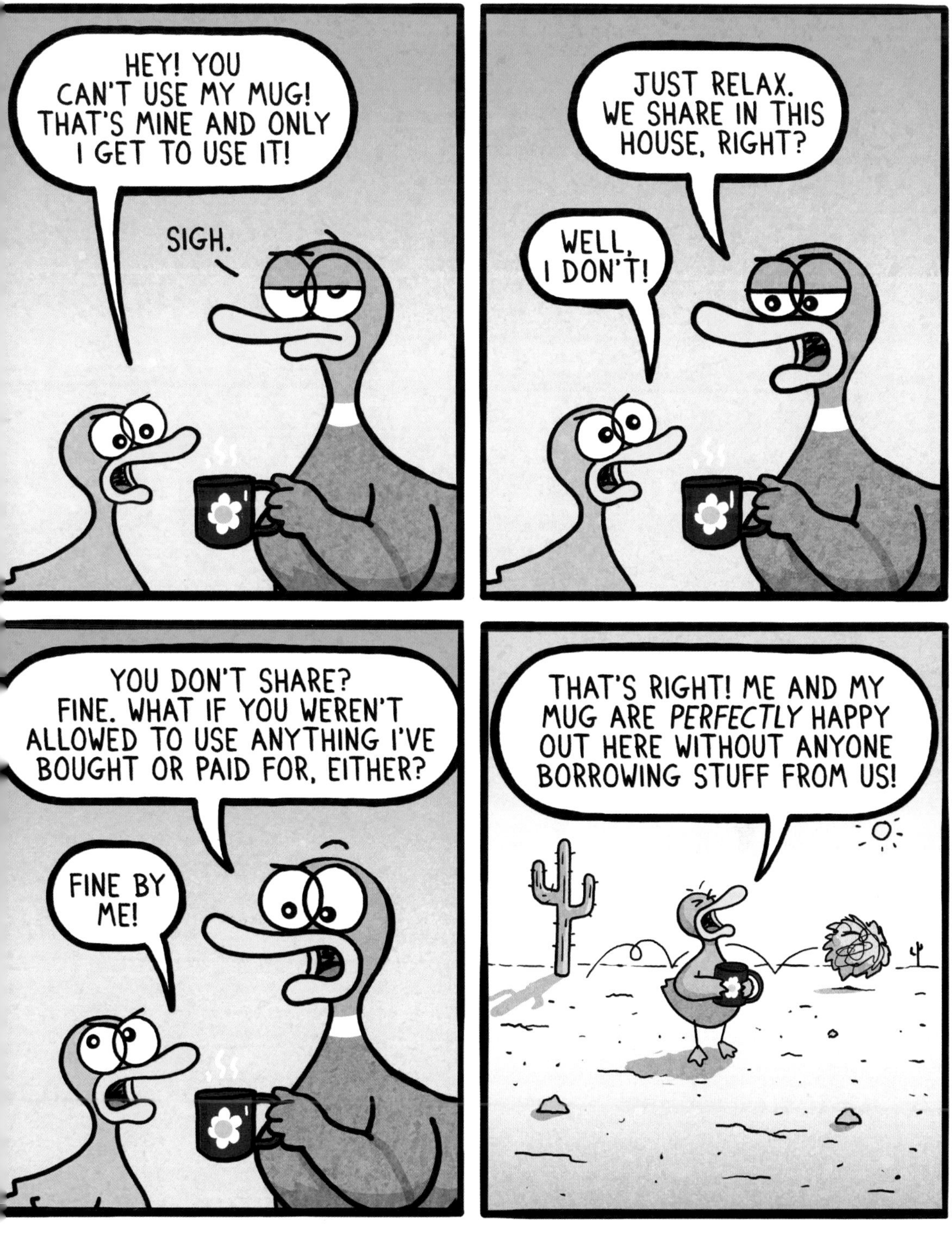
HEY! YOU CAN'T USE MY MUG! THAT'S MINE AND ONLY I GET TO USE IT!
SIGH.
JUST RELAX. WE SHARE IN THIS HOUSE, RIGHT?
WELL, I DON'T!
YOU DON'T SHARE? FINE. WHAT IF YOU WEREN'T ALLOWED TO USE ANYTHING I'VE BOUGHT OR PAID FOR, EITHER?
FINE BY ME!
THAT'S RIGHT! ME AND MY MUG ARE *PERFECTLY* HAPPY OUT HERE WITHOUT ANYONE BORROWING STUFF FROM US!

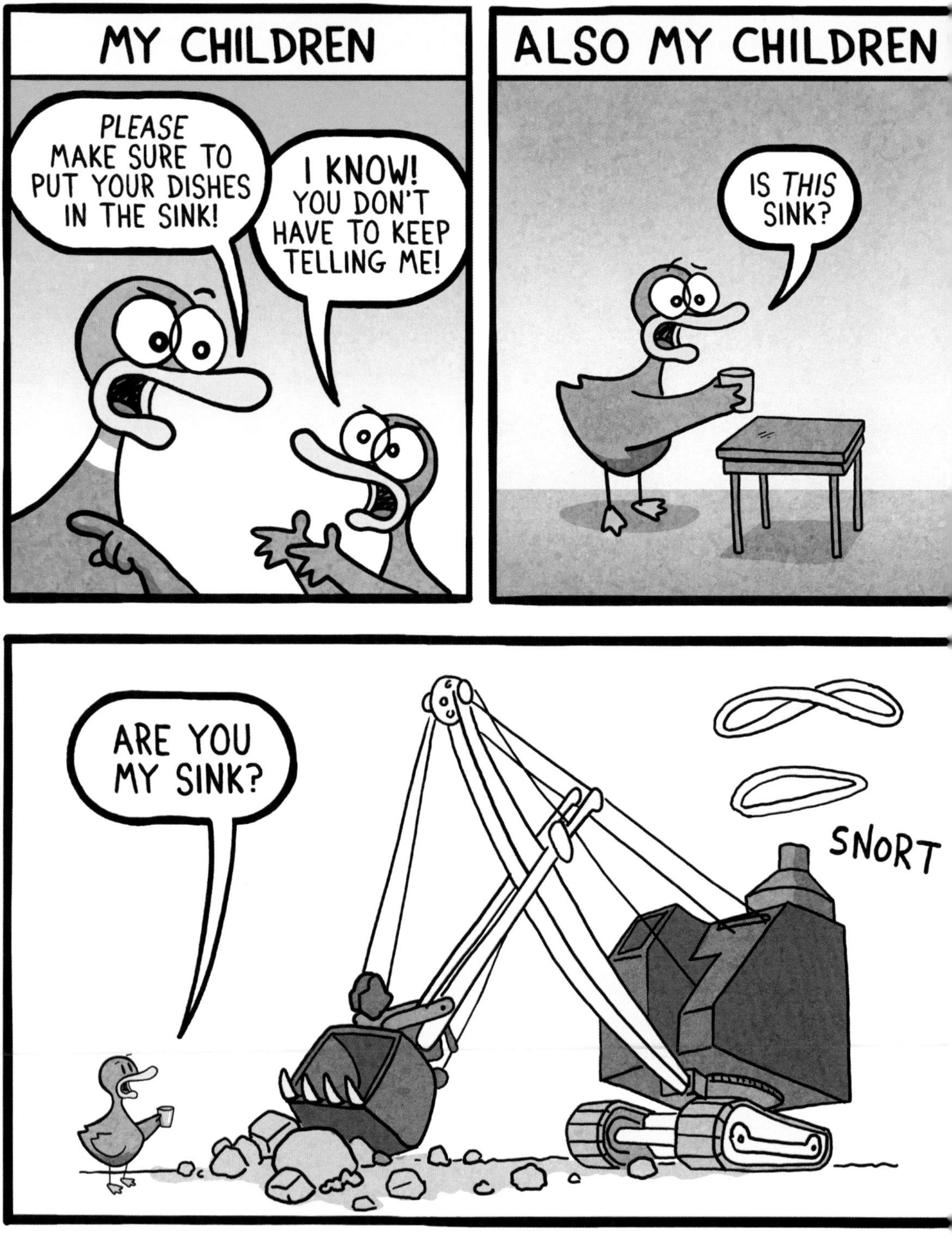
MY CHILDREN
PLEASE MAKE SURE TO PUT YOUR DISHES IN THE SINK!
I KNOW! YOU DON'T HAVE TO KEEP TELLING ME!
ALSO MY CHILDREN
IS THIS SINK?
ARE YOU MY SINK?
SNORT

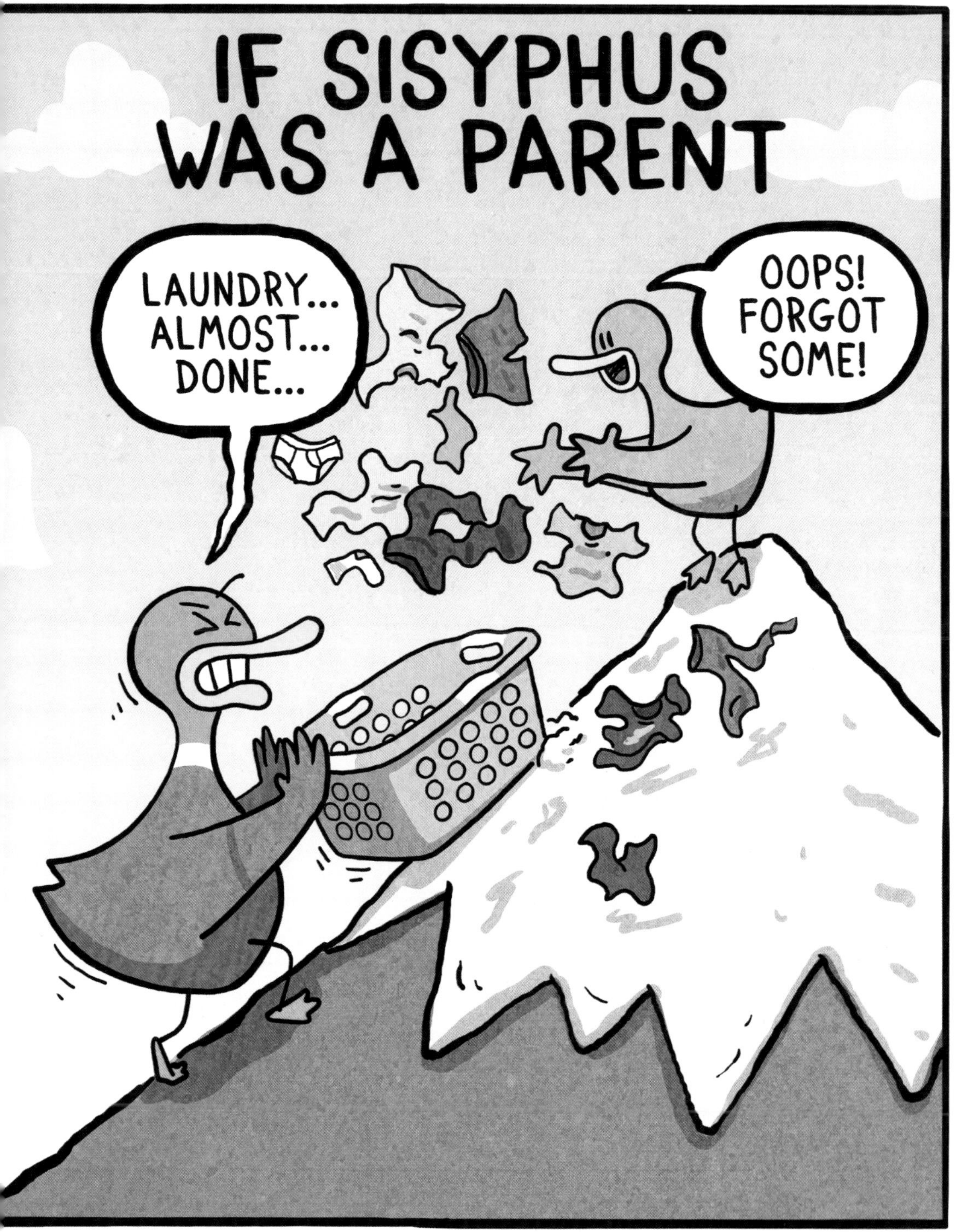
IF SISYPHUS WAS A PARENT
LAUNDRY... ALMOST... DONE...
OOPS! FORGOT SOME!

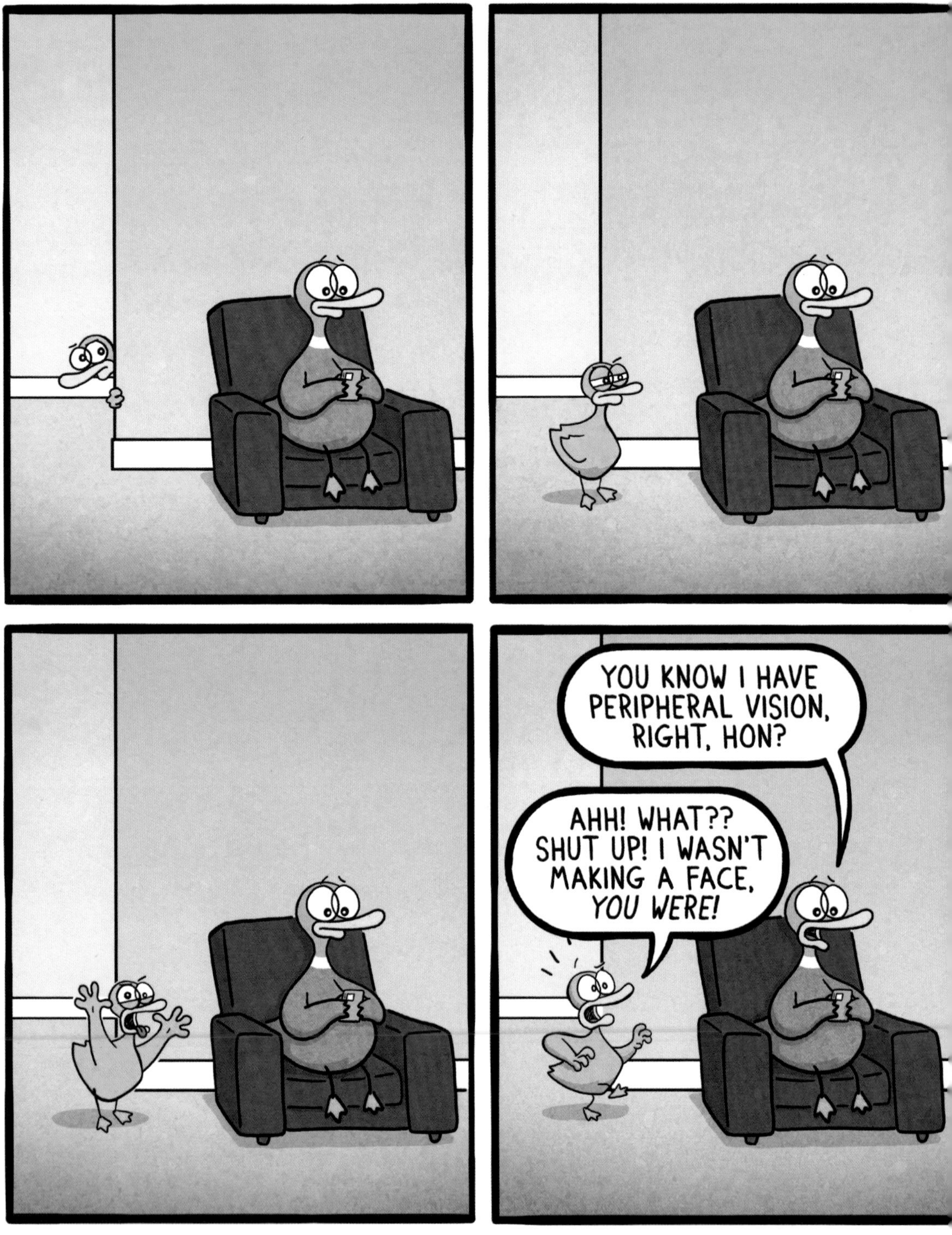
YOU KNOW I HAVE PERIPHERAL VISION, RIGHT, HON?
AHH! WHAT?? SHUT UP! I WASN'T MAKING A FACE, *YOU* WERE!

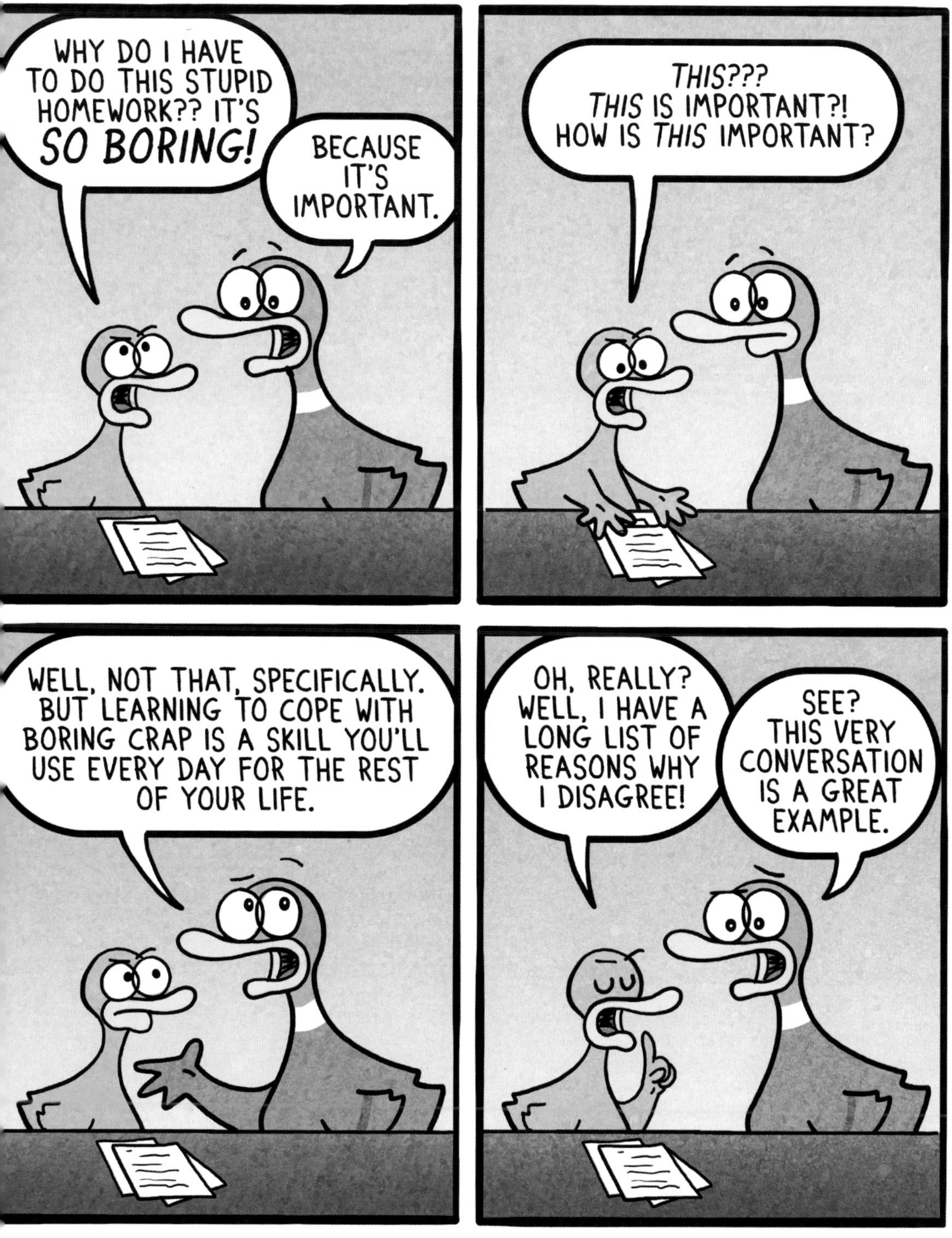
WHY DO I HAVE TO DO THIS STUPID HOMEWORK?? IT'S *SO BORING!*
BECAUSE IT'S IMPORTANT.
THIS??? *THIS* IS IMPORTANT?! HOW IS *THIS* IMPORTANT?
WELL, NOT THAT, SPECIFICALLY. BUT LEARNING TO COPE WITH BORING CRAP IS A SKILL YOU'LL USE EVERY DAY FOR THE REST OF YOUR LIFE.
OH, REALLY? WELL, I HAVE A LONG LIST OF REASONS WHY I DISAGREE!
SEE? THIS VERY CONVERSATION IS A GREAT EXAMPLE.

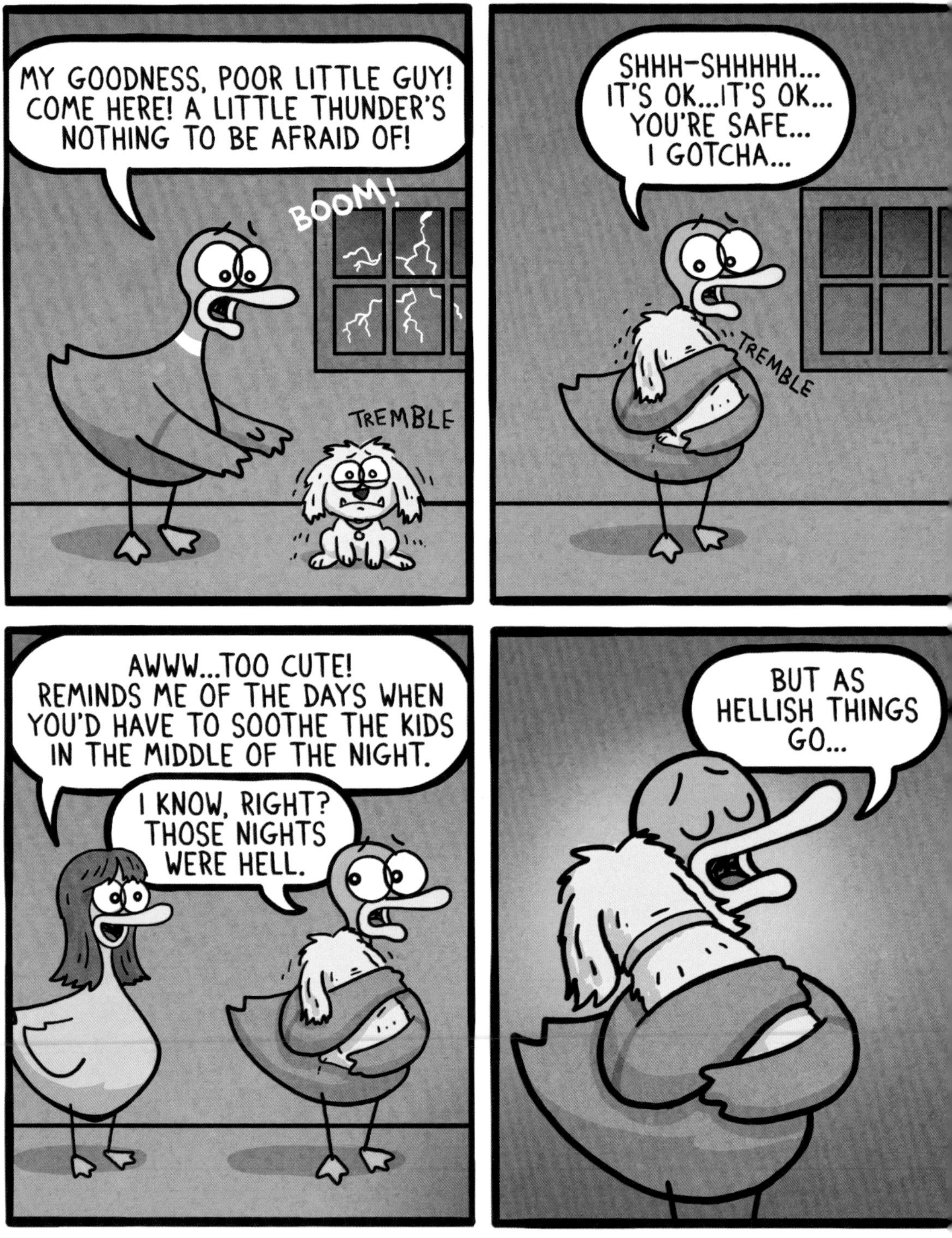
MY GOODNESS, POOR LITTLE GUY! COME HERE! A LITTLE THUNDER'S NOTHING TO BE AFRAID OF!
BOOM!
TREMBLE
SHHH-SHHHHH... IT'S OK...IT'S OK... YOU'RE SAFE... I GOTCHA...
TREMBLE
AWWW...TOO CUTE! REMINDS ME OF THE DAYS WHEN YOU'D HAVE TO SOOTHE THE KIDS IN THE MIDDLE OF THE NIGHT.
I KNOW, RIGHT? THOSE NIGHTS WERE HELL.
BUT AS HELLISH THINGS GO...

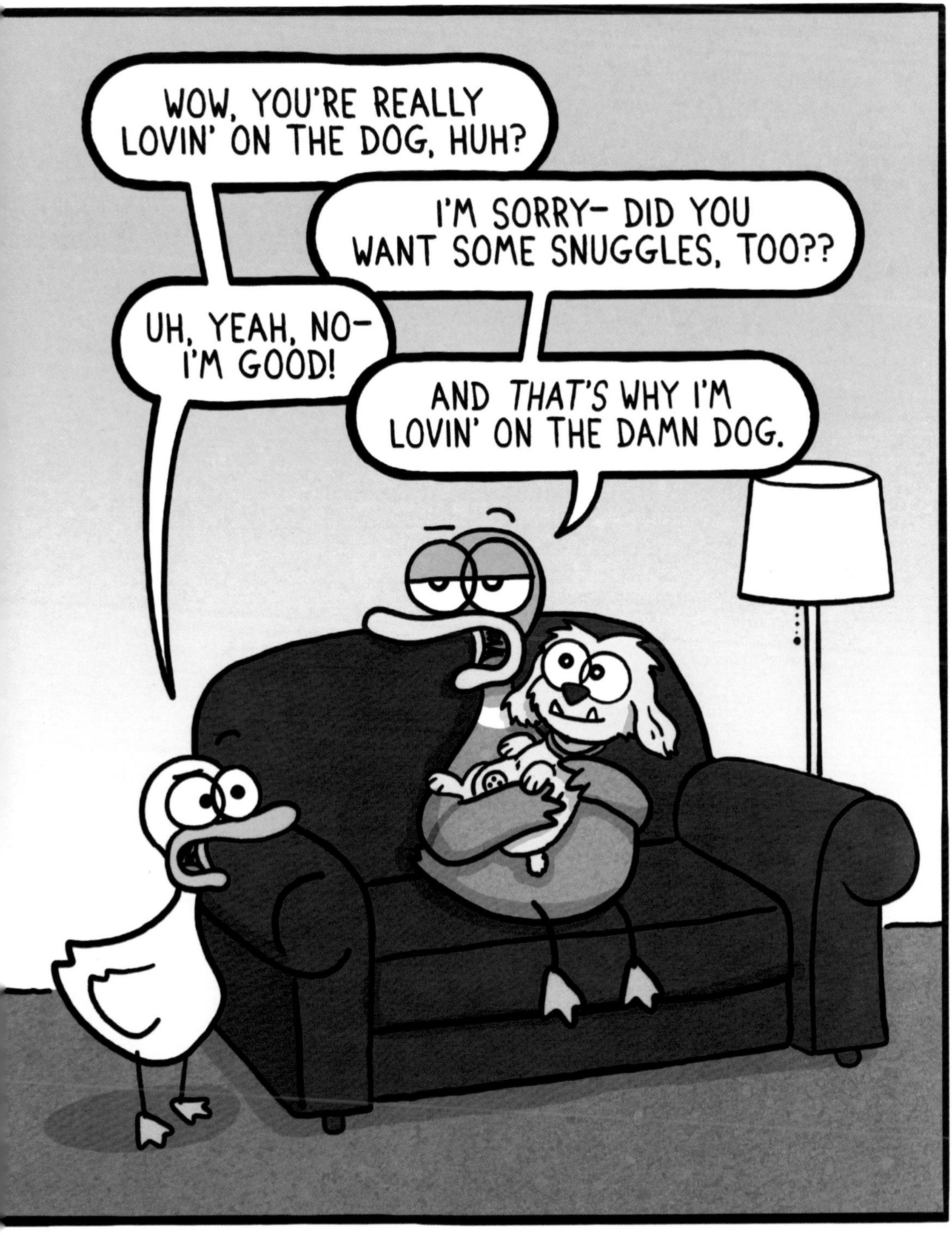
WOW, YOU'RE REALLY LOVIN' ON THE DOG, HUH?
I'M SORRY– DID YOU WANT SOME SNUGGLES, TOO??
UH, YEAH, NO– I'M GOOD!
AND *THAT'S* WHY I'M LOVIN' ON THE DAMN DOG.

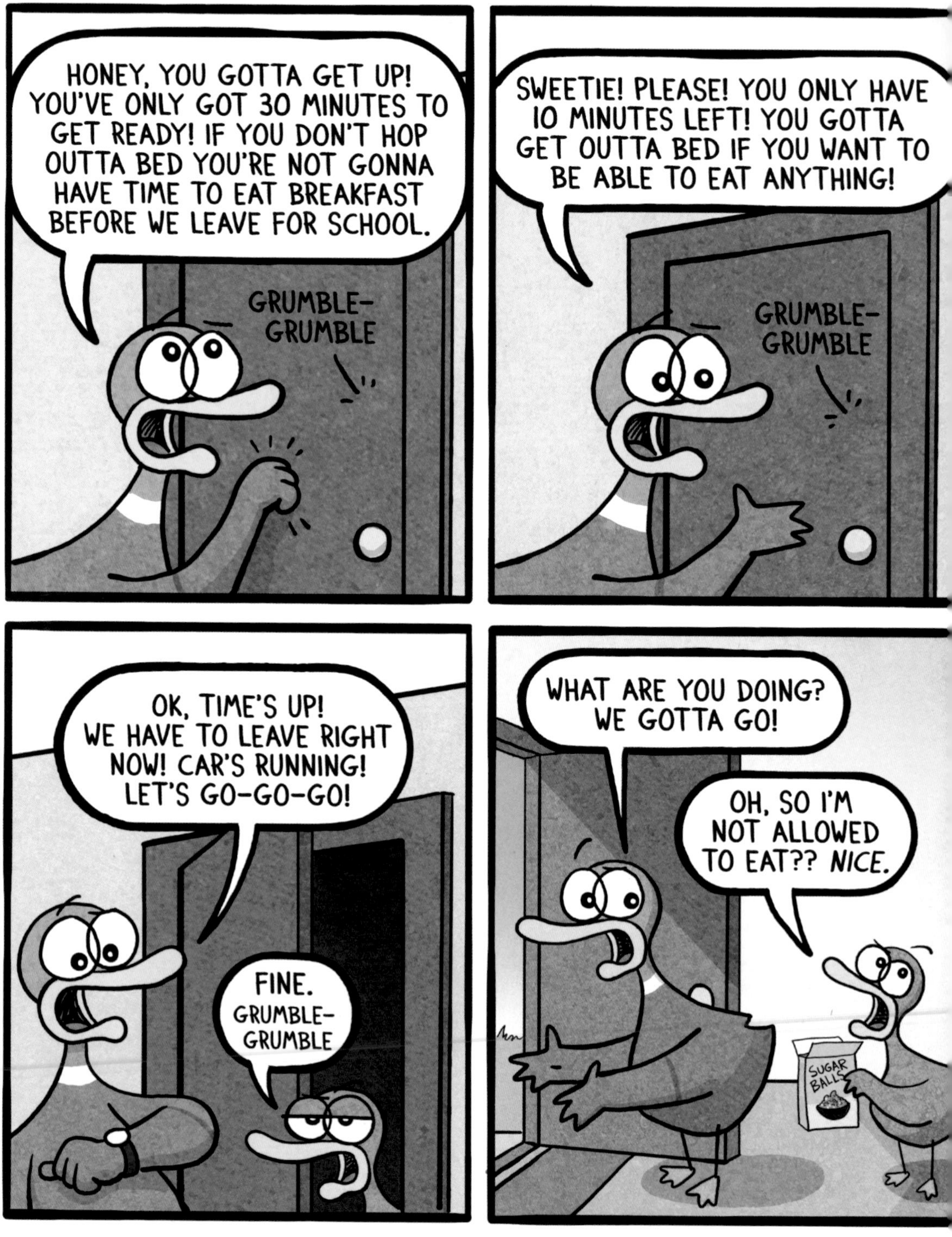
HONEY, YOU GOTTA GET UP! YOU'VE ONLY GOT 30 MINUTES TO GET READY! IF YOU DON'T HOP OUTTA BED YOU'RE NOT GONNA HAVE TIME TO EAT BREAKFAST BEFORE WE LEAVE FOR SCHOOL.
GRUMBLE-GRUMBLE
SWEETIE! PLEASE! YOU ONLY HAVE 10 MINUTES LEFT! YOU GOTTA GET OUTTA BED IF YOU WANT TO BE ABLE TO EAT ANYTHING!
GRUMBLE-GRUMBLE
OK, TIME'S UP! WE HAVE TO LEAVE RIGHT NOW! CAR'S RUNNING! LET'S GO-GO-GO!
FINE. GRUMBLE-GRUMBLE
WHAT ARE YOU DOING? WE GOTTA GO!
OH, SO I'M NOT ALLOWED TO EAT?? *NICE.*
SUGAR BALLS

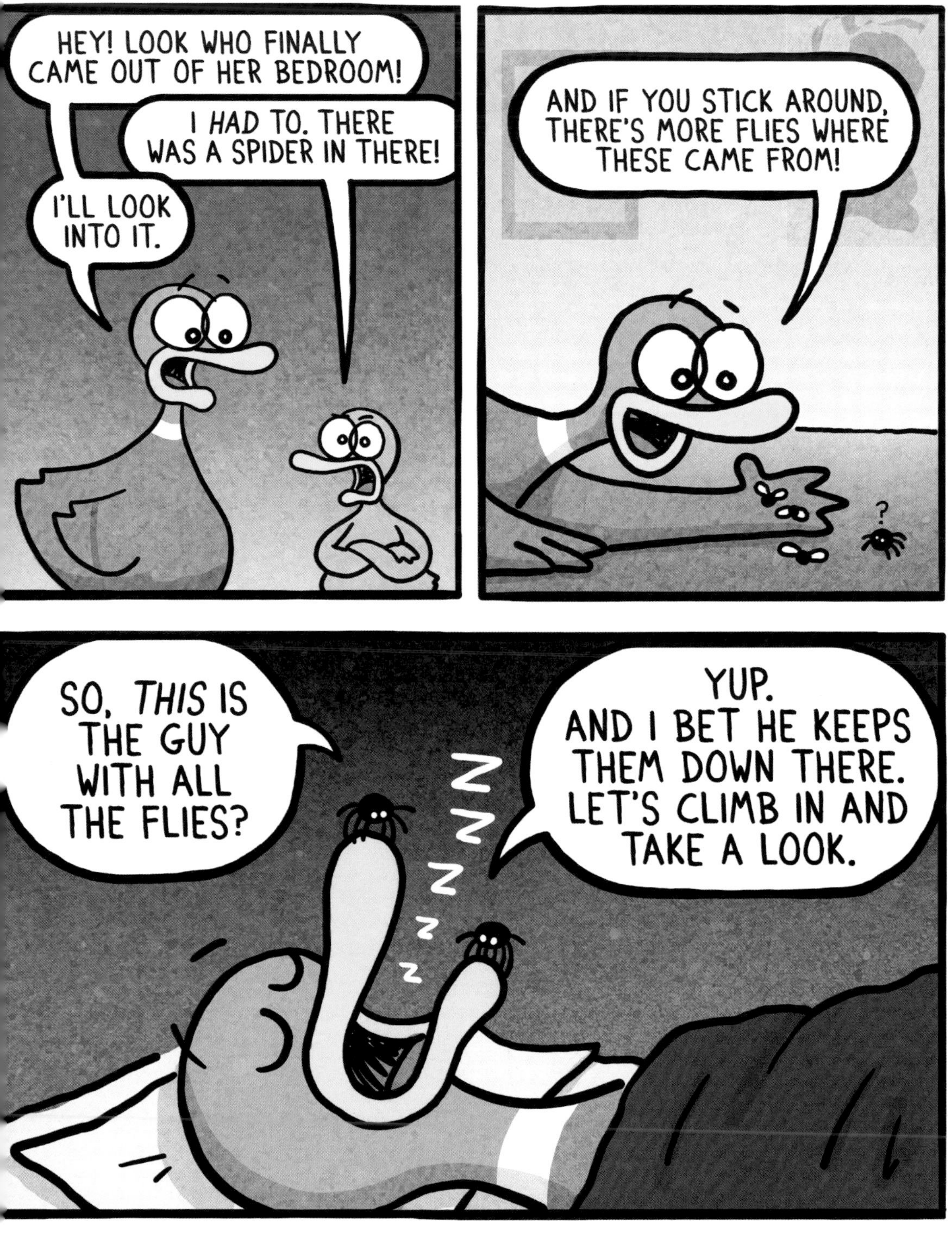
HEY! LOOK WHO FINALLY CAME OUT OF HER BEDROOM!
I *HAD* TO. THERE WAS A SPIDER IN THERE!
I'LL LOOK INTO IT.
AND IF YOU STICK AROUND, THERE'S MORE FLIES WHERE THESE CAME FROM!
?
SO, *THIS* IS THE GUY WITH ALL THE FLIES?
YUP. AND I BET HE KEEPS THEM DOWN THERE. LET'S CLIMB IN AND TAKE A LOOK.
Z Z Z Z Z

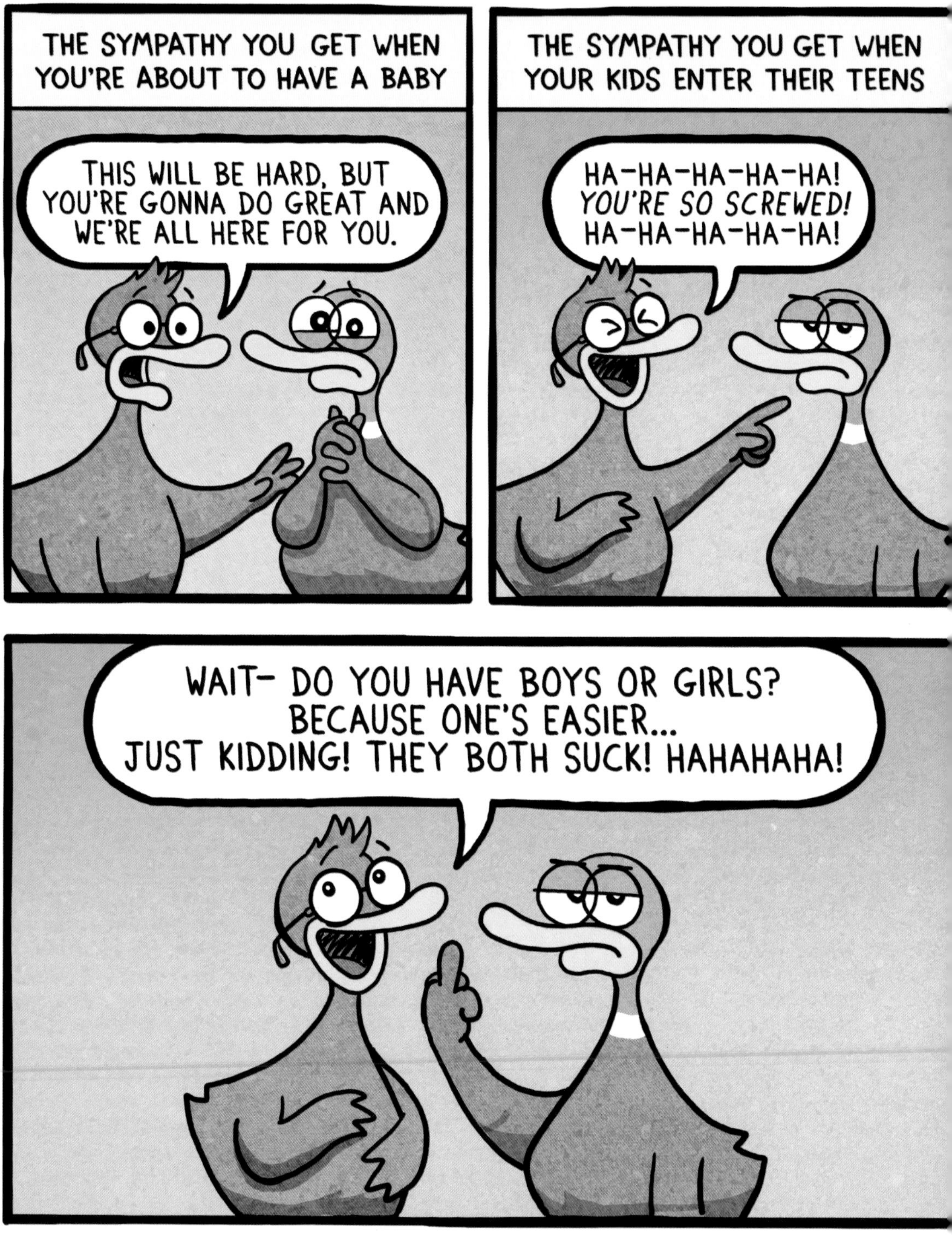
THE SYMPATHY YOU GET WHEN YOU'RE ABOUT TO HAVE A BABY
THIS WILL BE HARD, BUT YOU'RE GONNA DO GREAT AND WE'RE ALL HERE FOR YOU.
THE SYMPATHY YOU GET WHEN YOUR KIDS ENTER THEIR TEENS
HA-HA-HA-HA-HA! YOU'RE SO SCREWED! HA-HA-HA-HA-HA!
WAIT- DO YOU HAVE BOYS OR GIRLS? BECAUSE ONE'S EASIER... JUST KIDDING! THEY BOTH SUCK! HAHAHAHA!

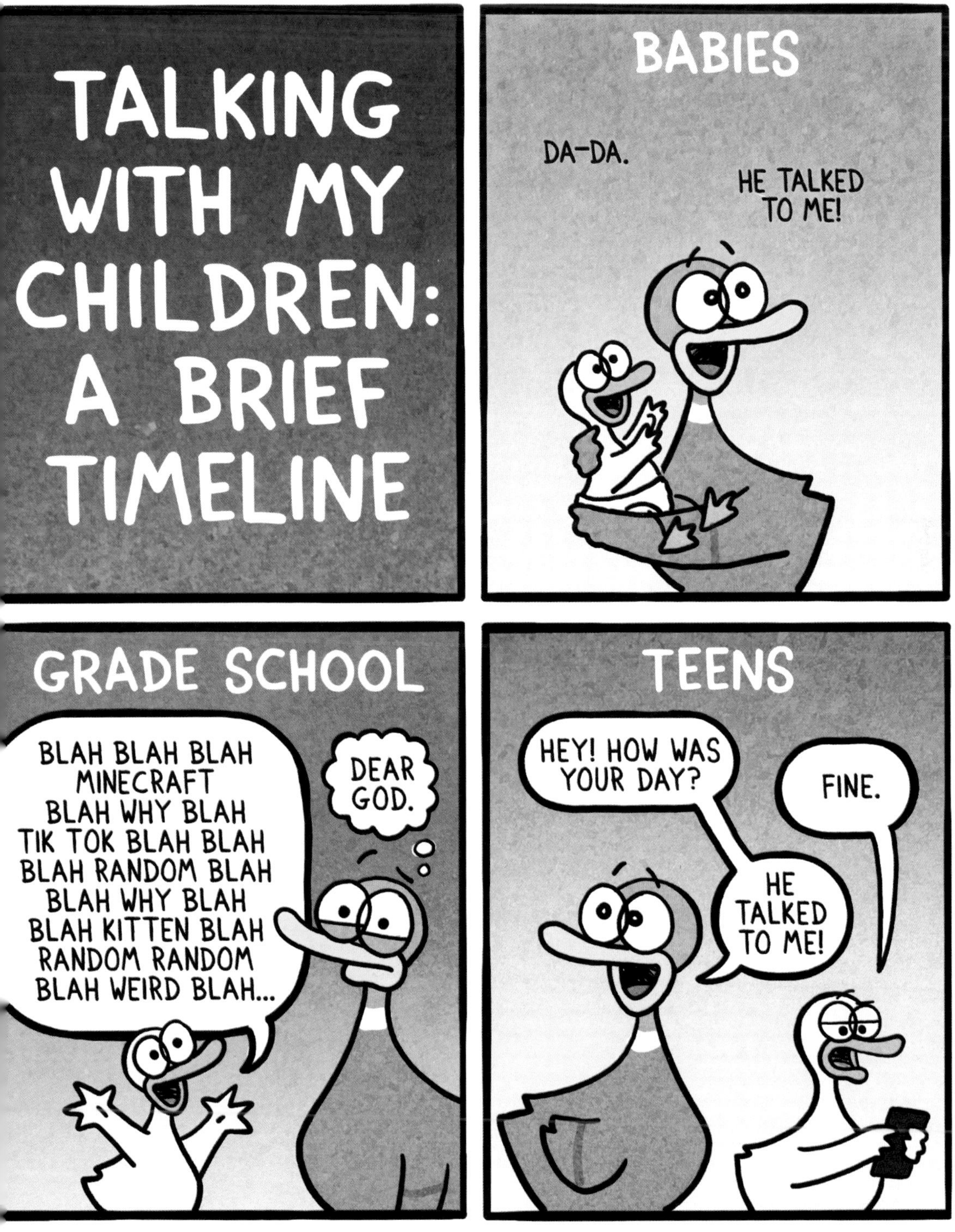
TALKING WITH MY CHILDREN: A BRIEF TIMELINE
BABIES
DA-DA.
HE TALKED TO ME!
GRADE SCHOOL
BLAH BLAH BLAH MINECRAFT BLAH WHY BLAH TIK TOK BLAH BLAH BLAH RANDOM BLAH BLAH WHY BLAH BLAH KITTEN BLAH RANDOM RANDOM BLAH WEIRD BLAH...
DEAR GOD.
TEENS
HEY! HOW WAS YOUR DAY?
FINE.
HE TALKED TO ME!

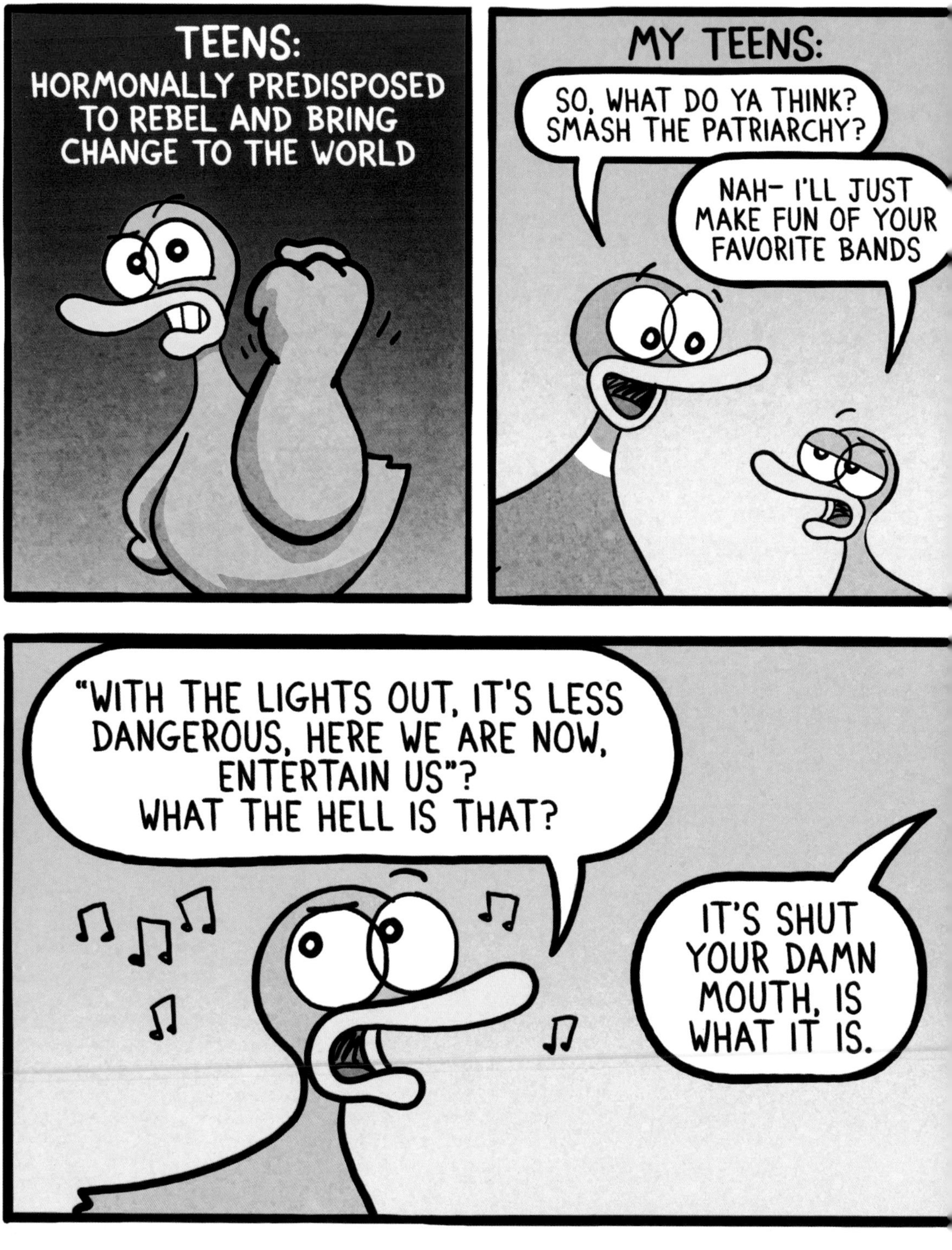
TEENS:
HORMONALLY PREDISPOSED TO REBEL AND BRING CHANGE TO THE WORLD
MY TEENS:
SO, WHAT DO YA THINK? SMASH THE PATRIARCHY?
NAH– I'LL JUST MAKE FUN OF YOUR FAVORITE BANDS
"WITH THE LIGHTS OUT, IT'S LESS DANGEROUS, HERE WE ARE NOW, ENTERTAIN US"? WHAT THE HELL IS THAT?
IT'S SHUT YOUR DAMN MOUTH, IS WHAT IT IS.

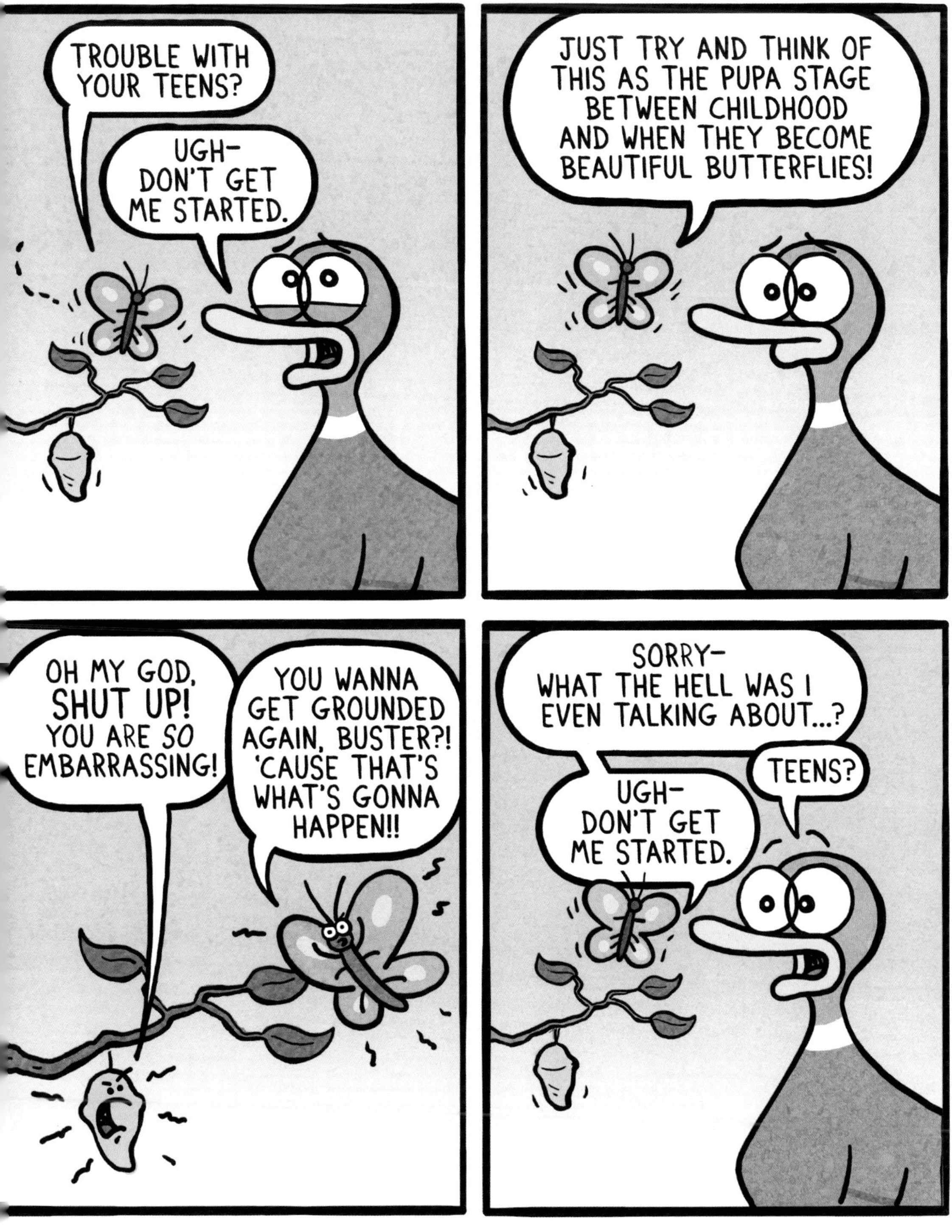

TROUBLE WITH YOUR TEENS?
UGH– DON'T GET ME STARTED.
JUST TRY AND THINK OF THIS AS THE PUPA STAGE BETWEEN CHILDHOOD AND WHEN THEY BECOME BEAUTIFUL BUTTERFLIES!
OH MY GOD, SHUT UP! YOU ARE *SO* EMBARRASSING!
YOU WANNA GET GROUNDED AGAIN, BUSTER?! 'CAUSE THAT'S WHAT'S GONNA HAPPEN!!
SORRY– WHAT THE HELL WAS I EVEN TALKING ABOUT...?
TEENS?
UGH– DON'T GET ME STARTED.

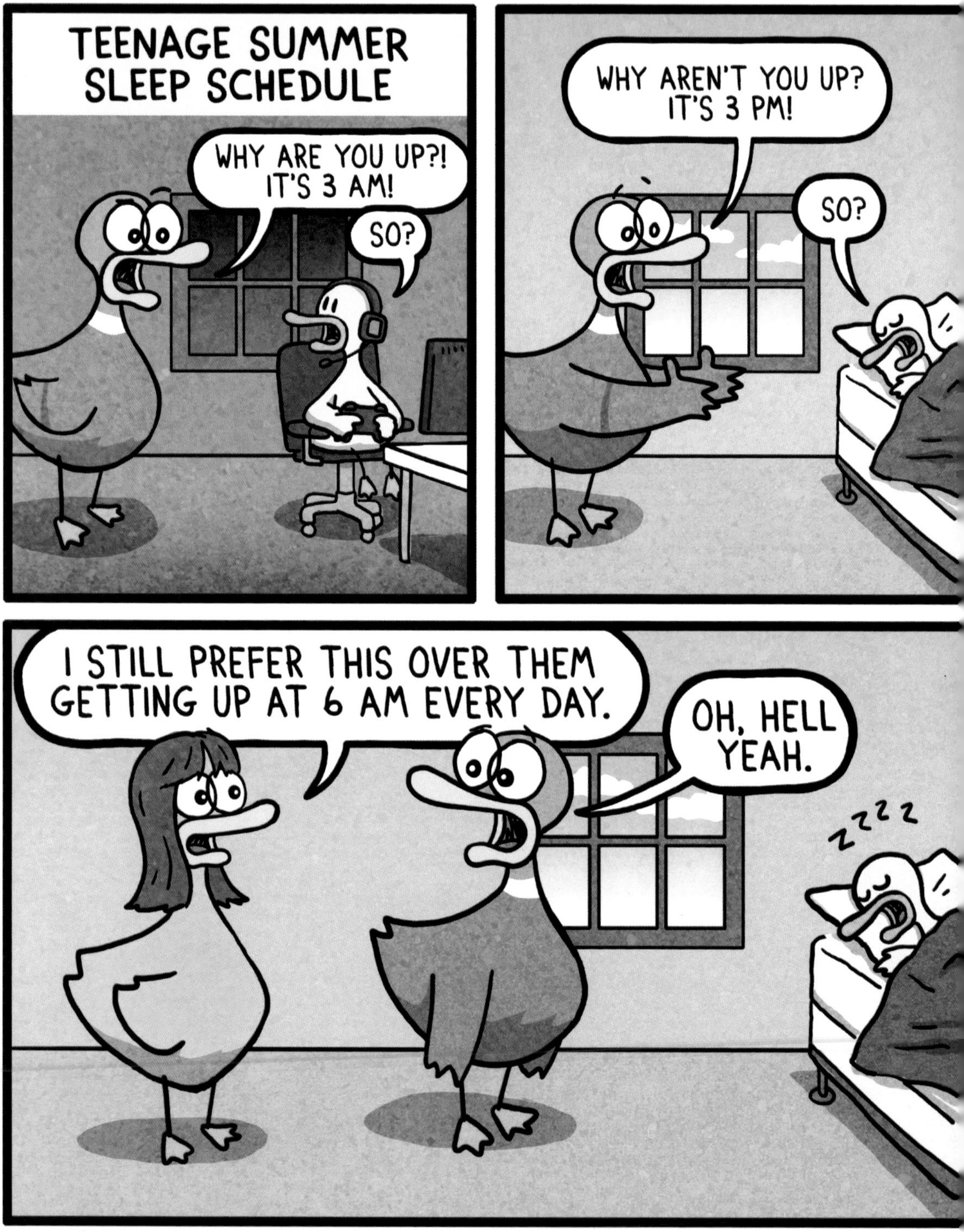
TEENAGE SUMMER SLEEP SCHEDULE
WHY ARE YOU UP?! IT'S 3 AM!
SO?
WHY AREN'T YOU UP? IT'S 3 PM!
SO?
I STILL PREFER THIS OVER THEM GETTING UP AT 6 AM EVERY DAY.
OH, HELL YEAH.
Z Z Z Z

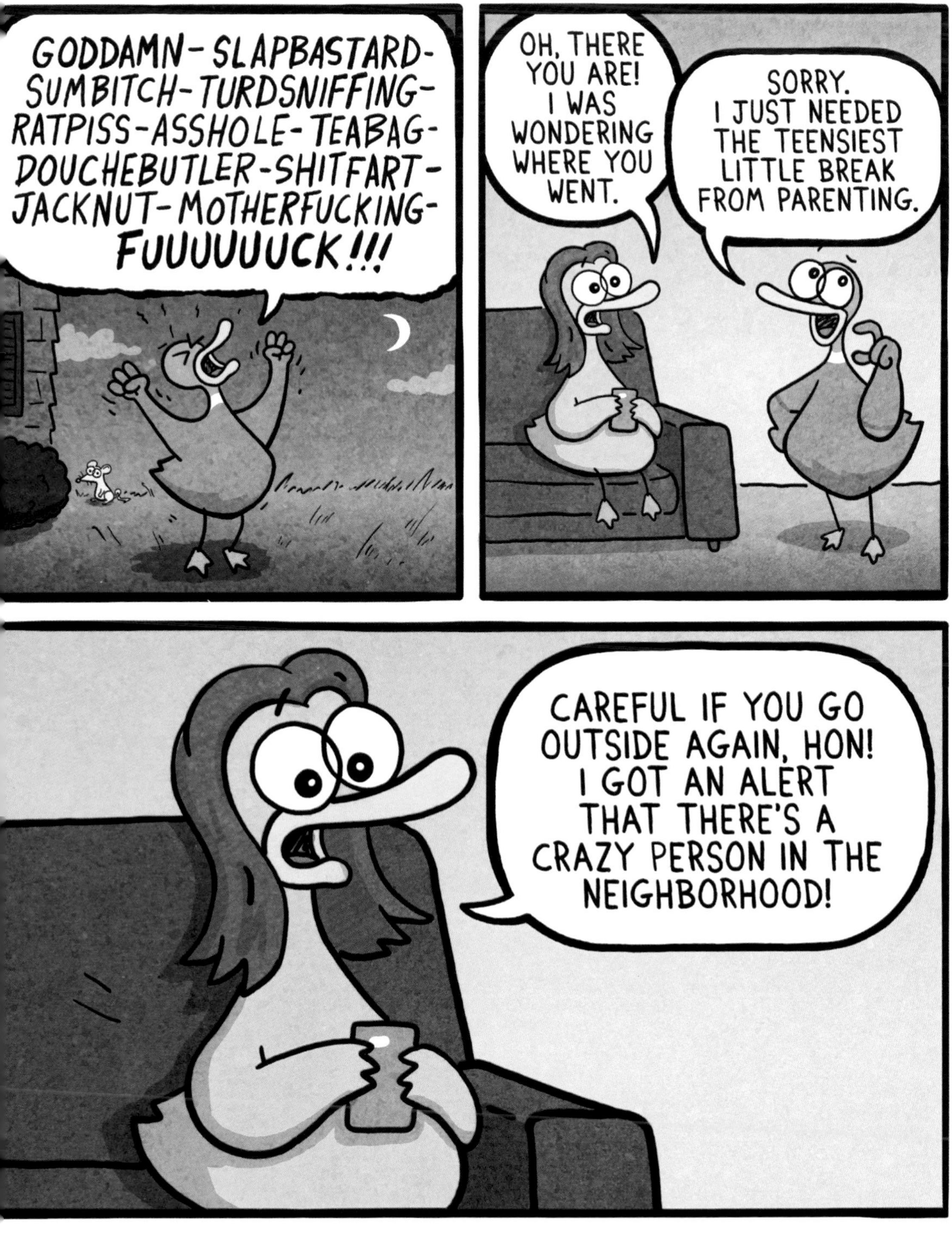
GODDAMN-SLAPBASTARD-SUMBITCH-TURDSNIFFING-RATPISS-ASSHOLE-TEABAG-DOUCHEBUTLER-SHITFART-JACKNUT-MOTHERFUCKING-FUUUUUUCK!!!
OH, THERE YOU ARE! I WAS WONDERING WHERE YOU WENT.
SORRY. I JUST NEEDED THE TEENSIEST LITTLE BREAK FROM PARENTING.
CAREFUL IF YOU GO OUTSIDE AGAIN, HON! I GOT AN ALERT THAT THERE'S A CRAZY PERSON IN THE NEIGHBORHOOD!

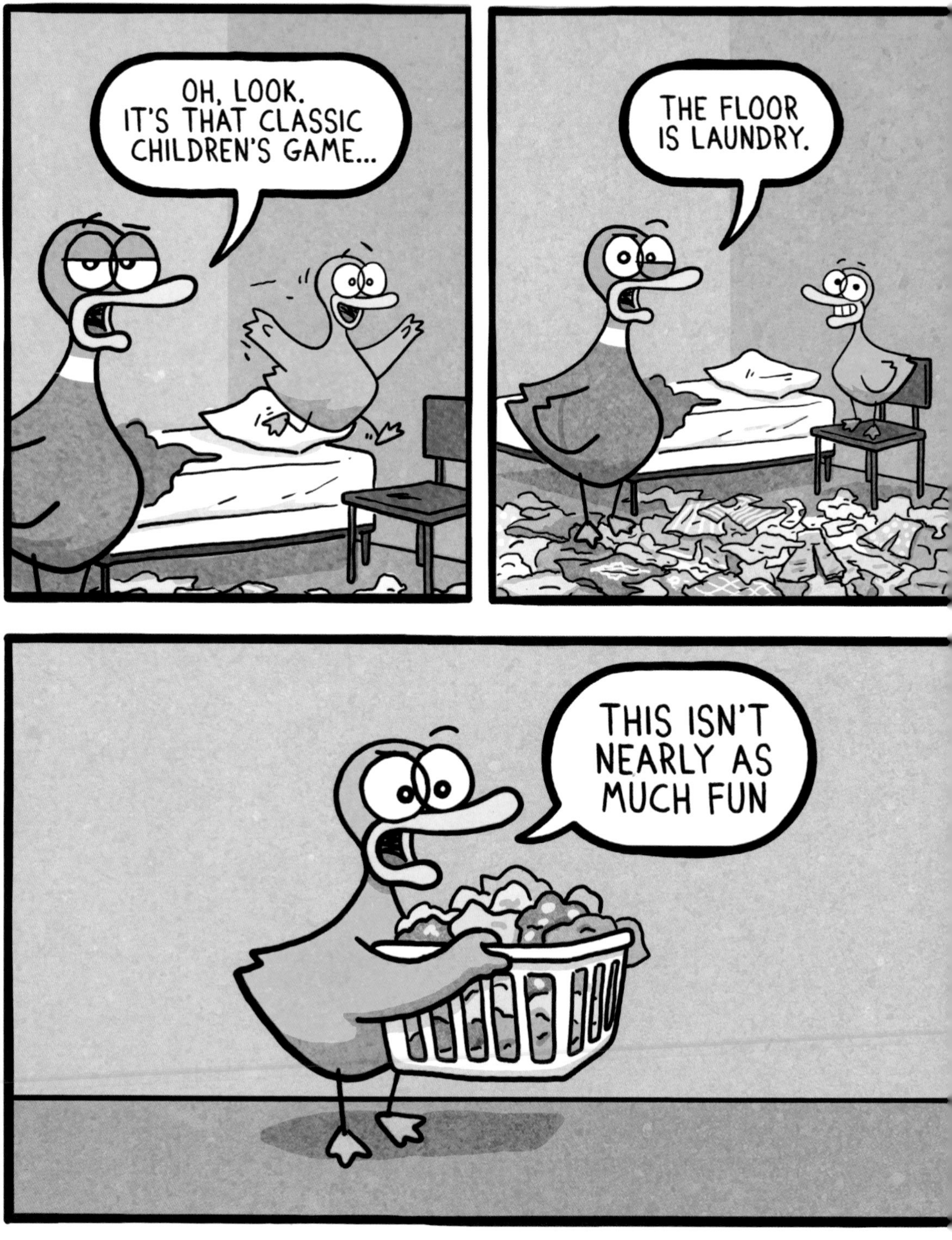
OH, LOOK.
IT'S THAT CLASSIC
CHILDREN'S GAME...
THE FLOOR
IS LAUNDRY.
THIS ISN'T
NEARLY AS
MUCH FUN

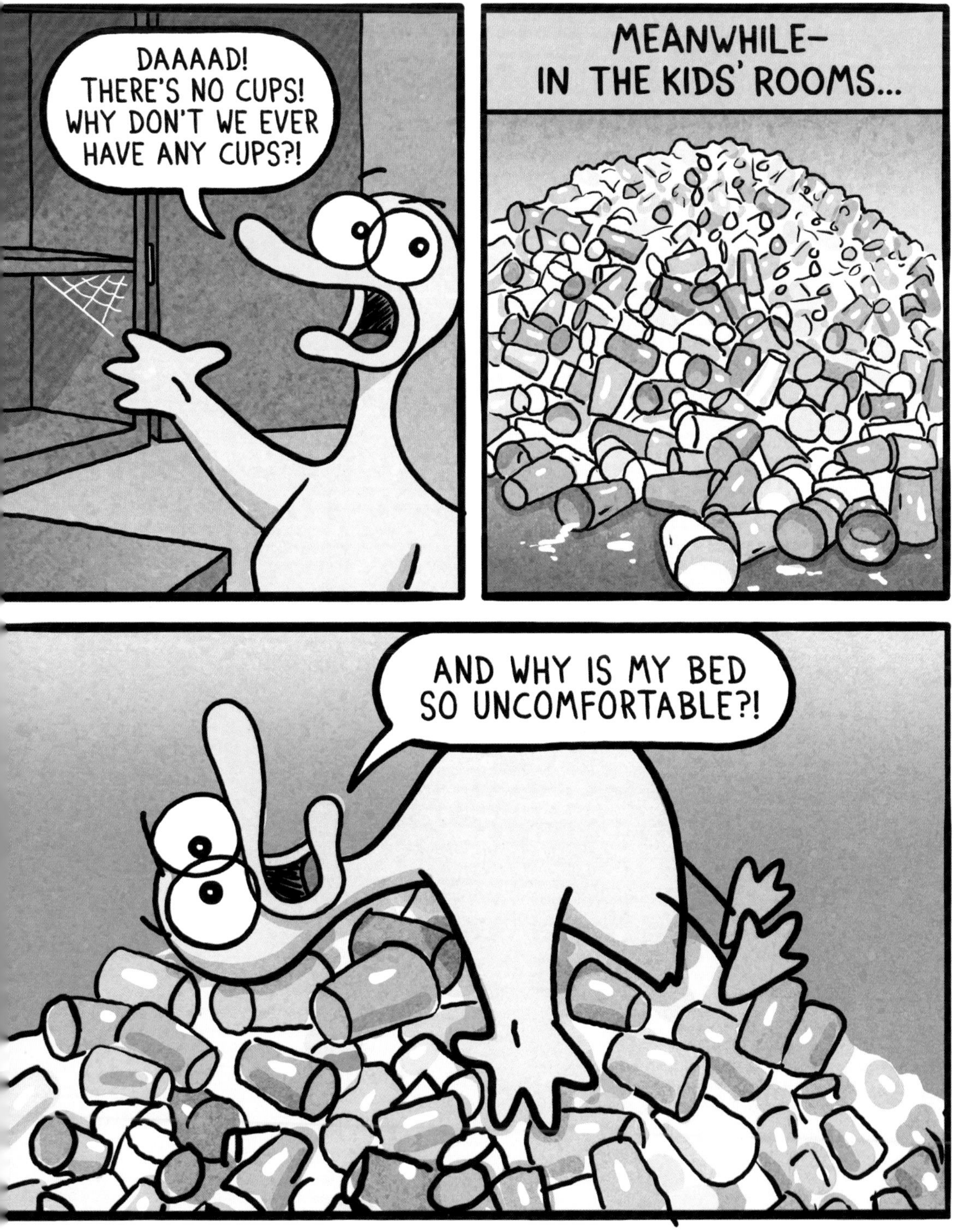
DAAAAD! THERE'S NO CUPS! WHY DON'T WE EVER HAVE ANY CUPS?!
MEANWHILE– IN THE KIDS' ROOMS...
AND WHY IS MY BED SO UNCOMFORTABLE?!

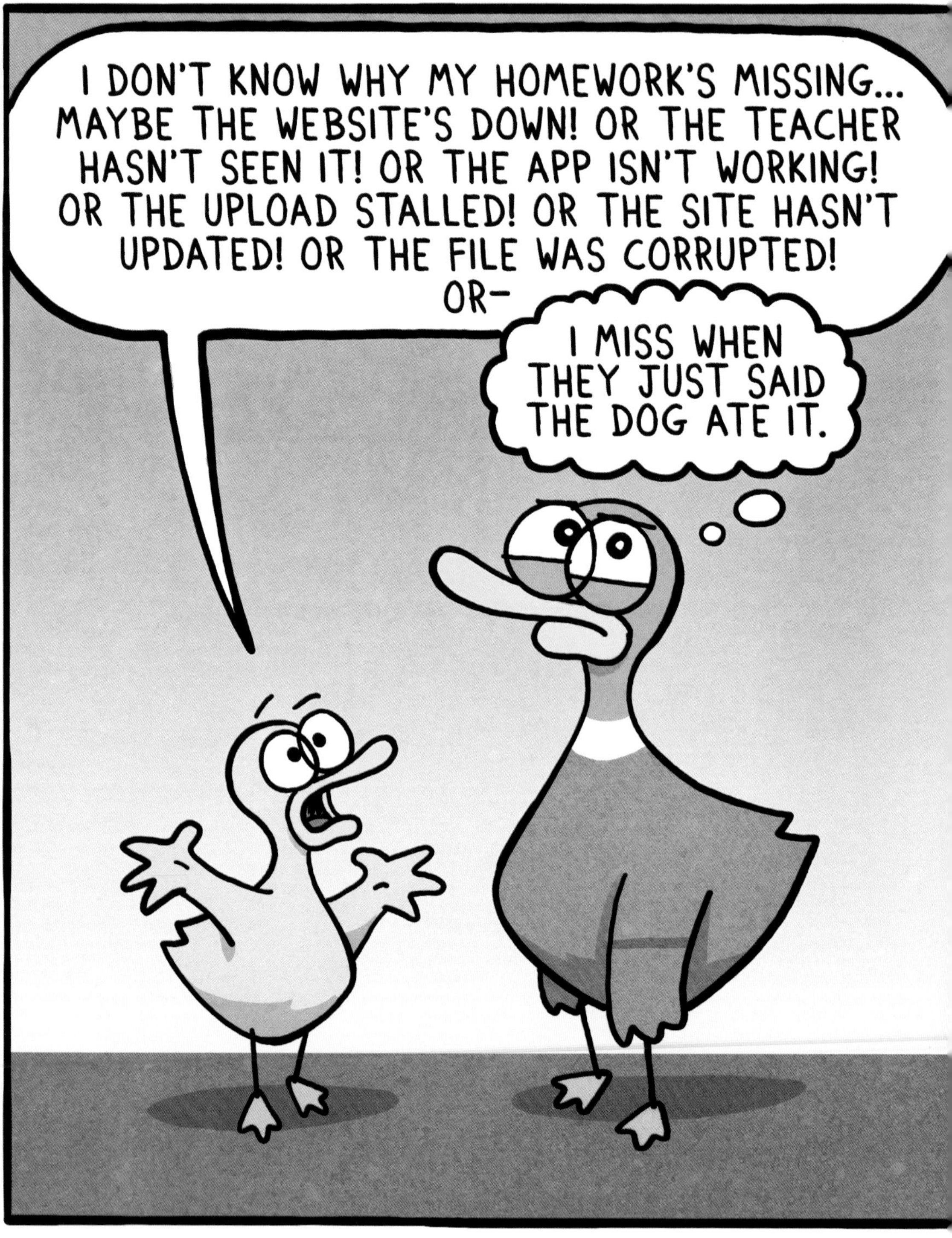
I DON'T KNOW WHY MY HOMEWORK'S MISSING... MAYBE THE WEBSITE'S DOWN! OR THE TEACHER HASN'T SEEN IT! OR THE APP ISN'T WORKING! OR THE UPLOAD STALLED! OR THE SITE HASN'T UPDATED! OR THE FILE WAS CORRUPTED! OR-
I MISS WHEN THEY JUST SAID THE DOG ATE IT.

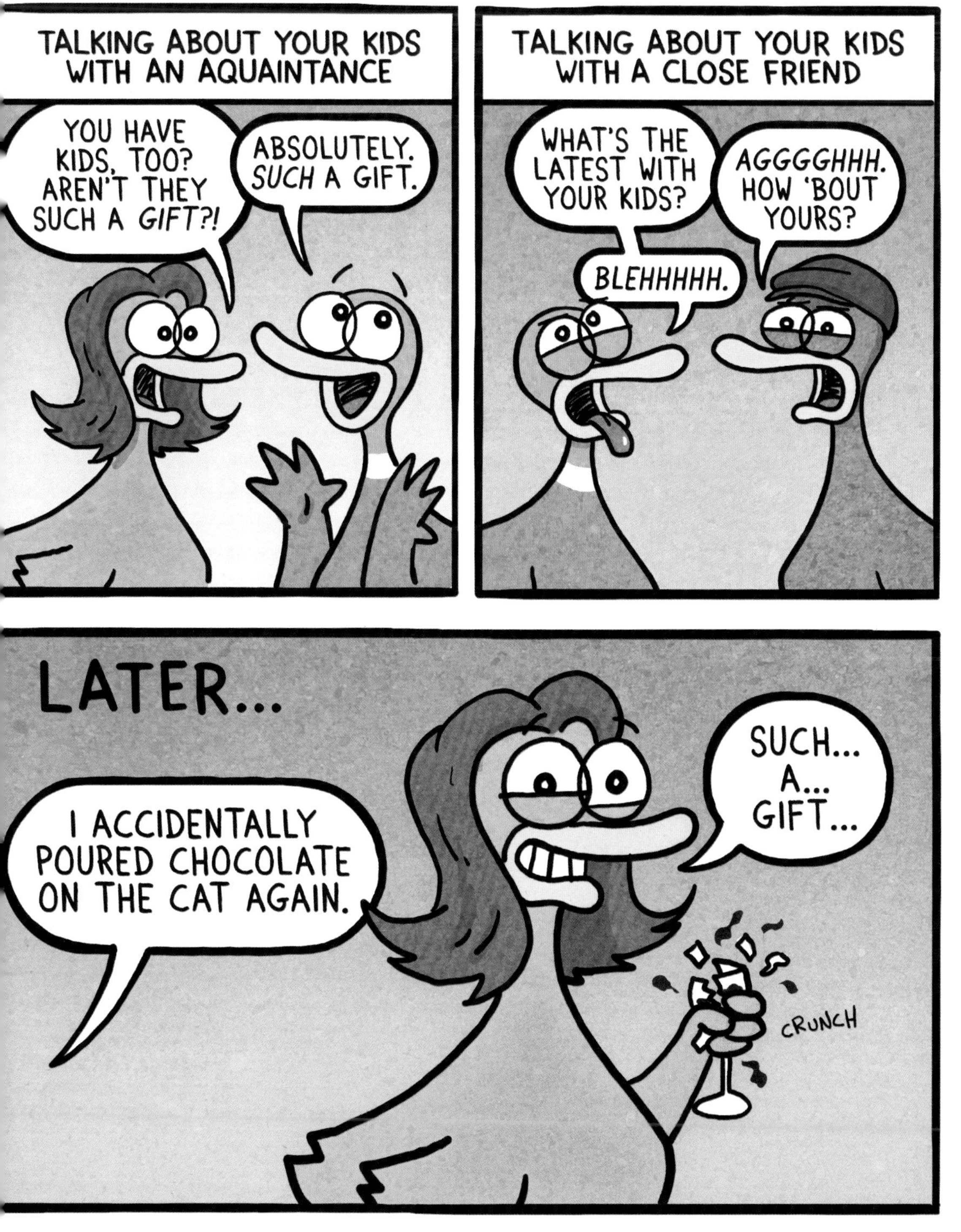
TALKING ABOUT YOUR KIDS WITH AN AQUAINTANCE
YOU HAVE KIDS, TOO? AREN'T THEY SUCH A *GIFT*?!
ABSOLUTELY. *SUCH* A GIFT.
TALKING ABOUT YOUR KIDS WITH A CLOSE FRIEND
WHAT'S THE LATEST WITH YOUR KIDS?
BLEHHHHH.
AGGGGHHH. HOW 'BOUT YOURS?
LATER...
I ACCIDENTALLY POURED CHOCOLATE ON THE CAT AGAIN.
SUCH... A... GIFT...
CRUNCH

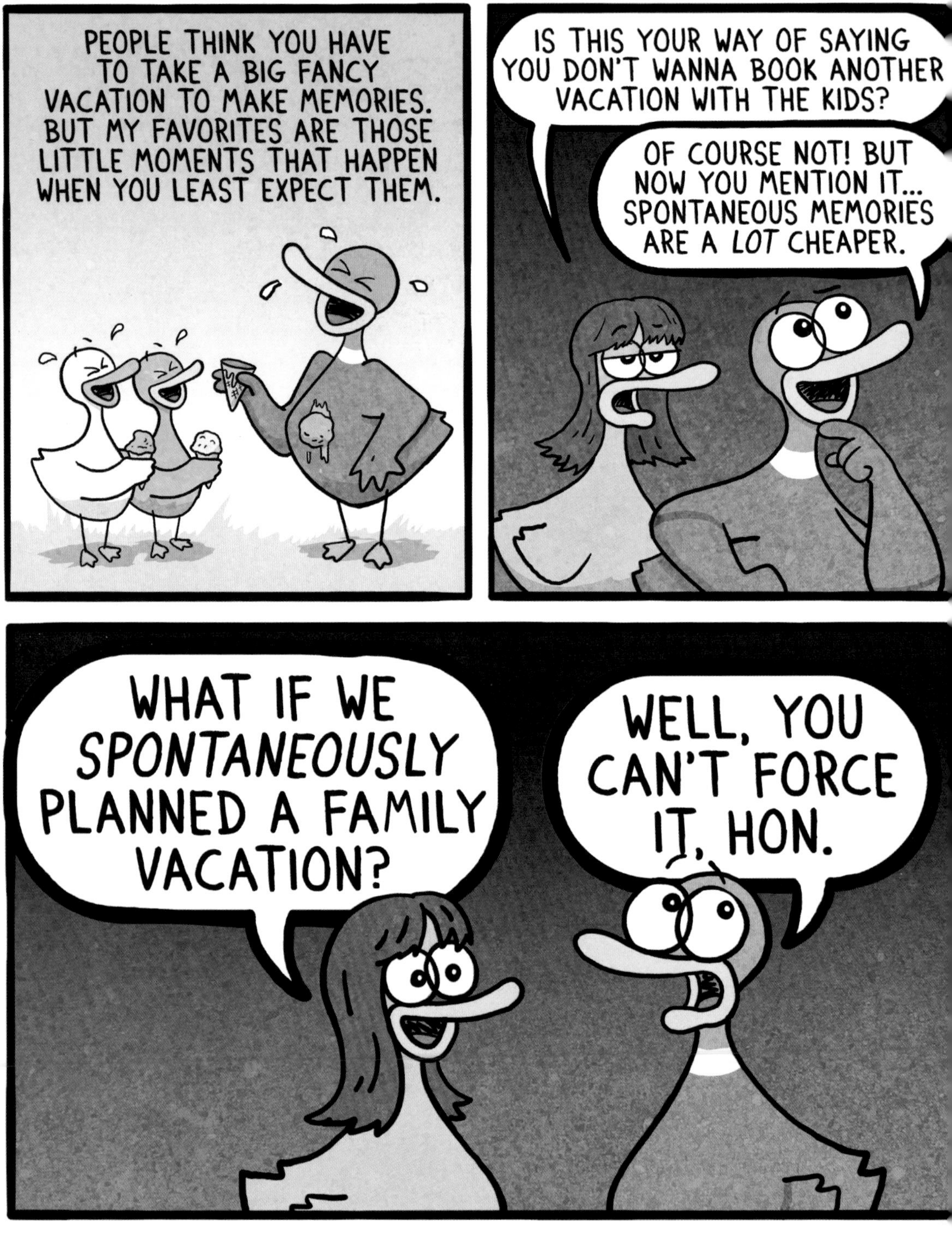
PEOPLE THINK YOU HAVE TO TAKE A BIG FANCY VACATION TO MAKE MEMORIES. BUT MY FAVORITES ARE THOSE LITTLE MOMENTS THAT HAPPEN WHEN YOU LEAST EXPECT THEM.
IS THIS YOUR WAY OF SAYING YOU DON'T WANNA BOOK ANOTHER VACATION WITH THE KIDS?
OF COURSE NOT! BUT NOW YOU MENTION IT... SPONTANEOUS MEMORIES ARE A *LOT* CHEAPER.
WHAT IF WE *SPONTANEOUSLY* PLANNED A FAMILY VACATION?
WELL, YOU CAN'T FORCE IT, HON.

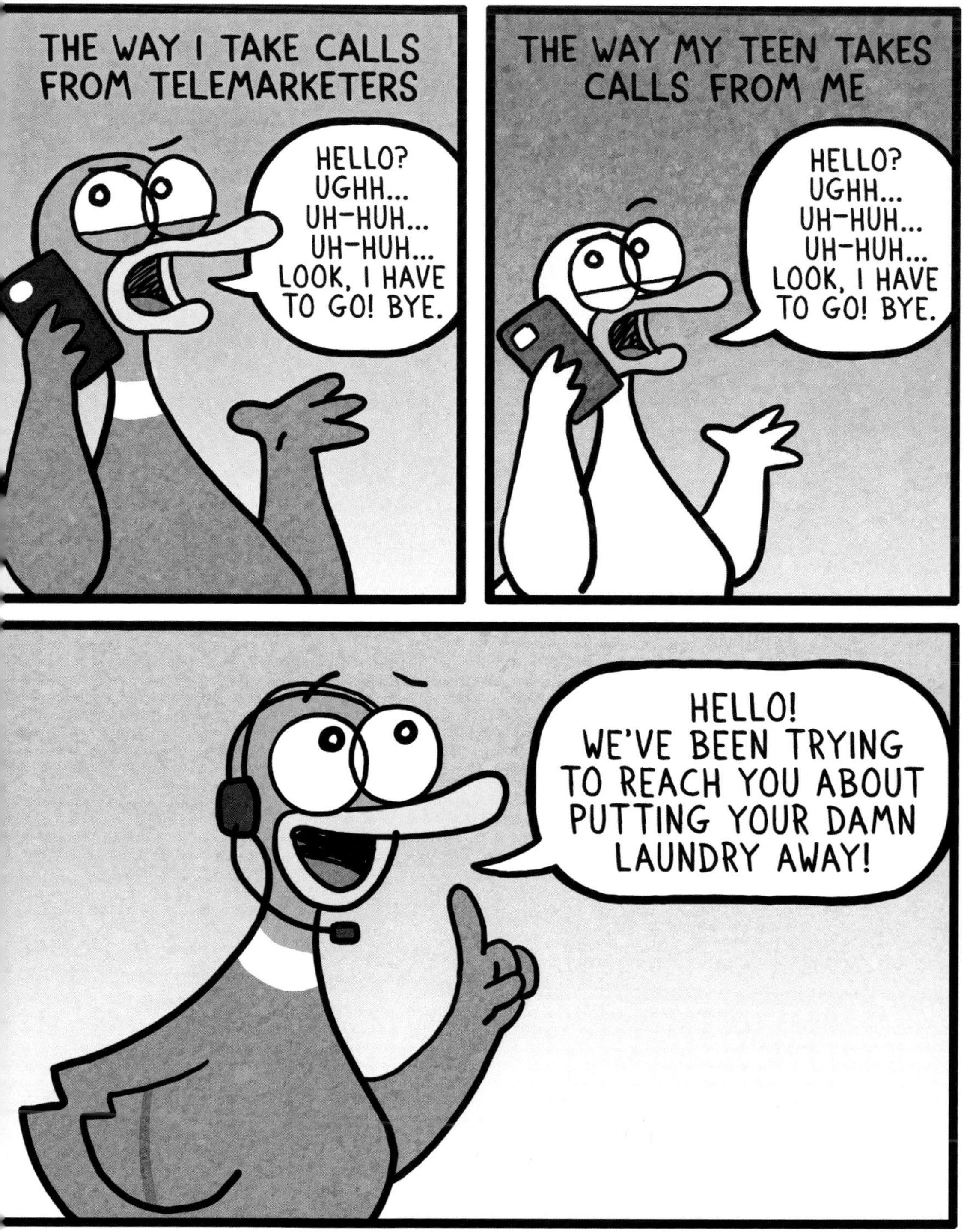
THE WAY I TAKE CALLS FROM TELEMARKETERS
HELLO? UGHH... UH-HUH... UH-HUH... LOOK, I HAVE TO GO! BYE.
THE WAY MY TEEN TAKES CALLS FROM ME
HELLO? UGHH... UH-HUH... UH-HUH... LOOK, I HAVE TO GO! BYE.
HELLO! WE'VE BEEN TRYING TO REACH YOU ABOUT PUTTING YOUR DAMN LAUNDRY AWAY!

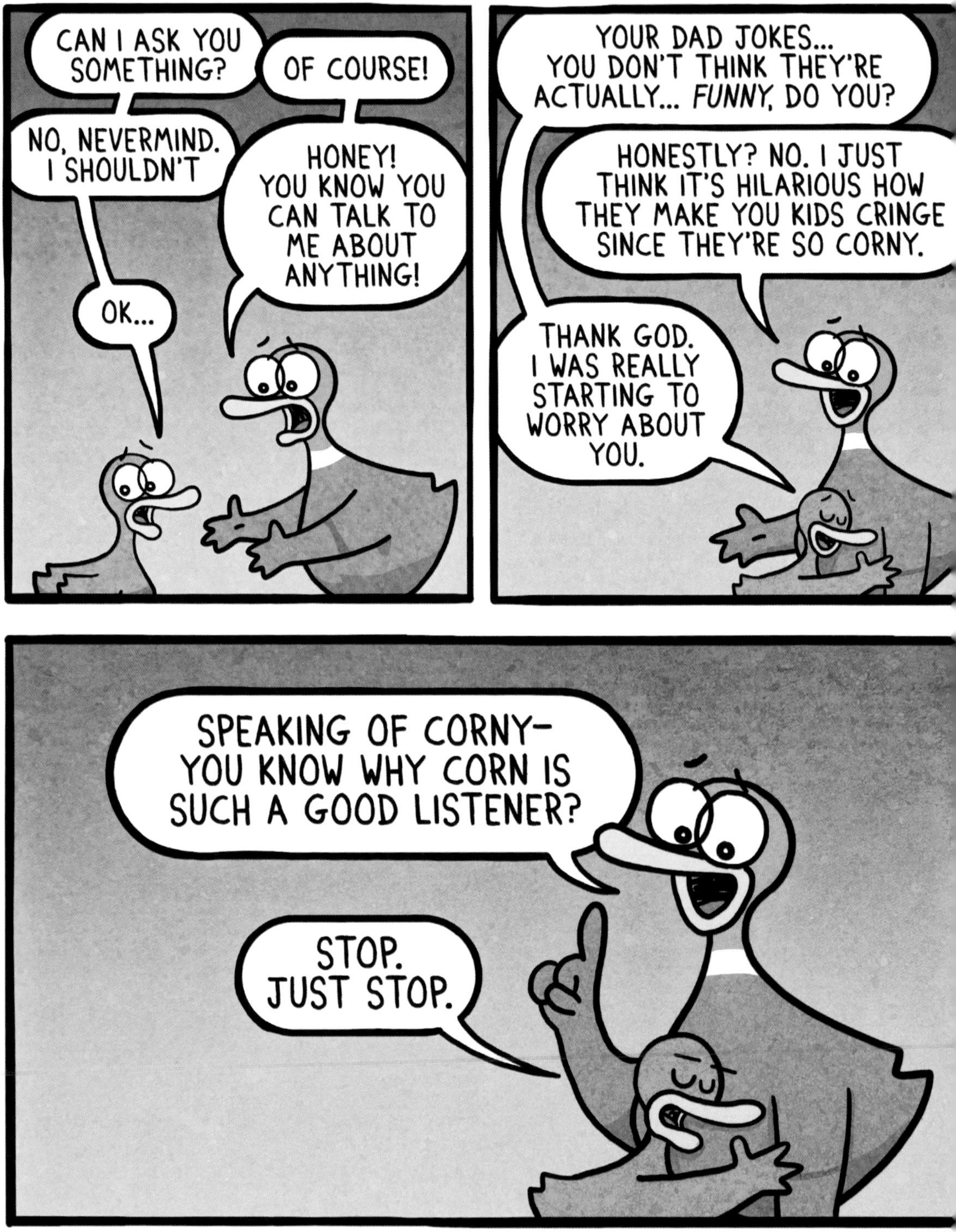
CAN I ASK YOU SOMETHING?
OF COURSE!
NO, NEVERMIND. I SHOULDN'T
HONEY! YOU KNOW YOU CAN TALK TO ME ABOUT ANYTHING!
OK...
YOUR DAD JOKES... YOU DON'T THINK THEY'RE ACTUALLY... *FUNNY*, DO YOU?
HONESTLY? NO. I JUST THINK IT'S HILARIOUS HOW THEY MAKE YOU KIDS CRINGE SINCE THEY'RE SO CORNY.
THANK GOD. I WAS REALLY STARTING TO WORRY ABOUT YOU.
SPEAKING OF CORNY- YOU KNOW WHY CORN IS SUCH A GOOD LISTENER?
STOP. JUST STOP.

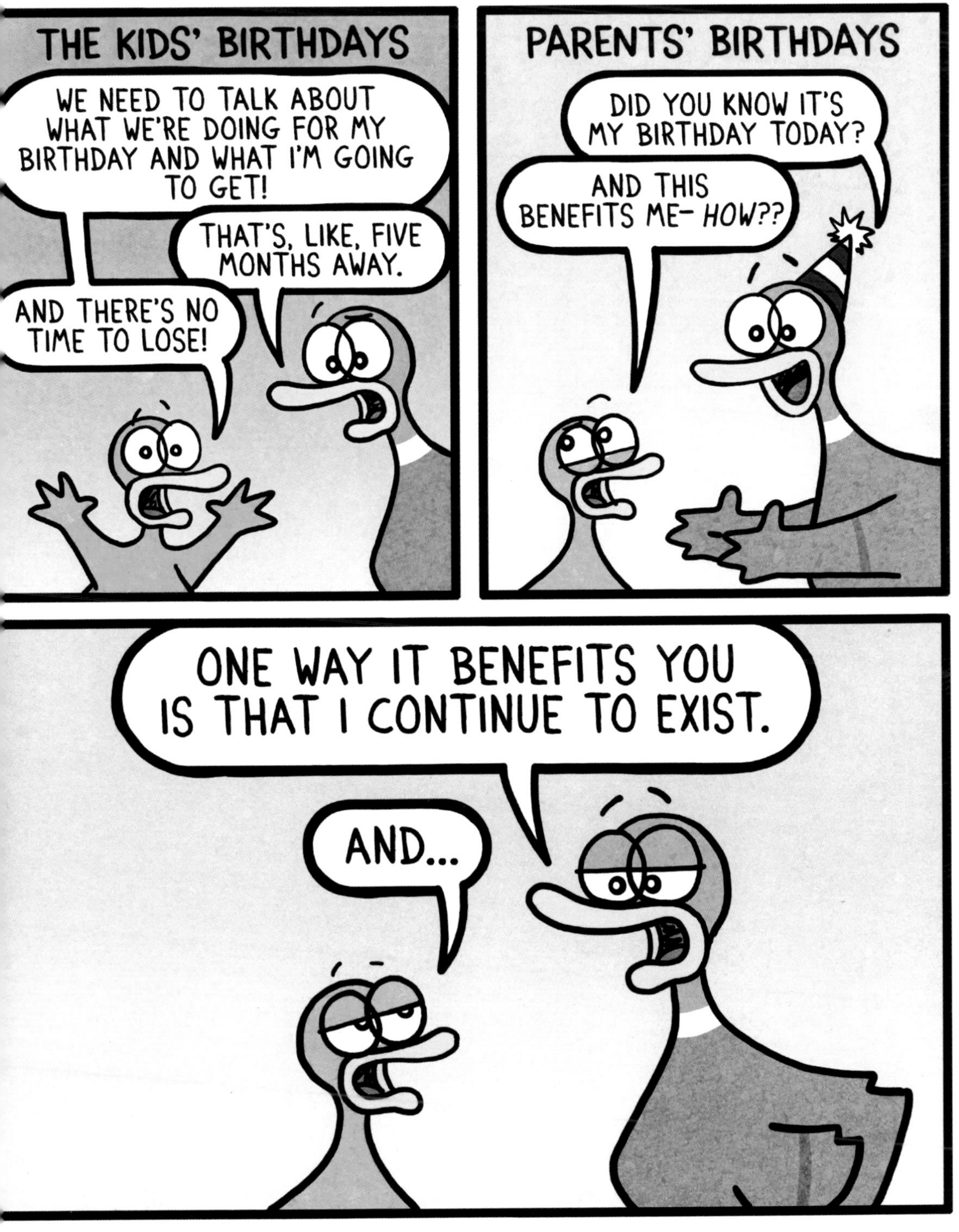

THE KIDS' BIRTHDAYS
WE NEED TO TALK ABOUT WHAT WE'RE DOING FOR MY BIRTHDAY AND WHAT I'M GOING TO GET!
THAT'S, LIKE, FIVE MONTHS AWAY.
AND THERE'S NO TIME TO LOSE!
PARENTS' BIRTHDAYS
DID YOU KNOW IT'S MY BIRTHDAY TODAY?
AND THIS BENEFITS ME– *HOW*??
ONE WAY IT BENEFITS YOU IS THAT I CONTINUE TO EXIST.
AND...

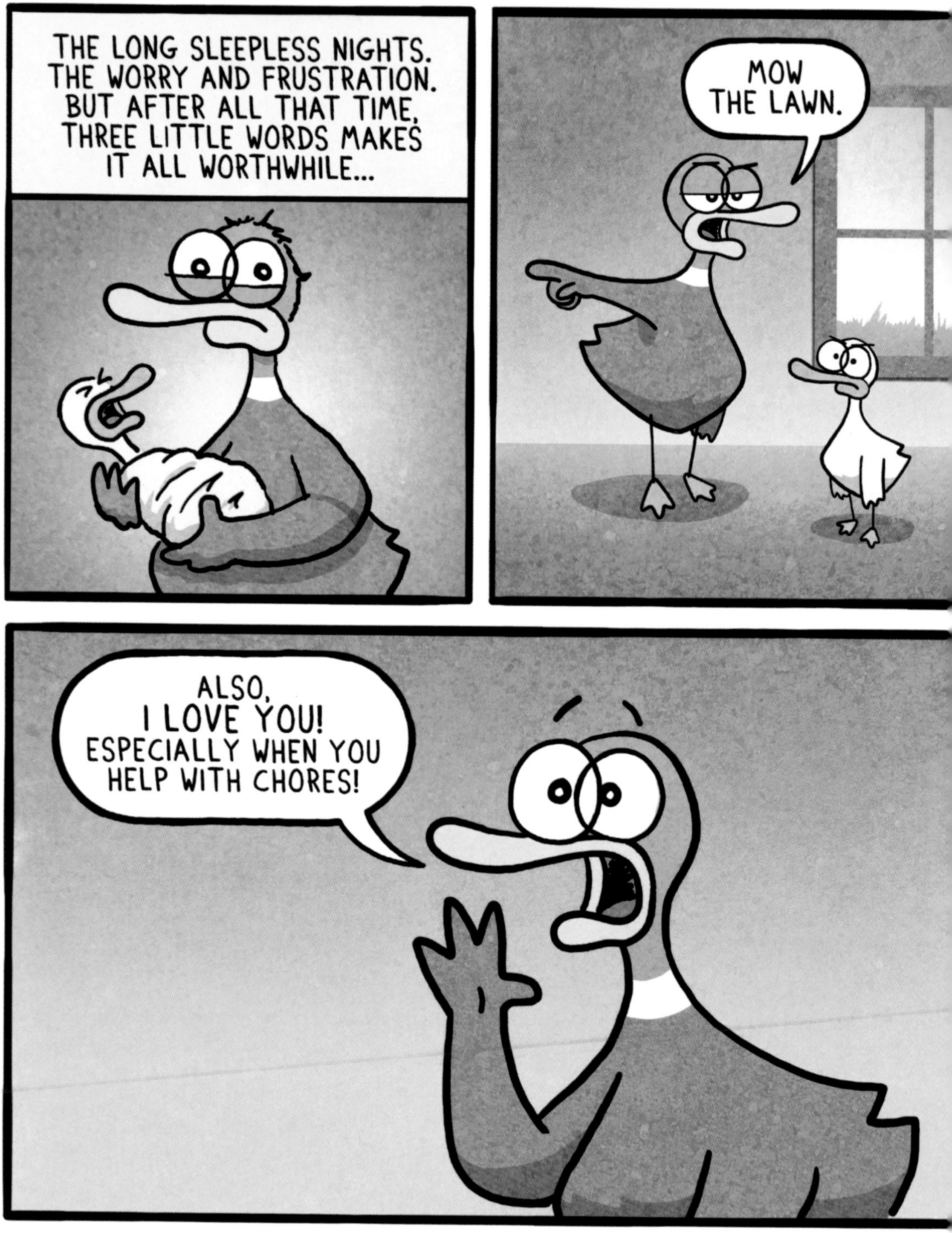
THE LONG SLEEPLESS NIGHTS. THE WORRY AND FRUSTRATION. BUT AFTER ALL THAT TIME, THREE LITTLE WORDS MAKES IT ALL WORTHWHILE...
MOW THE LAWN.
ALSO, I LOVE YOU! ESPECIALLY WHEN YOU HELP WITH CHORES!

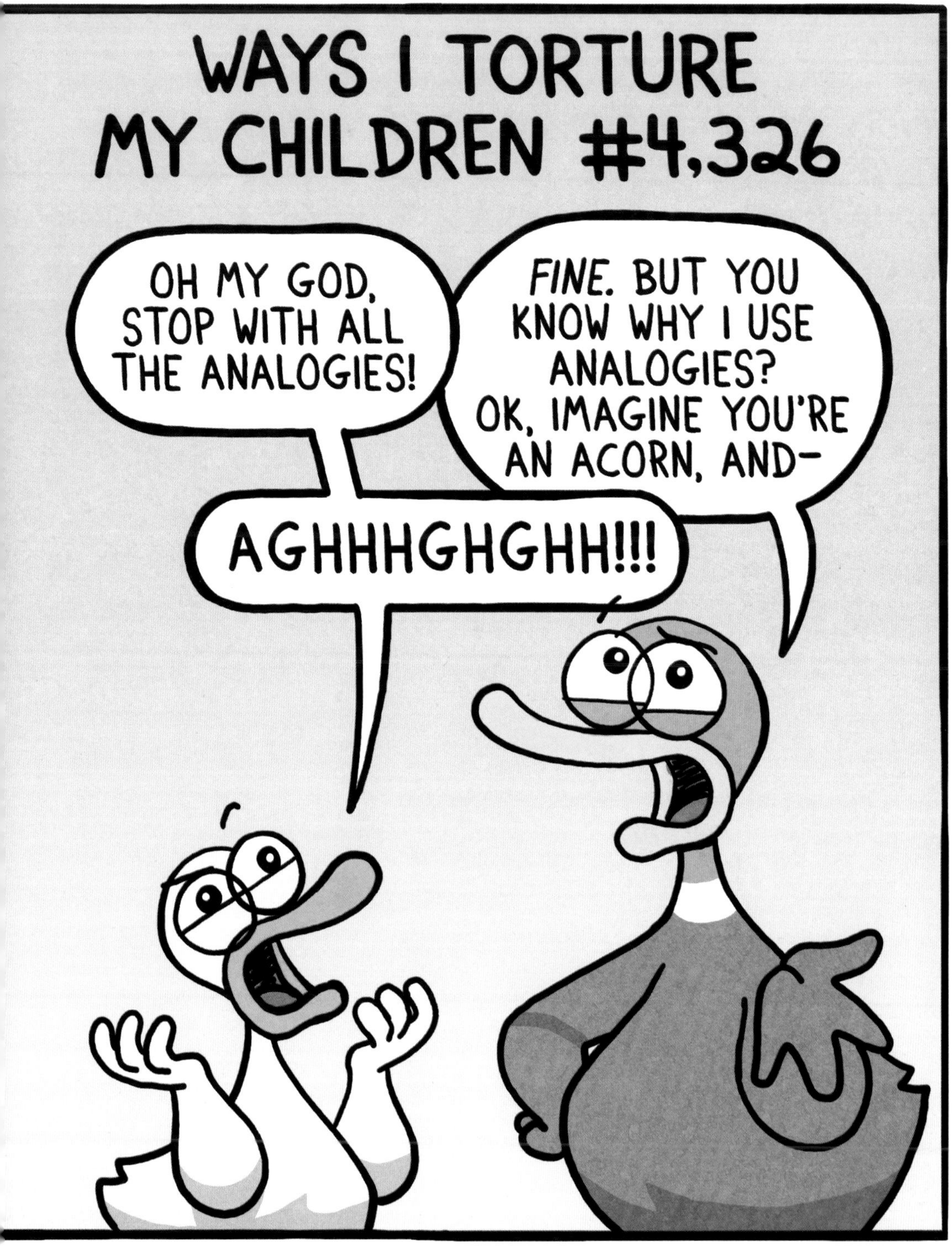
WAYS I TORTURE MY CHILDREN #4,326
OH MY GOD, STOP WITH ALL THE ANALOGIES!
FINE. BUT YOU KNOW WHY I USE ANALOGIES? OK, IMAGINE YOU'RE AN ACORN, AND–
AGHHHGHGHH!!!

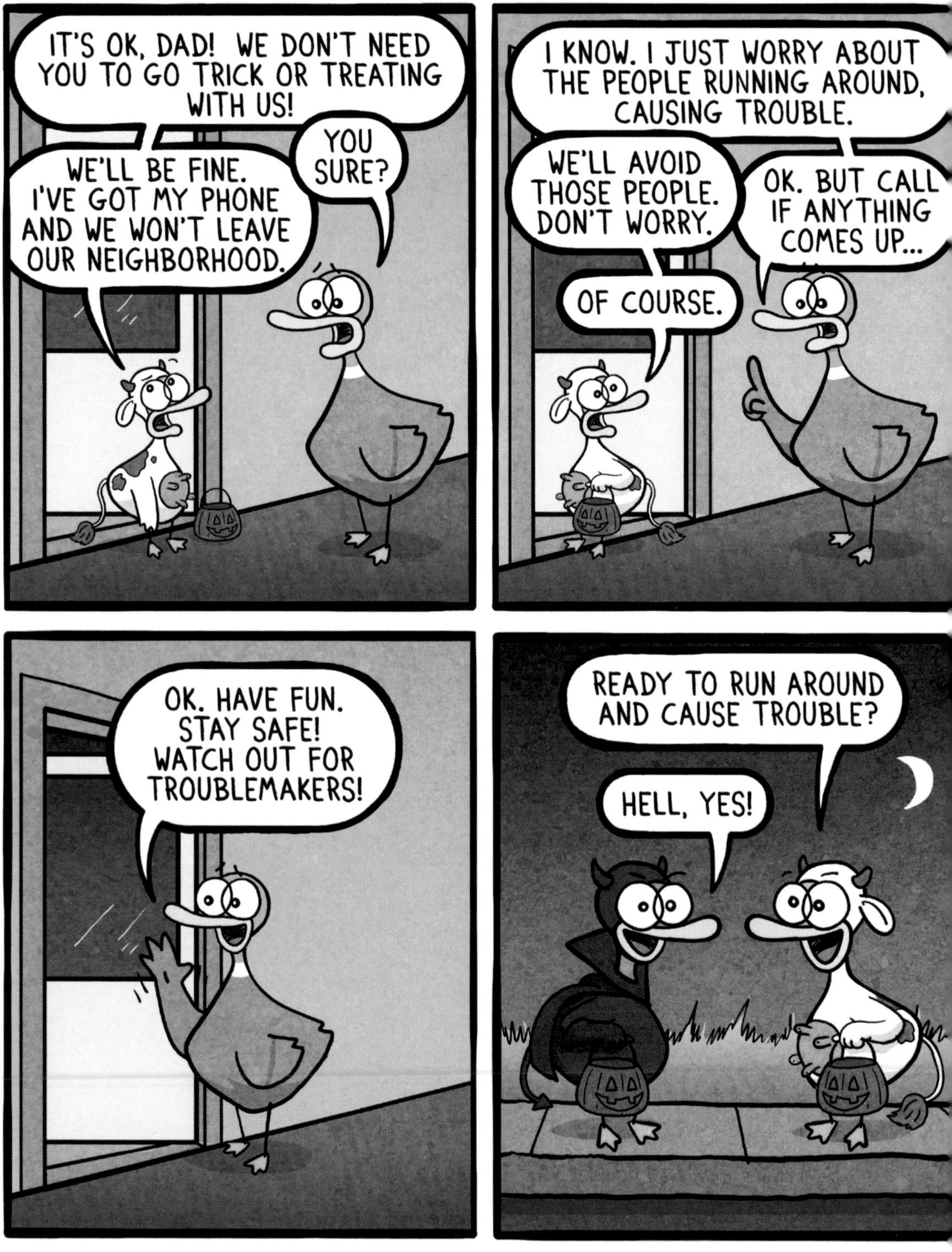
IT'S OK, DAD! WE DON'T NEED YOU TO GO TRICK OR TREATING WITH US!
WE'LL BE FINE. I'VE GOT MY PHONE AND WE WON'T LEAVE OUR NEIGHBORHOOD.
YOU SURE?
I KNOW. I JUST WORRY ABOUT THE PEOPLE RUNNING AROUND, CAUSING TROUBLE.
WE'LL AVOID THOSE PEOPLE. DON'T WORRY.
OK. BUT CALL IF ANYTHING COMES UP...
OF COURSE.
OK. HAVE FUN. STAY SAFE! WATCH OUT FOR TROUBLEMAKERS!
READY TO RUN AROUND AND CAUSE TROUBLE?
HELL, YES!

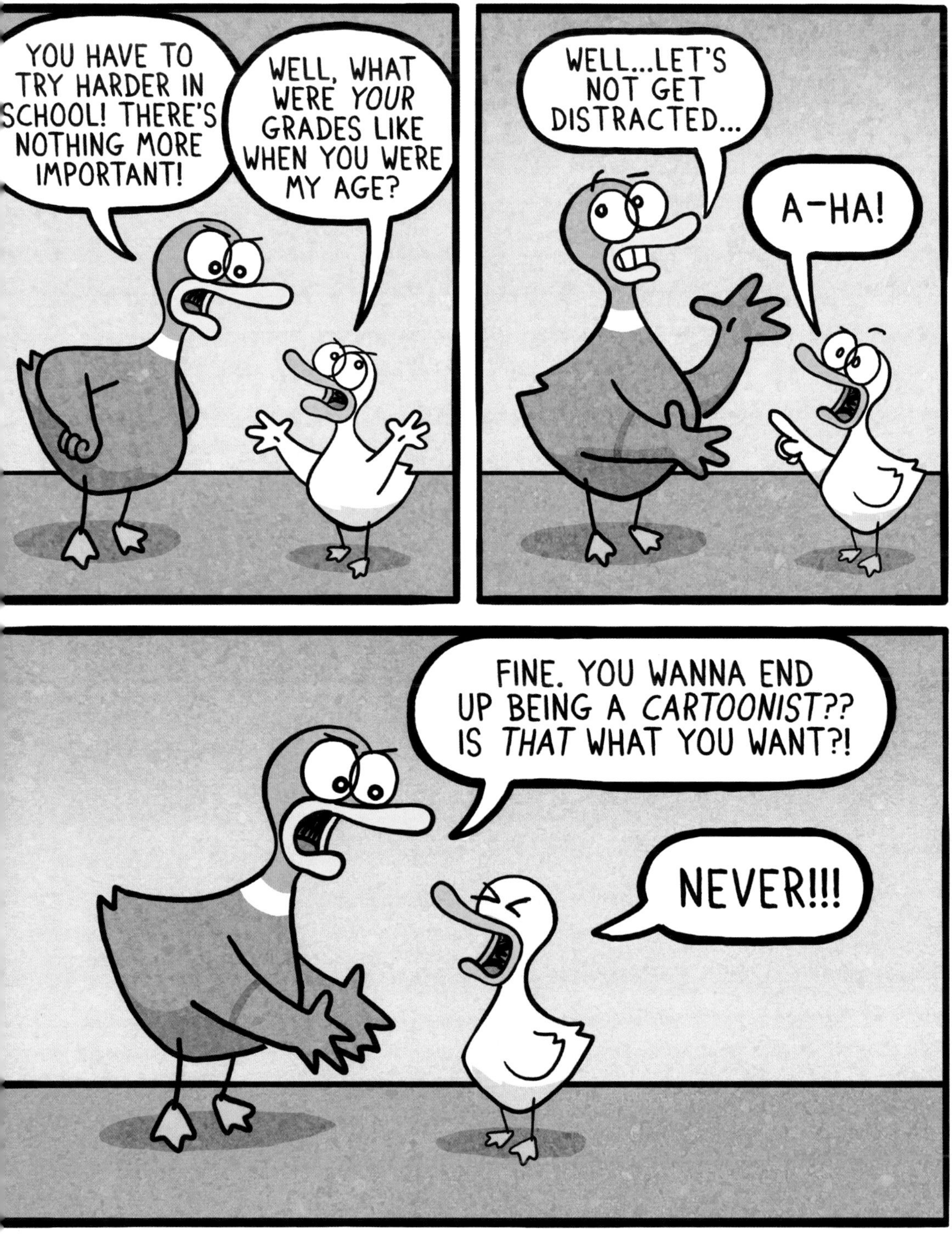
YOU HAVE TO TRY HARDER IN SCHOOL! THERE'S NOTHING MORE IMPORTANT!
WELL, WHAT WERE *YOUR* GRADES LIKE WHEN YOU WERE MY AGE?
WELL...LET'S NOT GET DISTRACTED...
A-HA!
FINE. YOU WANNA END UP BEING A *CARTOONIST*?? IS *THAT* WHAT YOU WANT?!
NEVER!!!

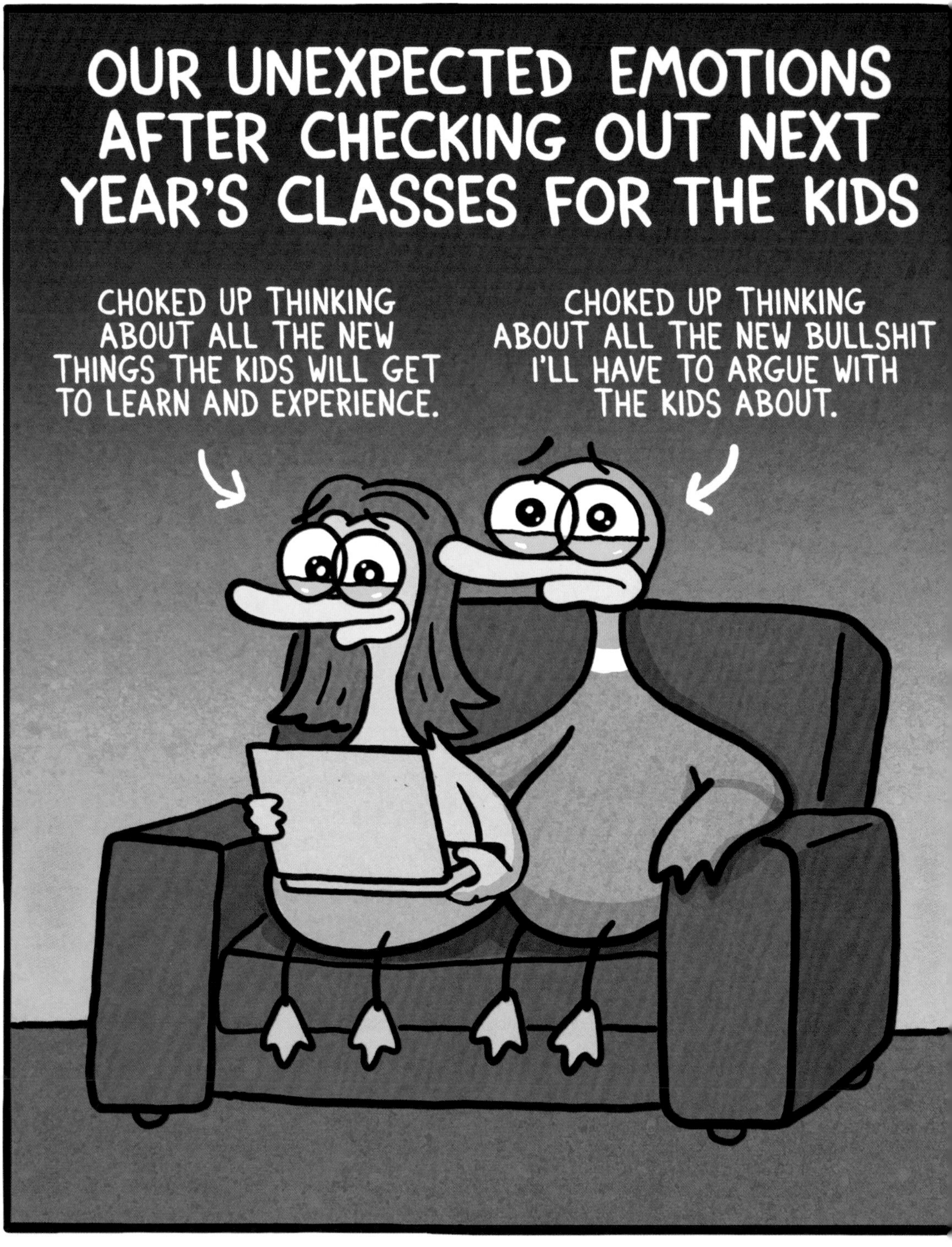
OUR UNEXPECTED EMOTIONS AFTER CHECKING OUT NEXT YEAR'S CLASSES FOR THE KIDS
CHOKED UP THINKING ABOUT ALL THE NEW THINGS THE KIDS WILL GET TO LEARN AND EXPERIENCE.
CHOKED UP THINKING ABOUT ALL THE NEW BULLSHIT I'LL HAVE TO ARGUE WITH THE KIDS ABOUT.

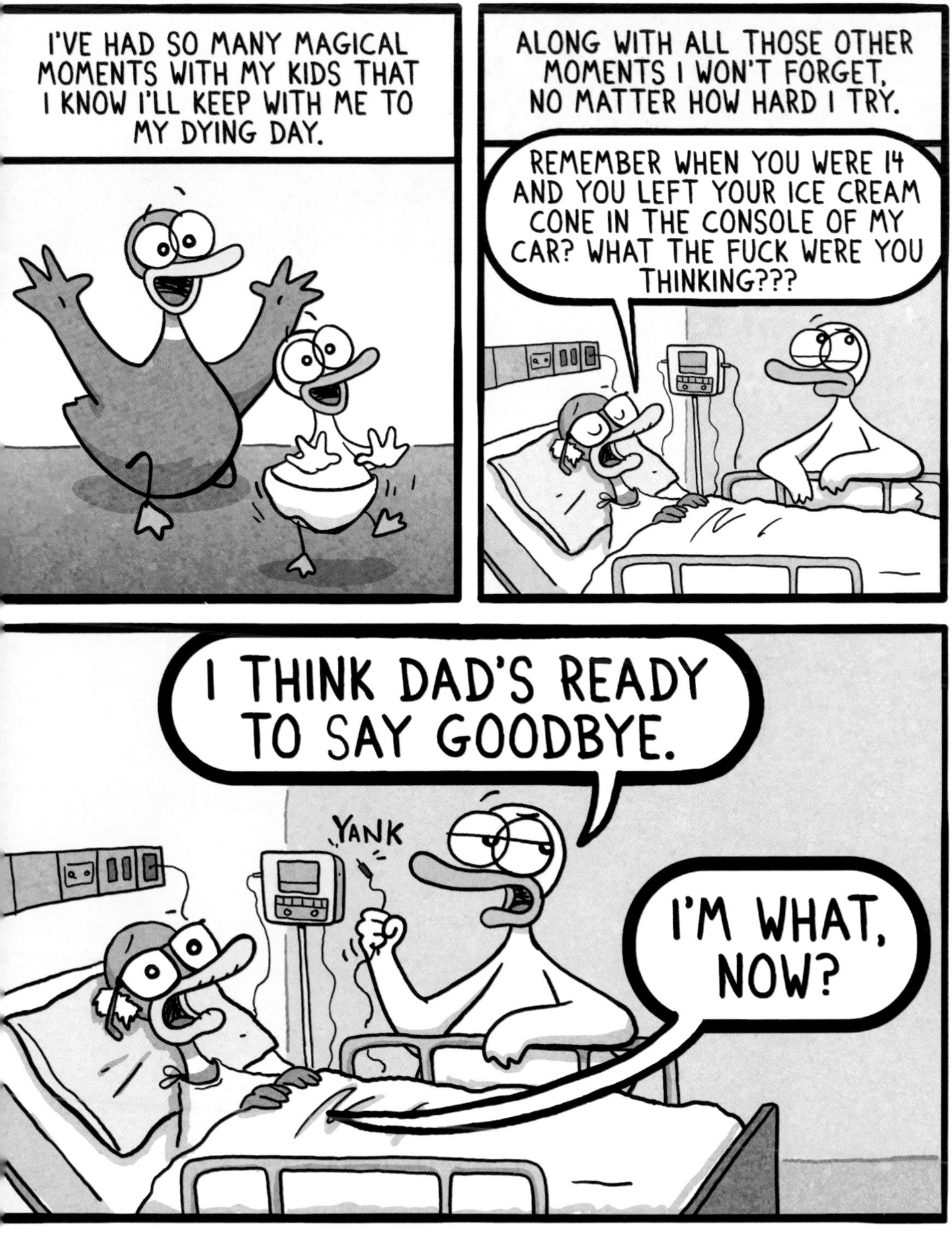
I'VE HAD SO MANY MAGICAL MOMENTS WITH MY KIDS THAT I KNOW I'LL KEEP WITH ME TO MY DYING DAY.
ALONG WITH ALL THOSE OTHER MOMENTS I WON'T FORGET, NO MATTER HOW HARD I TRY.
REMEMBER WHEN YOU WERE 14 AND YOU LEFT YOUR ICE CREAM CONE IN THE CONSOLE OF MY CAR? WHAT THE FUCK WERE YOU THINKING???
I THINK DAD'S READY TO SAY GOODBYE.
YANK
I'M WHAT, NOW?

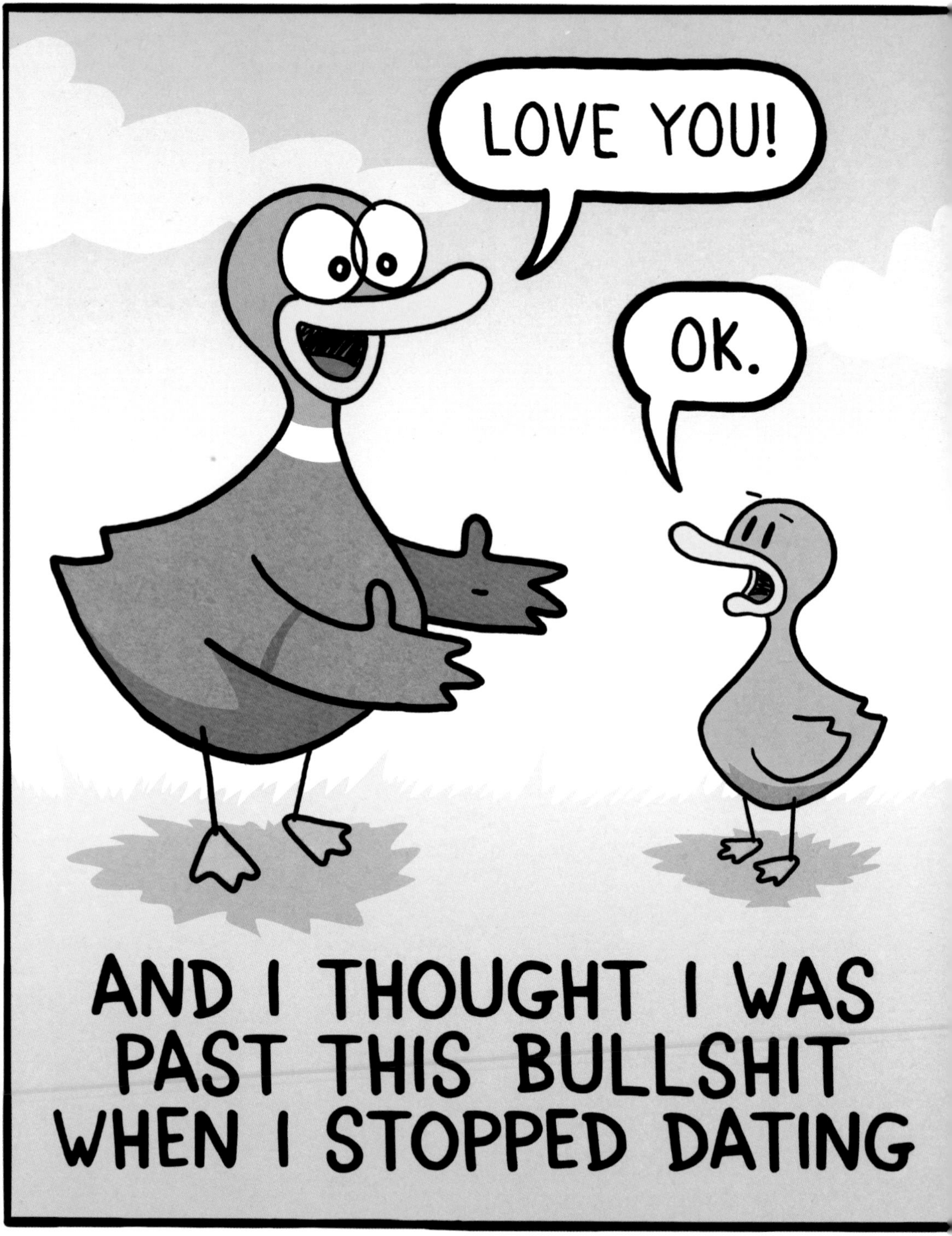
LOVE YOU!
OK.
AND I THOUGHT I WAS PAST THIS BULLSHIT WHEN I STOPPED DATING

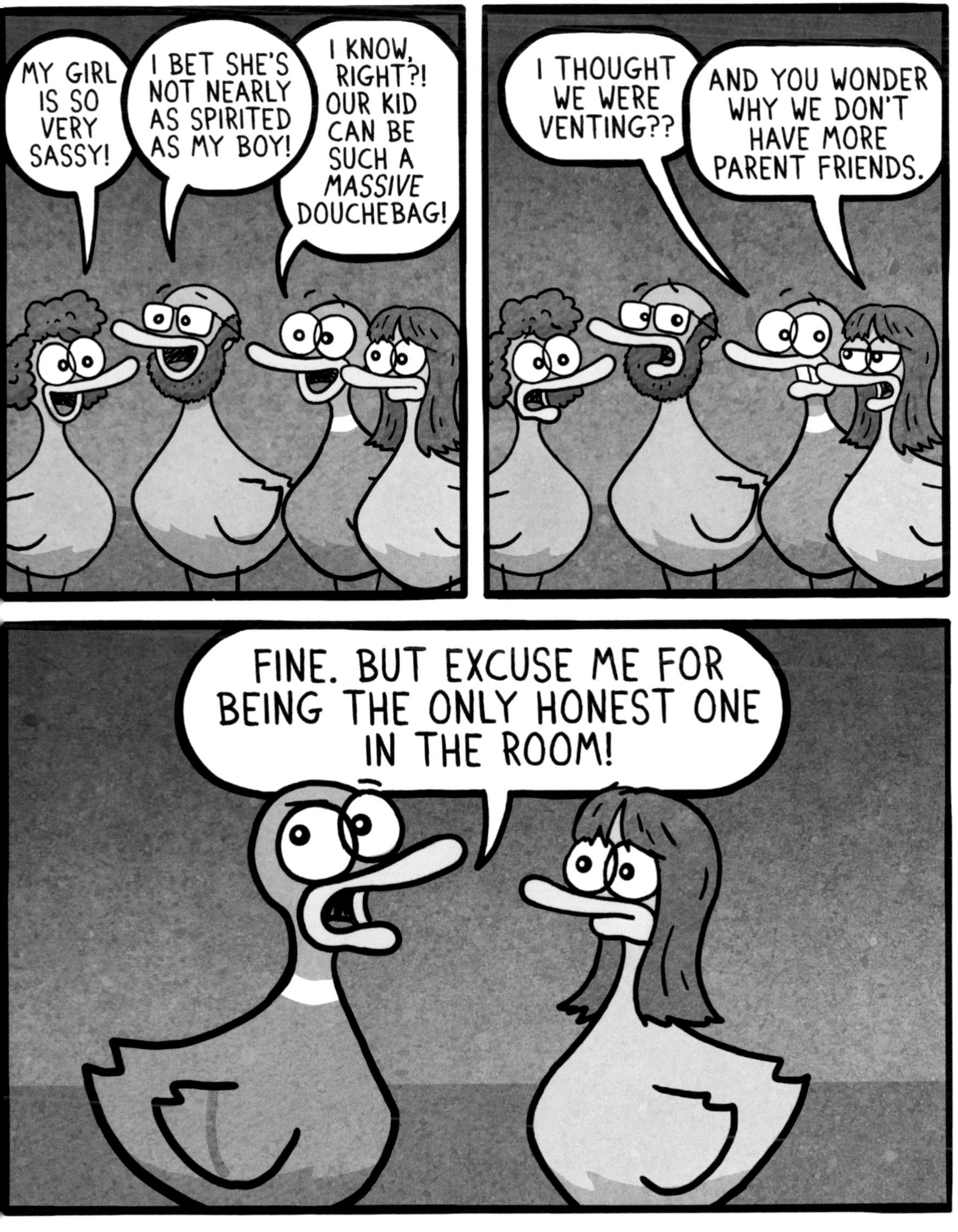
MY GIRL IS SO VERY SASSY!
I BET SHE'S NOT NEARLY AS SPIRITED AS MY BOY!
I KNOW, RIGHT?! OUR KID CAN BE SUCH A *MASSIVE* DOUCHEBAG!
I THOUGHT WE WERE VENTING??
AND YOU WONDER WHY WE DON'T HAVE MORE PARENT FRIENDS.
FINE. BUT EXCUSE ME FOR BEING THE ONLY HONEST ONE IN THE ROOM!

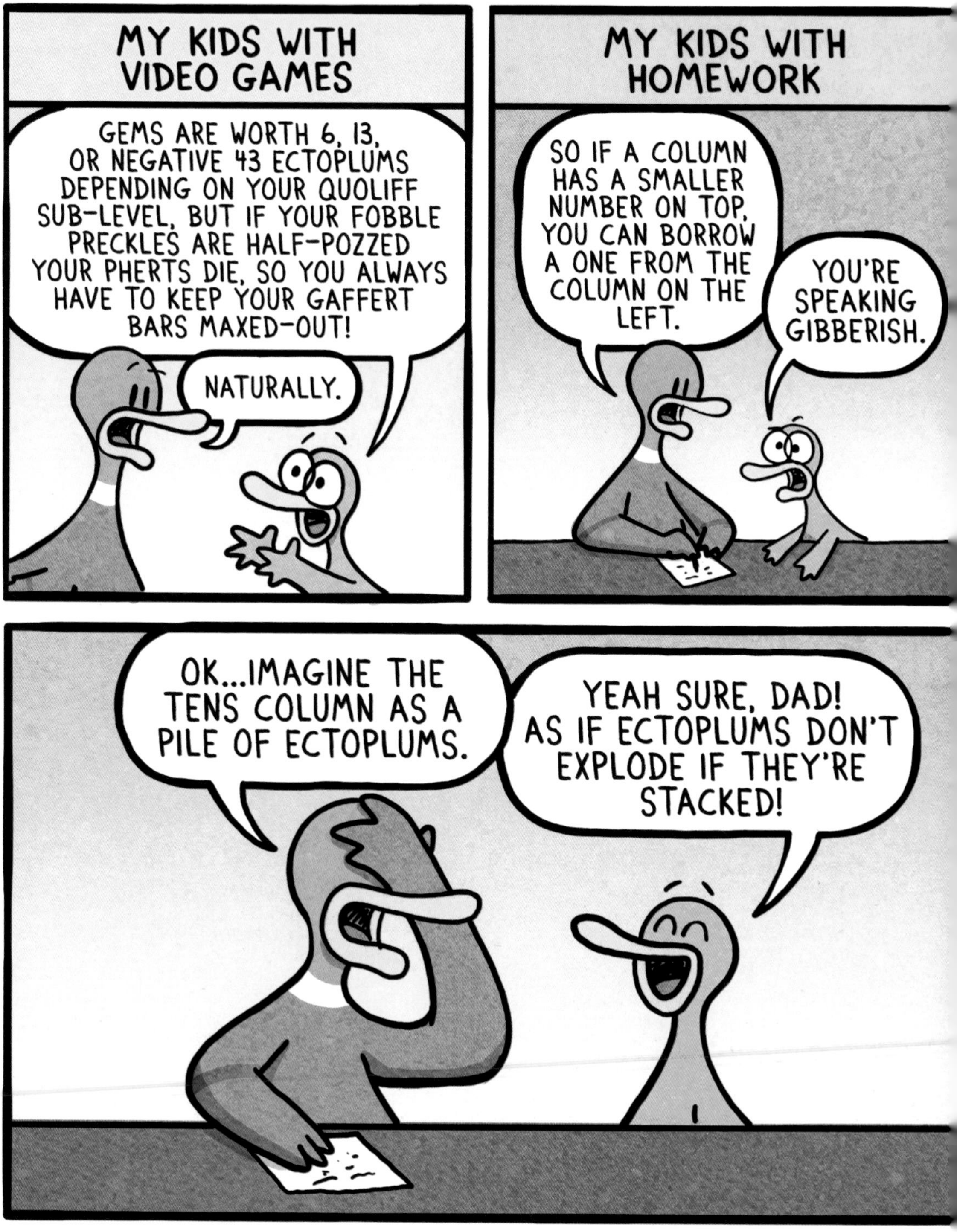
MY KIDS WITH VIDEO GAMES
GEMS ARE WORTH 6, 13, OR NEGATIVE 43 ECTOPLUMS DEPENDING ON YOUR QUOLIFF SUB-LEVEL, BUT IF YOUR FOBBLE PRECKLES ARE HALF-POZZED YOUR PHERTS DIE, SO YOU ALWAYS HAVE TO KEEP YOUR GAFFERT BARS MAXED-OUT!
NATURALLY.
MY KIDS WITH HOMEWORK
SO IF A COLUMN HAS A SMALLER NUMBER ON TOP, YOU CAN BORROW A ONE FROM THE COLUMN ON THE LEFT.
YOU'RE SPEAKING GIBBERISH.
OK...IMAGINE THE TENS COLUMN AS A PILE OF ECTOPLUMS.
YEAH SURE, DAD! AS IF ECTOPLUMS DON'T EXPLODE IF THEY'RE STACKED!

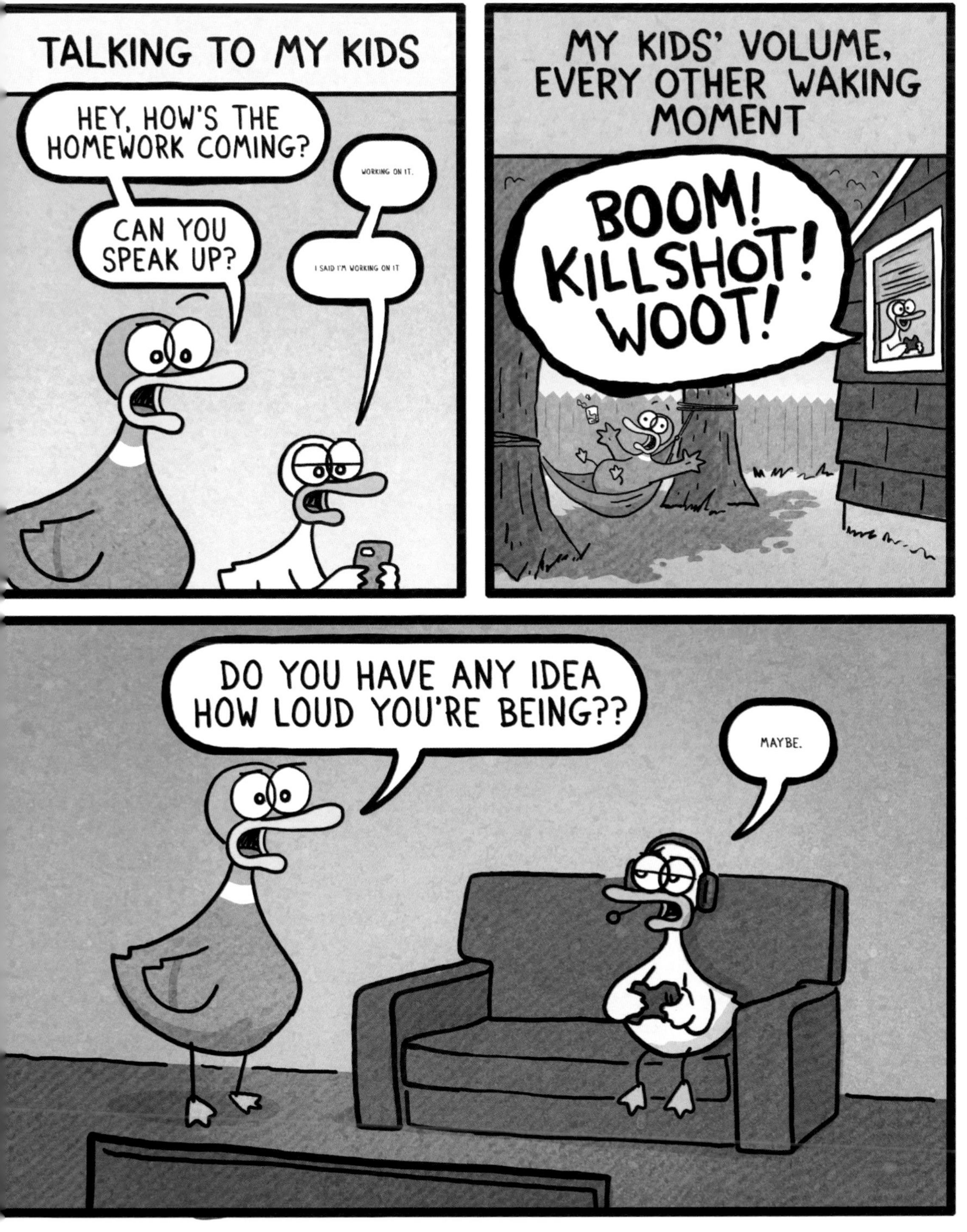
TALKING TO MY KIDS
HEY, HOW'S THE HOMEWORK COMING?
WORKING ON IT.
CAN YOU SPEAK UP?
I SAID I'M WORKING ON IT
MY KIDS' VOLUME, EVERY OTHER WAKING MOMENT
BOOM! KILLSHOT! WOOT!
DO YOU HAVE ANY IDEA HOW LOUD YOU'RE BEING??
MAYBE.

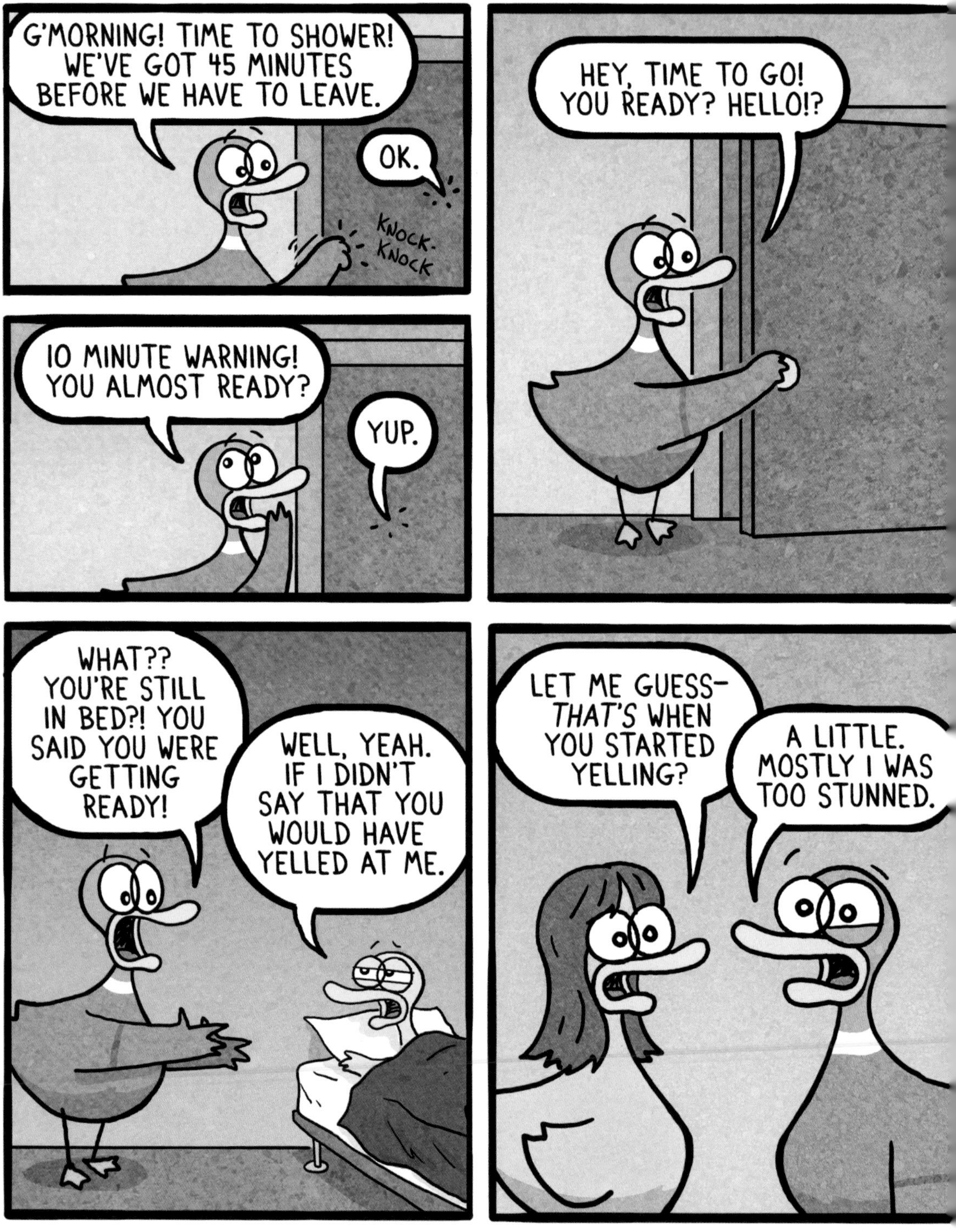
G'MORNING! TIME TO SHOWER! WE'VE GOT 45 MINUTES BEFORE WE HAVE TO LEAVE.
OK.
KNOCK-KNOCK
10 MINUTE WARNING! YOU ALMOST READY?
YUP.
HEY, TIME TO GO! YOU READY? HELLO!?
WHAT?? YOU'RE STILL IN BED?! YOU SAID YOU WERE GETTING READY!
WELL, YEAH. IF I DIDN'T SAY THAT YOU WOULD HAVE YELLED AT ME.
LET ME GUESS—*THAT'S* WHEN YOU STARTED YELLING?
A LITTLE. MOSTLY I WAS TOO STUNNED.

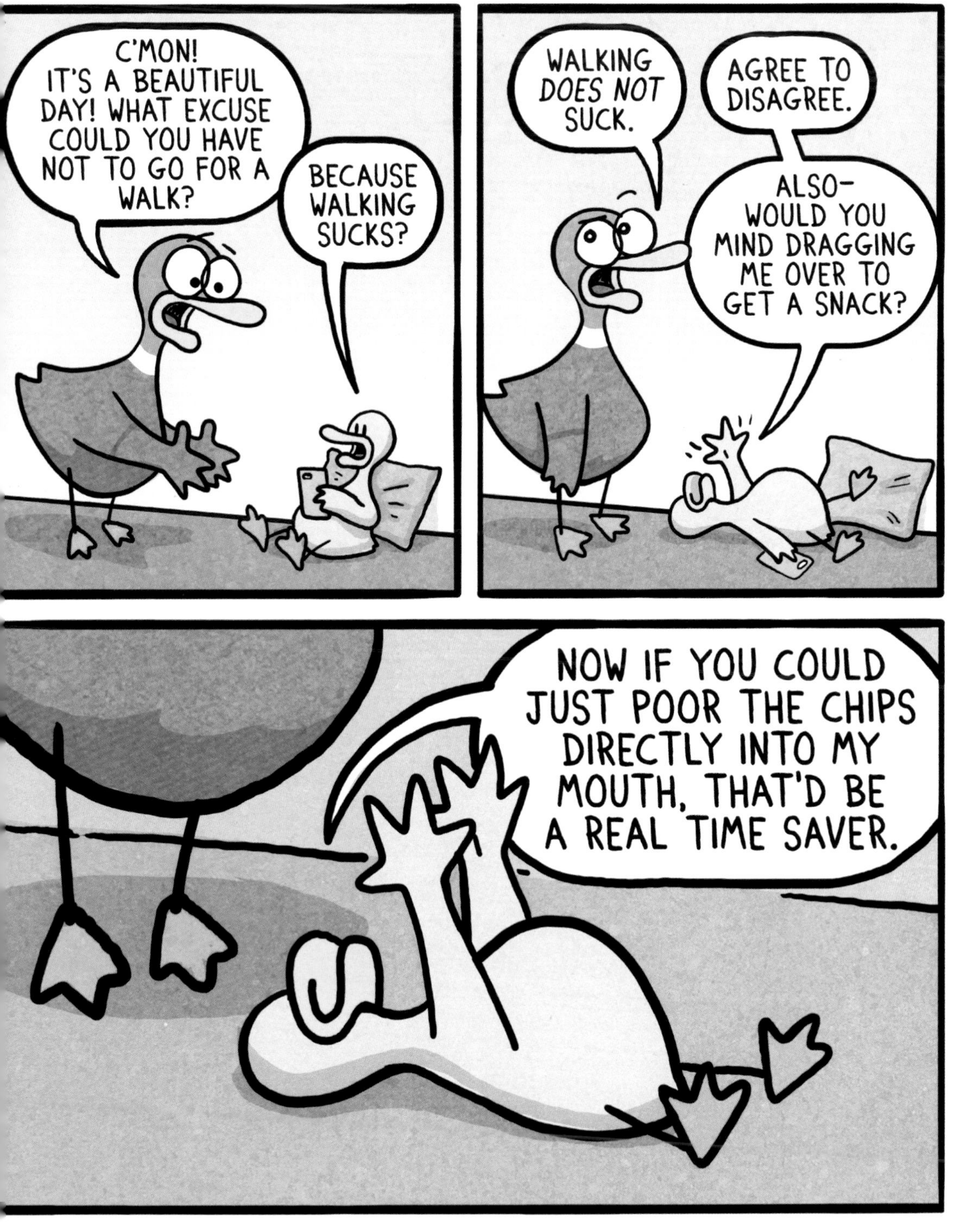
C'MON! IT'S A BEAUTIFUL DAY! WHAT EXCUSE COULD YOU HAVE NOT TO GO FOR A WALK?
BECAUSE WALKING SUCKS?
WALKING *DOES NOT* SUCK.
AGREE TO DISAGREE.
ALSO– WOULD YOU MIND DRAGGING ME OVER TO GET A SNACK?
NOW IF YOU COULD JUST POOR THE CHIPS DIRECTLY INTO MY MOUTH, THAT'D BE A REAL TIME SAVER.

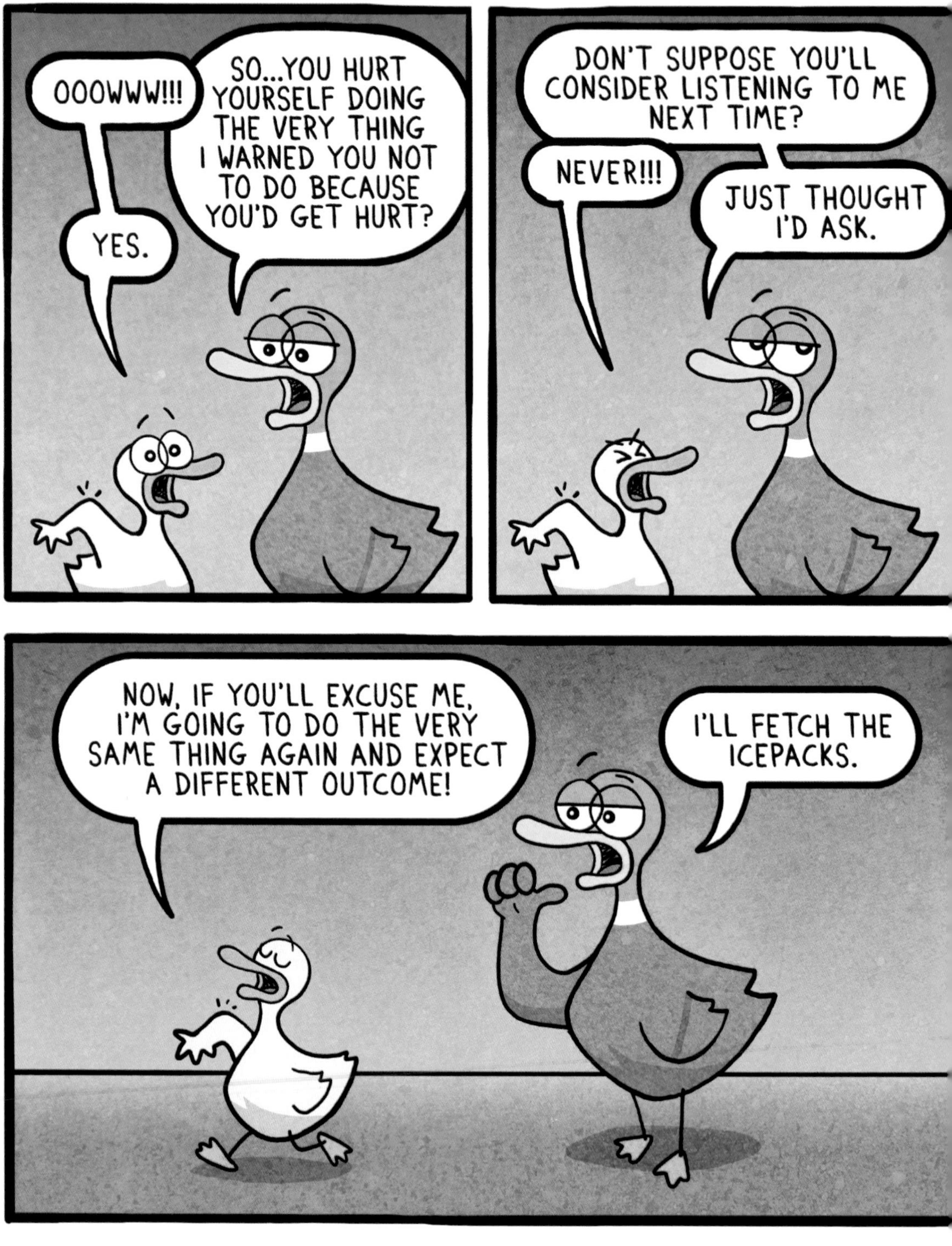
OOOWWW!!!
SO...YOU HURT YOURSELF DOING THE VERY THING I WARNED YOU NOT TO DO BECAUSE YOU'D GET HURT?
YES.
DON'T SUPPOSE YOU'LL CONSIDER LISTENING TO ME NEXT TIME?
NEVER!!!
JUST THOUGHT I'D ASK.
NOW, IF YOU'LL EXCUSE ME, I'M GOING TO DO THE VERY SAME THING AGAIN AND EXPECT A DIFFERENT OUTCOME!
I'LL FETCH THE ICEPACKS.

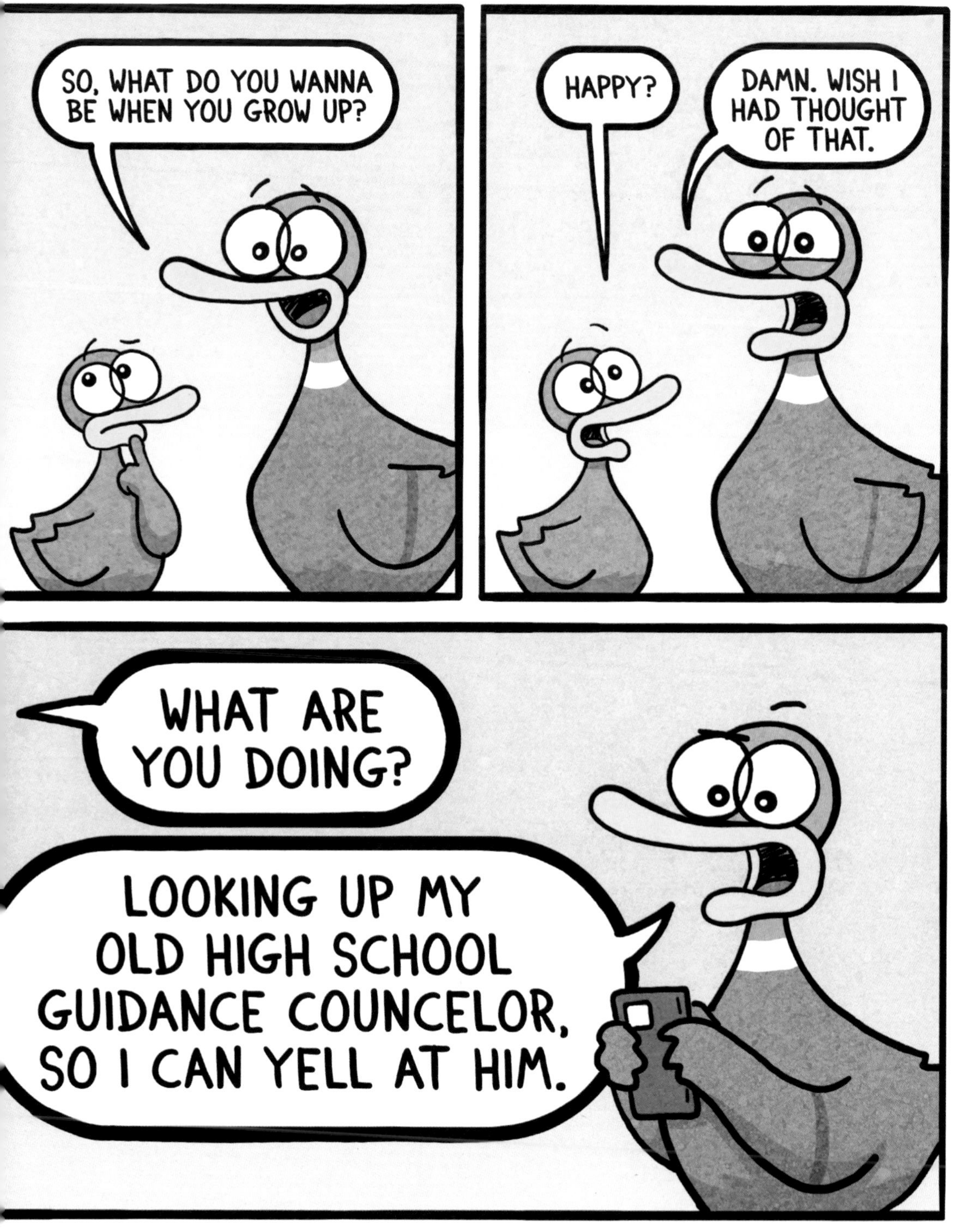
SO, WHAT DO YOU WANNA BE WHEN YOU GROW UP?
HAPPY?
DAMN. WISH I HAD THOUGHT OF THAT.
WHAT ARE YOU DOING?
LOOKING UP MY OLD HIGH SCHOOL GUIDANCE COUNCELOR, SO I CAN YELL AT HIM.

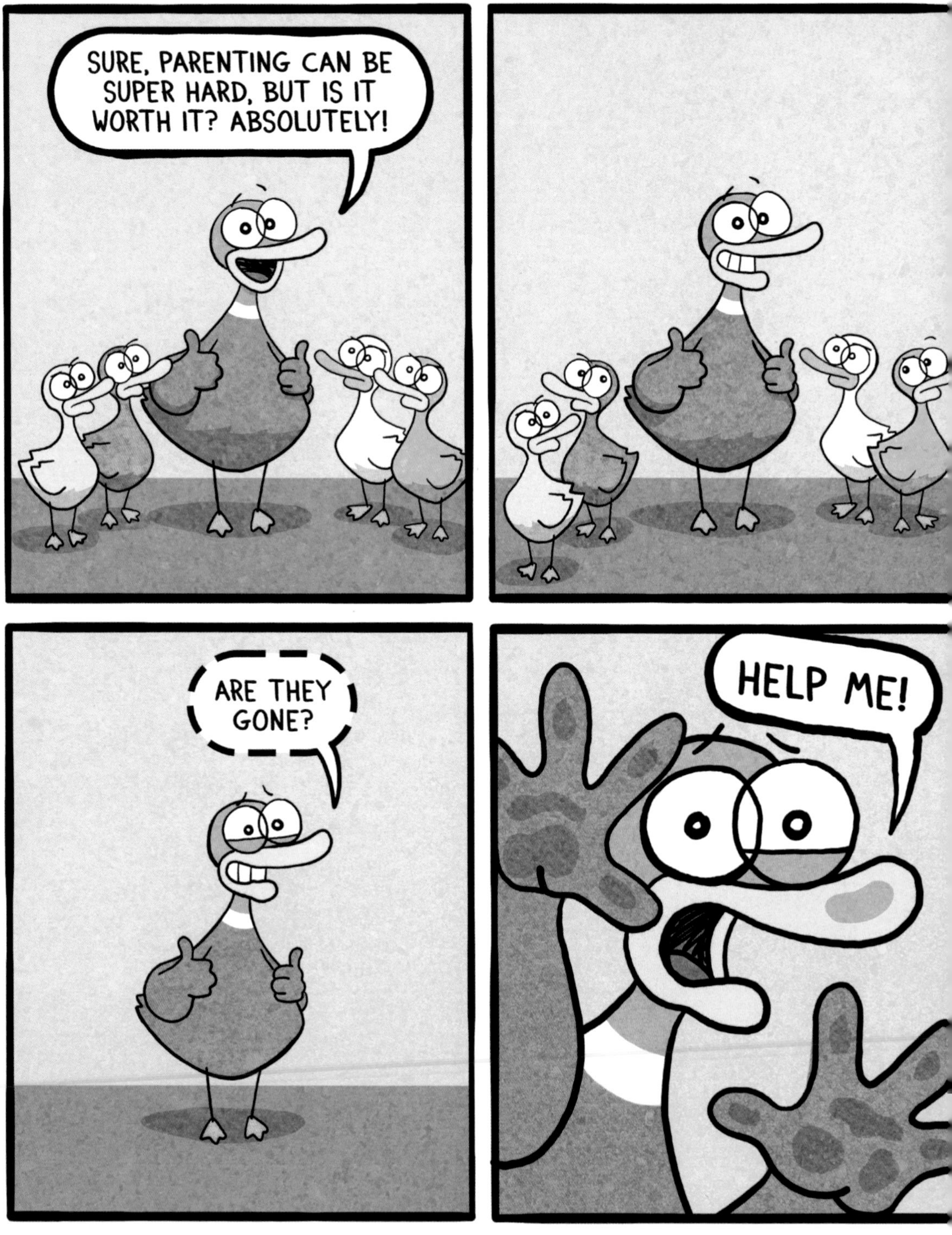
SURE, PARENTING CAN BE SUPER HARD, BUT IS IT WORTH IT? ABSOLUTELY!
ARE THEY GONE?
HELP ME!

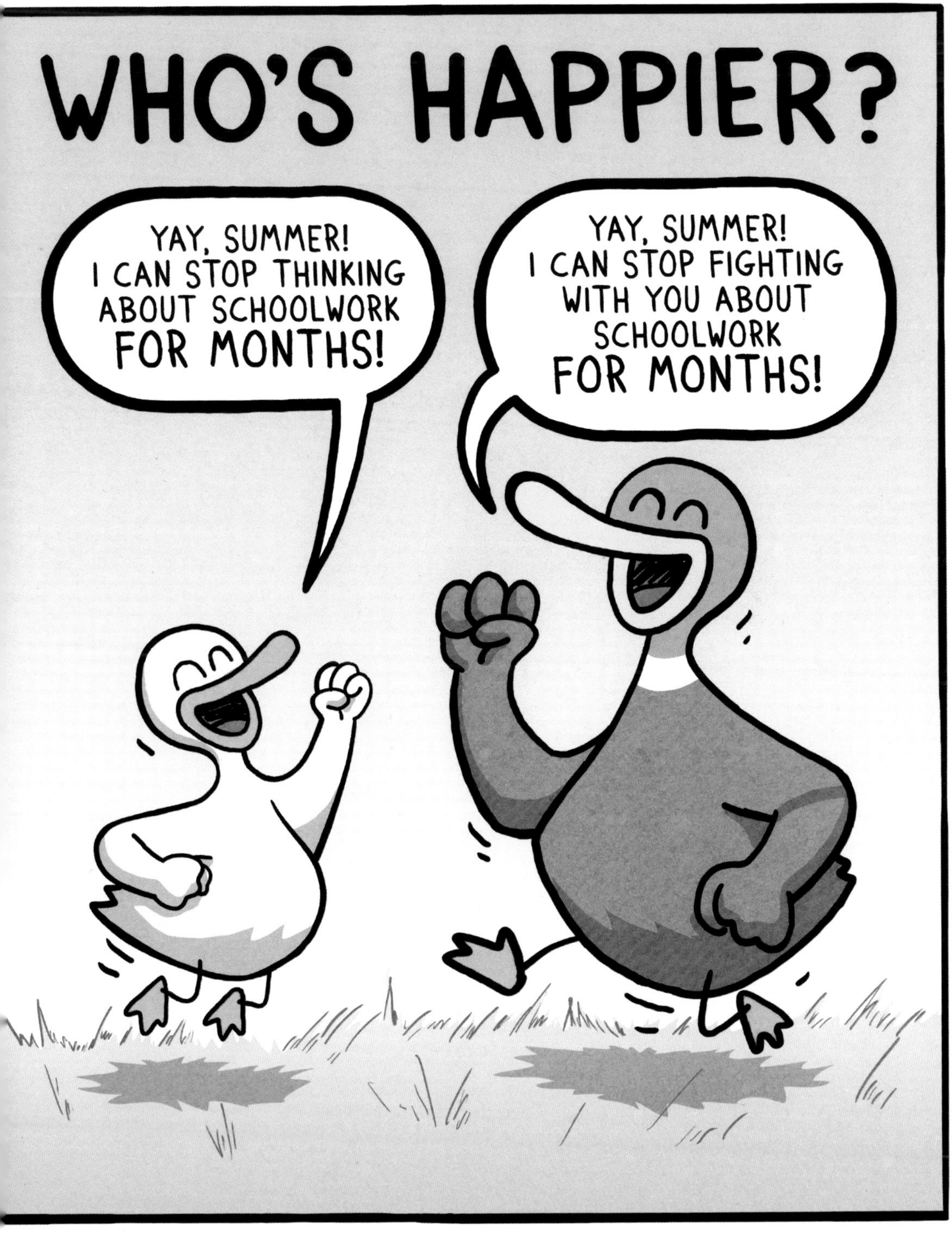
WHO'S HAPPIER?
YAY, SUMMER! I CAN STOP THINKING ABOUT SCHOOLWORK FOR MONTHS!
YAY, SUMMER! I CAN STOP FIGHTING WITH YOU ABOUT SCHOOLWORK FOR MONTHS!

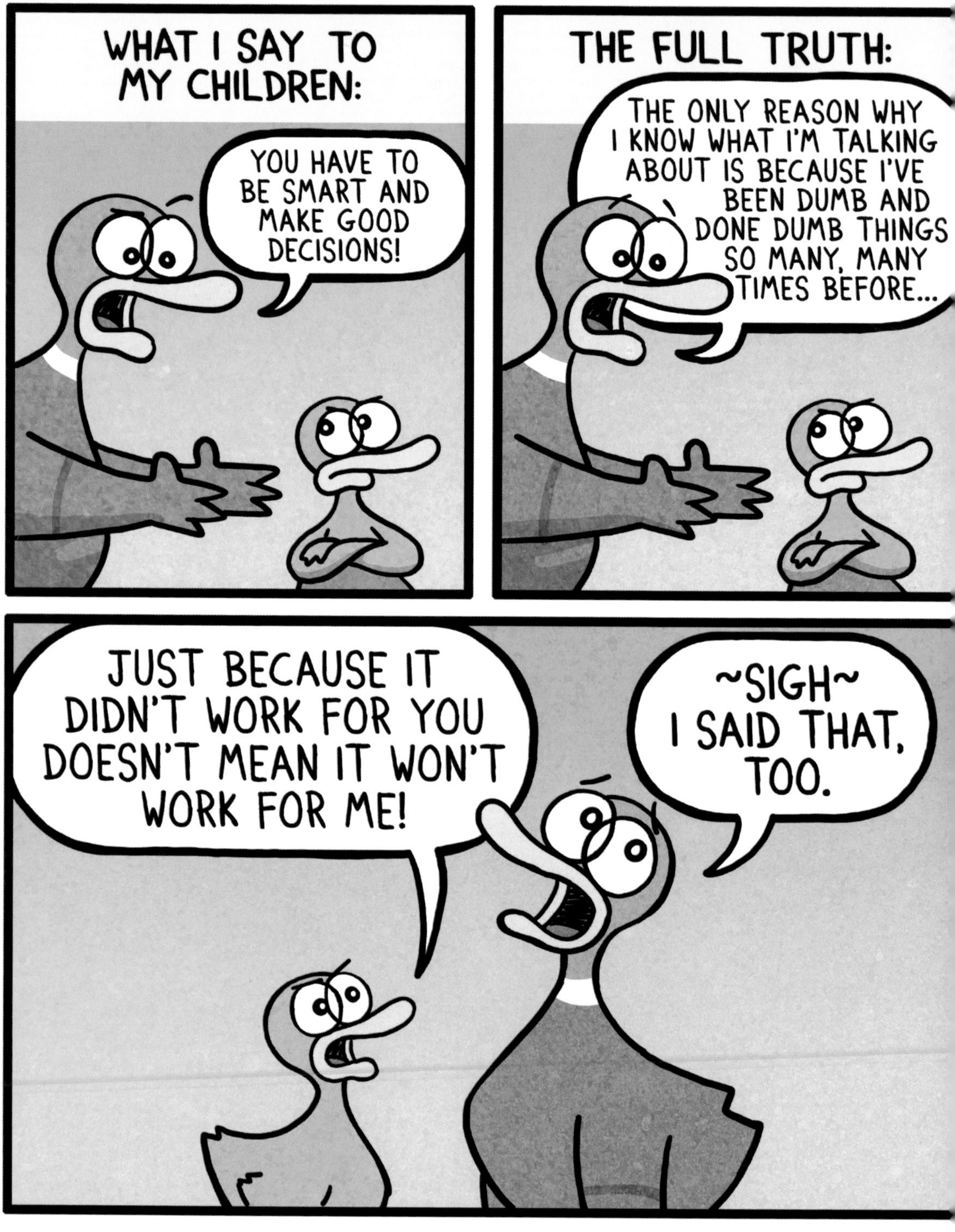
WHAT I SAY TO MY CHILDREN:
YOU HAVE TO BE SMART AND MAKE GOOD DECISIONS!
THE FULL TRUTH:
THE ONLY REASON WHY I KNOW WHAT I'M TALKING ABOUT IS BECAUSE I'VE BEEN DUMB AND DONE DUMB THINGS SO MANY, MANY TIMES BEFORE...
JUST BECAUSE IT DIDN'T WORK FOR YOU DOESN'T MEAN IT WON'T WORK FOR ME!
~SIGH~ I SAID THAT, TOO.

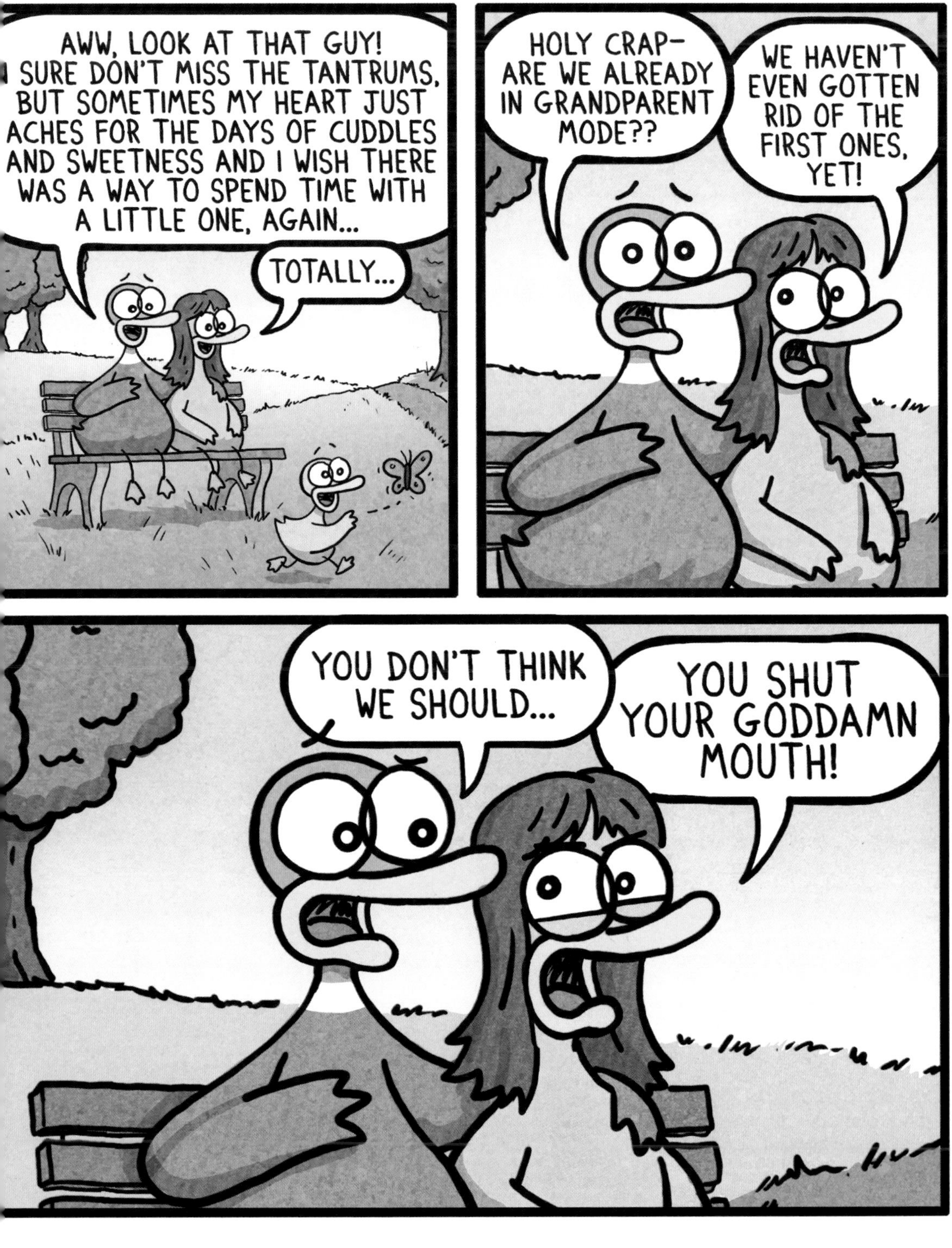
AWW, LOOK AT THAT GUY! I SURE DON'T MISS THE TANTRUMS, BUT SOMETIMES MY HEART JUST ACHES FOR THE DAYS OF CUDDLES AND SWEETNESS AND I WISH THERE WAS A WAY TO SPEND TIME WITH A LITTLE ONE, AGAIN...
TOTALLY...
HOLY CRAP– ARE WE ALREADY IN GRANDPARENT MODE??
WE HAVEN'T EVEN GOTTEN RID OF THE FIRST ONES, YET!
YOU DON'T THINK WE SHOULD...
YOU SHUT YOUR GODDAMN MOUTH!

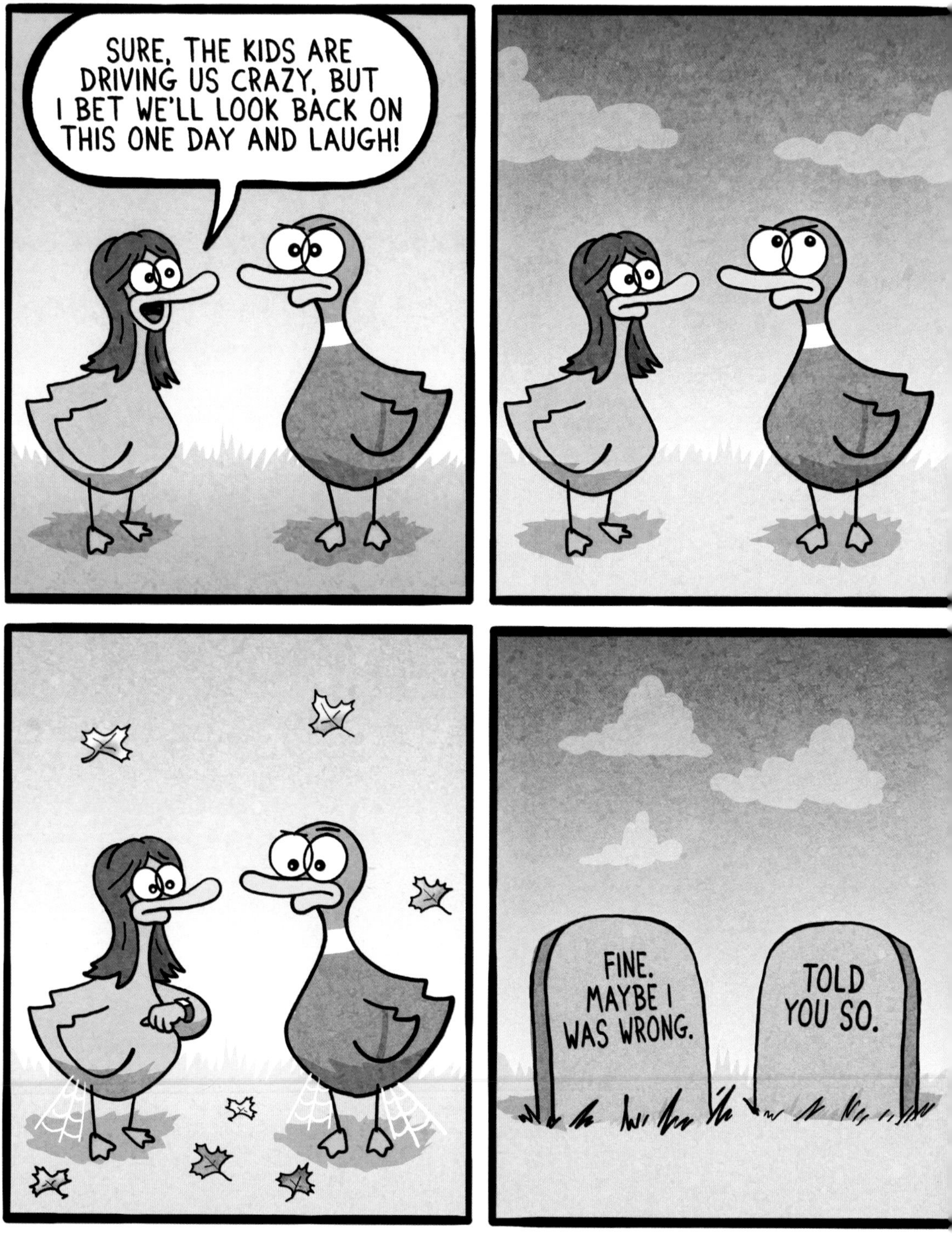
SURE, THE KIDS ARE DRIVING US CRAZY, BUT I BET WE'LL LOOK BACK ON THIS ONE DAY AND LAUGH!
FINE. MAYBE I WAS WRONG.
TOLD YOU SO.

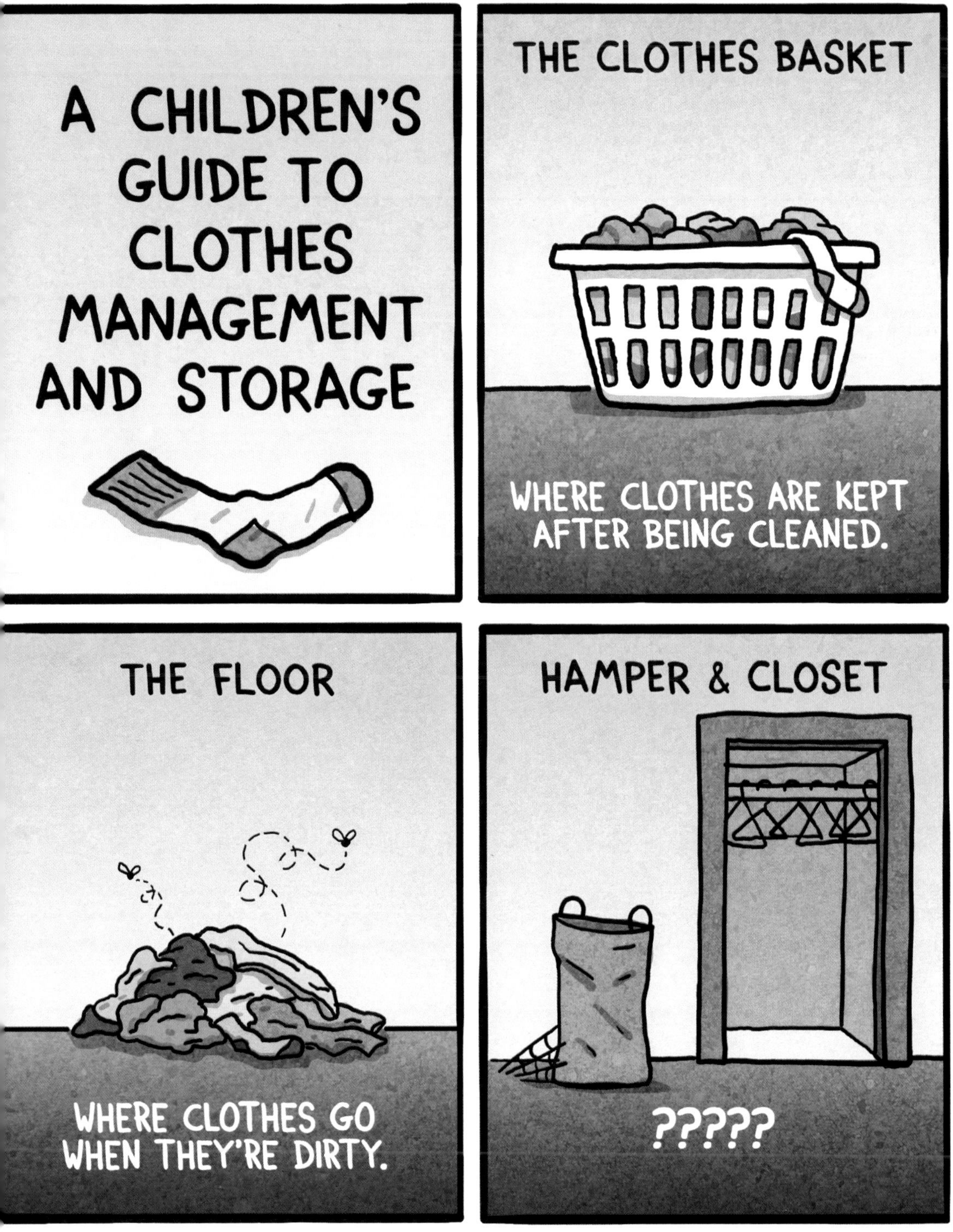
A CHILDREN'S GUIDE TO CLOTHES MANAGEMENT AND STORAGE
THE CLOTHES BASKET
WHERE CLOTHES ARE KEPT AFTER BEING CLEANED.
THE FLOOR
WHERE CLOTHES GO WHEN THEY'RE DIRTY.
HAMPER & CLOSET
?????

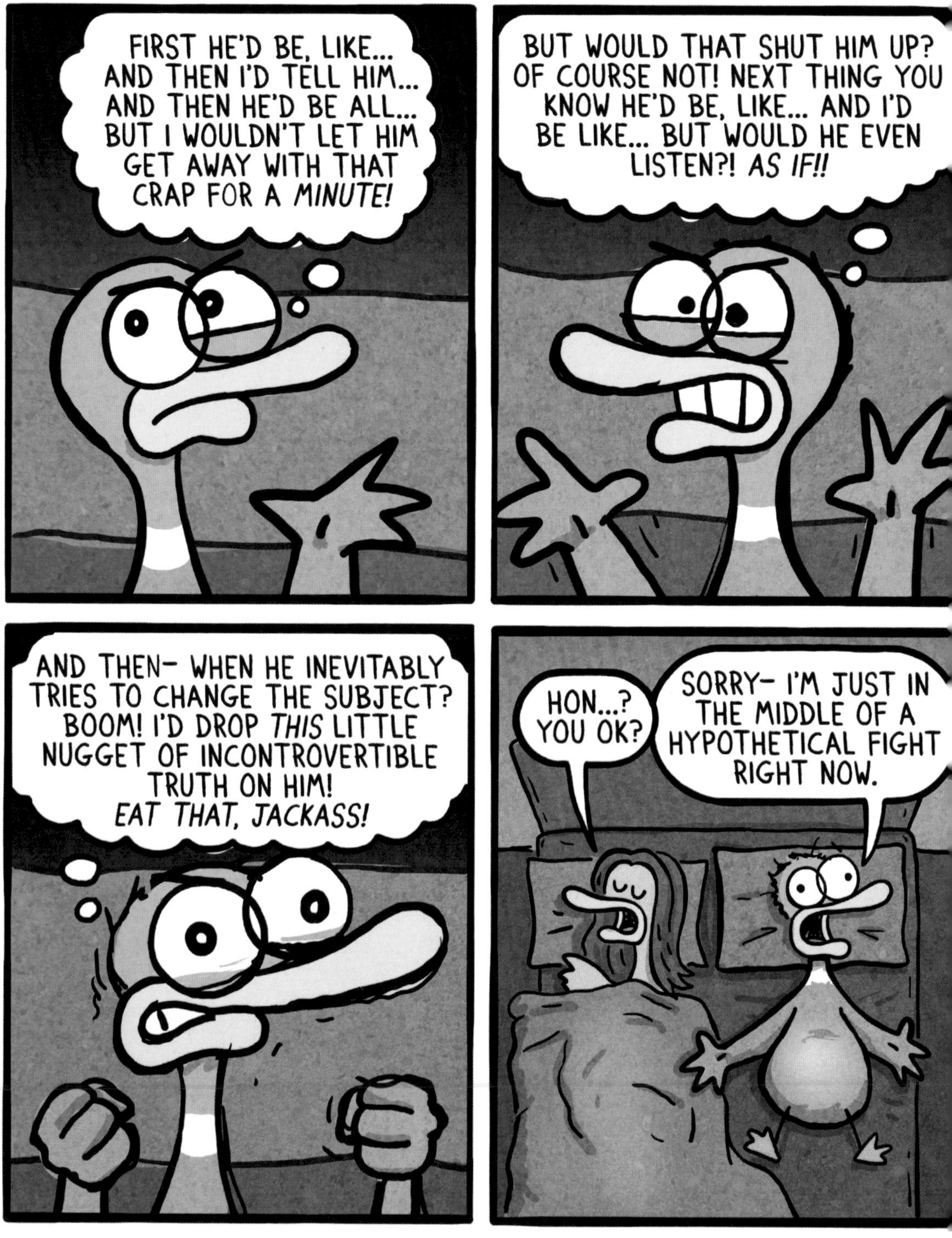
FIRST HE'D BE, LIKE... AND THEN I'D TELL HIM... AND THEN HE'D BE ALL... BUT I WOULDN'T LET HIM GET AWAY WITH THAT CRAP FOR A *MINUTE!*
BUT WOULD THAT SHUT HIM UP? OF COURSE NOT! NEXT THING YOU KNOW HE'D BE, LIKE... AND I'D BE LIKE... BUT WOULD HE EVEN LISTEN?! *AS IF!!*
AND THEN– WHEN HE INEVITABLY TRIES TO CHANGE THE SUBJECT? BOOM! I'D DROP *THIS* LITTLE NUGGET OF INCONTROVERTIBLE TRUTH ON HIM! *EAT THAT, JACKASS!*
HON...? YOU OK?
SORRY– I'M JUST IN THE MIDDLE OF A HYPOTHETICAL FIGHT RIGHT NOW.

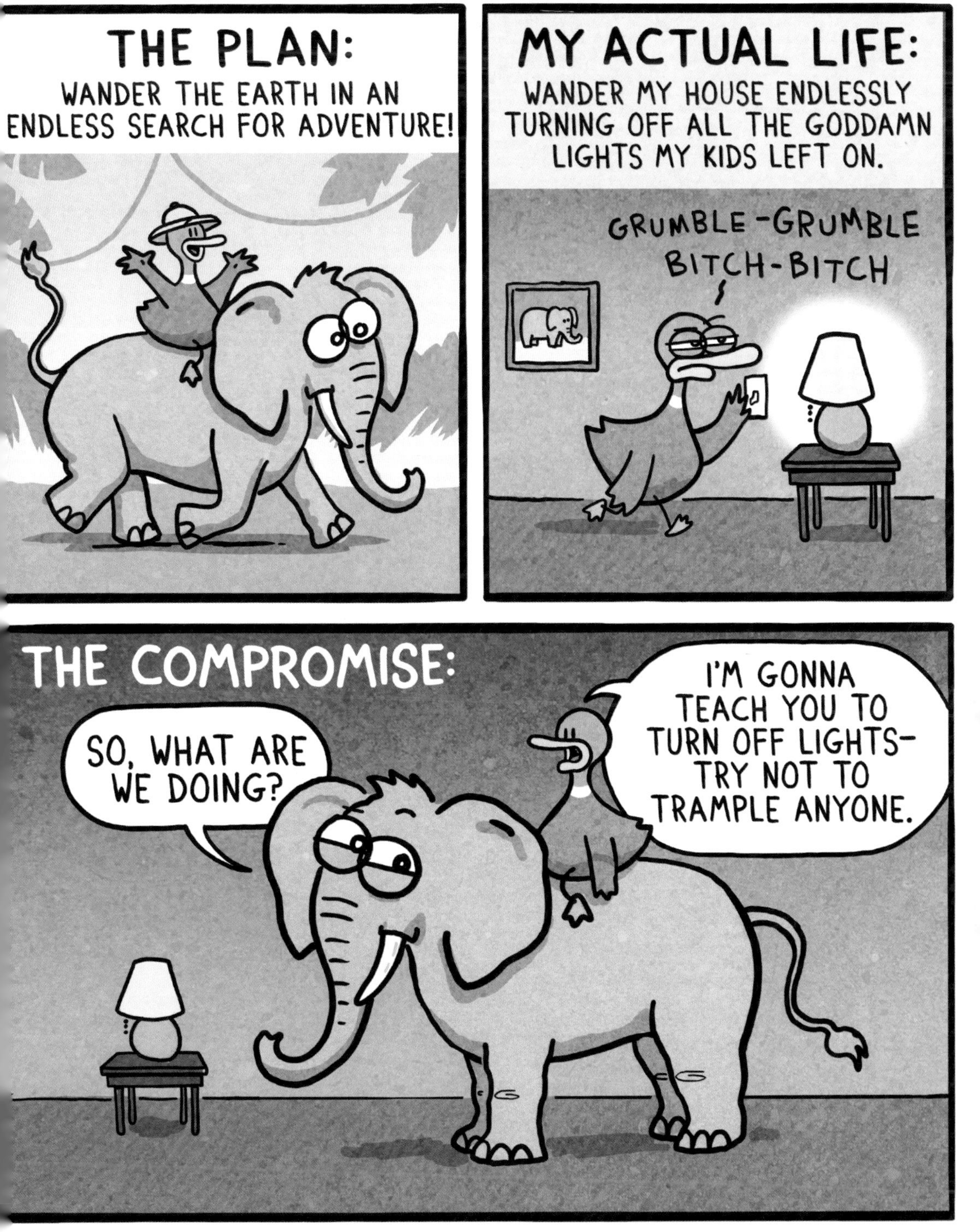
THE PLAN:
WANDER THE EARTH IN AN ENDLESS SEARCH FOR ADVENTURE!
MY ACTUAL LIFE:
WANDER MY HOUSE ENDLESSLY TURNING OFF ALL THE GODDAMN LIGHTS MY KIDS LEFT ON.
GRUMBLE-GRUMBLE BITCH-BITCH
THE COMPROMISE:
SO, WHAT ARE WE DOING?
I'M GONNA TEACH YOU TO TURN OFF LIGHTS- TRY NOT TO TRAMPLE ANYONE.

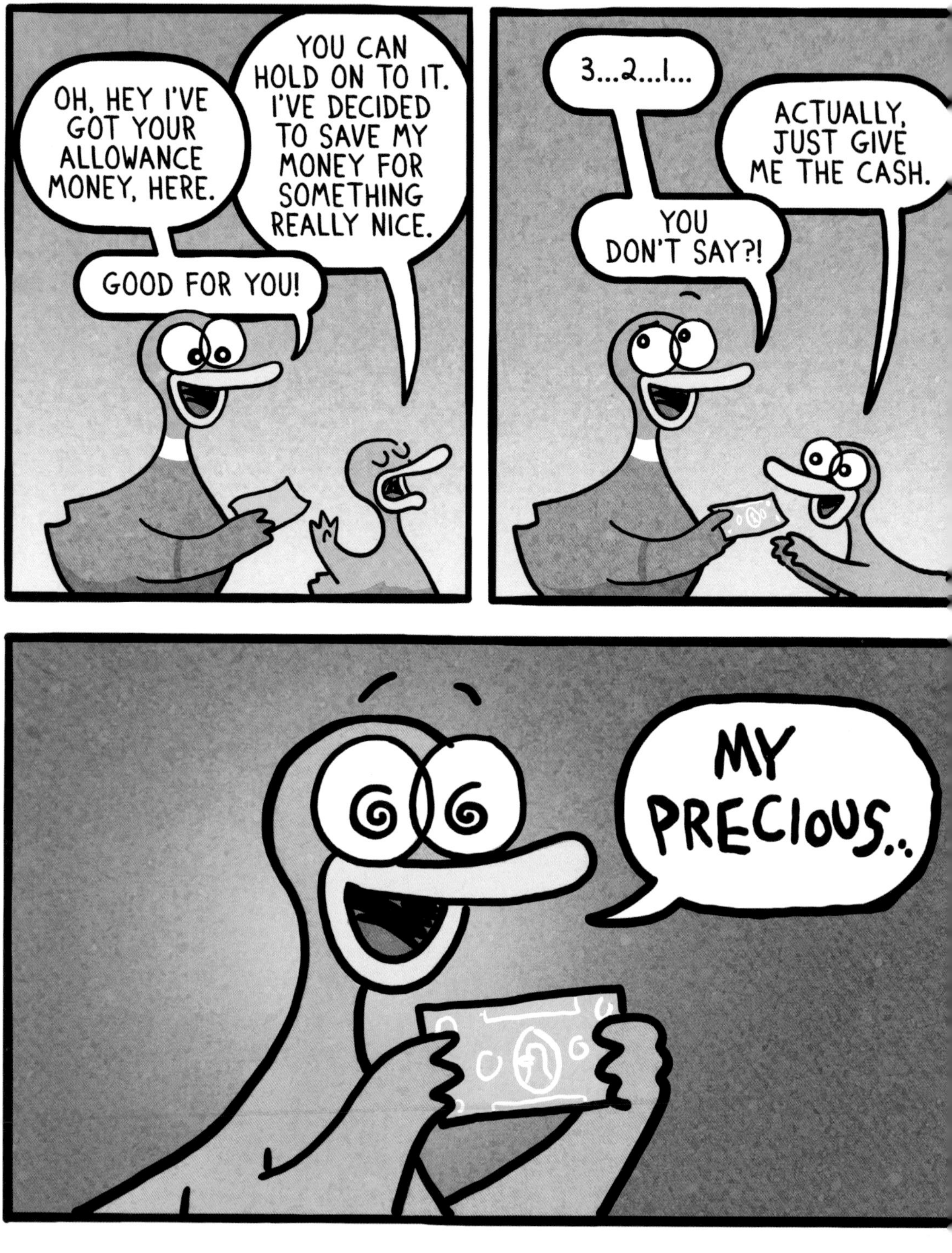

OH, HEY I'VE GOT YOUR ALLOWANCE MONEY, HERE.
YOU CAN HOLD ON TO IT. I'VE DECIDED TO SAVE MY MONEY FOR SOMETHING REALLY NICE.
GOOD FOR YOU!
3...2...1...
ACTUALLY, JUST GIVE ME THE CASH.
YOU DON'T SAY?!
MY PRECIOUS...

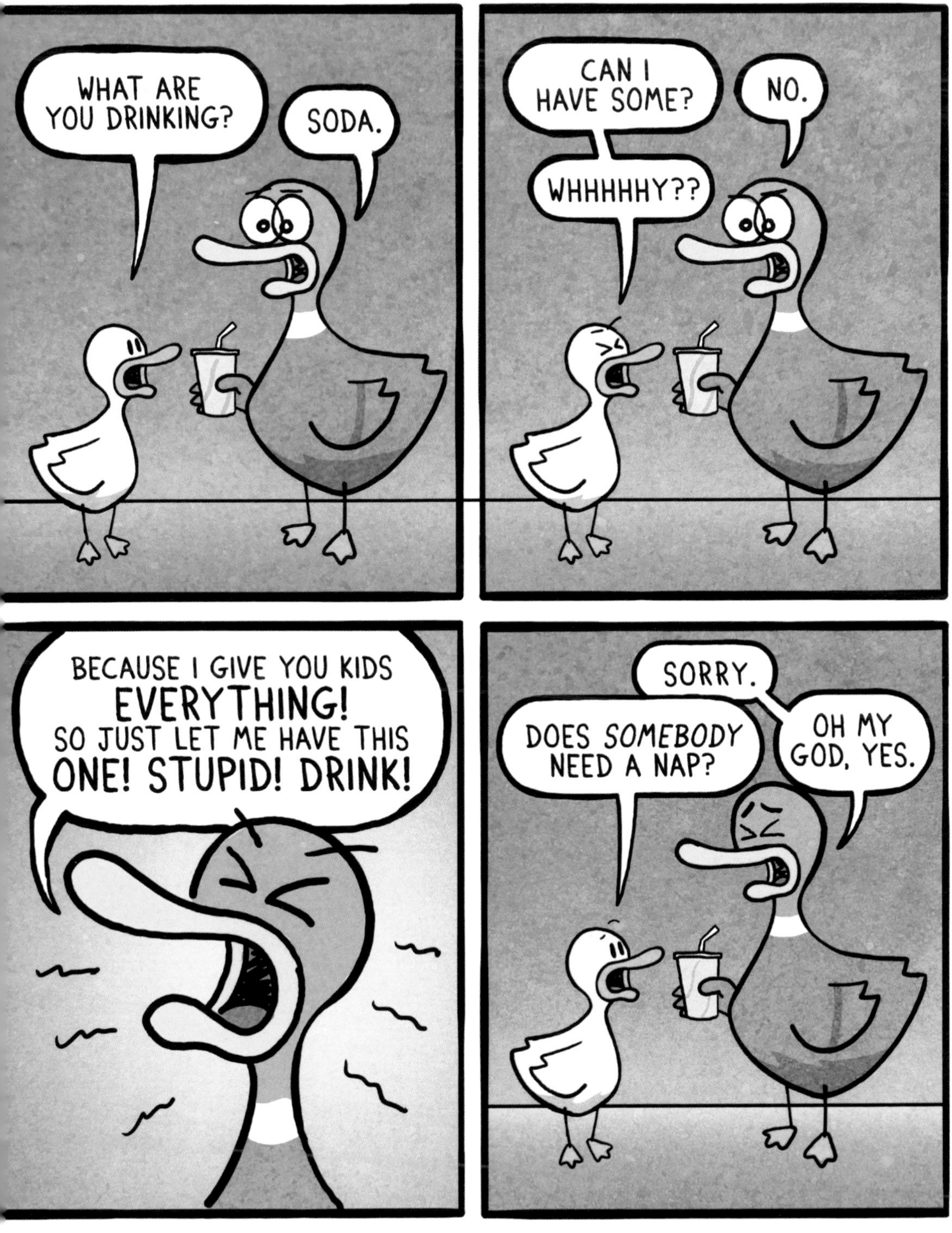
WHAT ARE YOU DRINKING?
SODA.
CAN I HAVE SOME?
NO.
WHHHHHY??
BECAUSE I GIVE YOU KIDS EVERYTHING! SO JUST LET ME HAVE THIS ONE! STUPID! DRINK!
DOES SOMEBODY NEED A NAP?
OH MY GOD, YES.
SORRY.

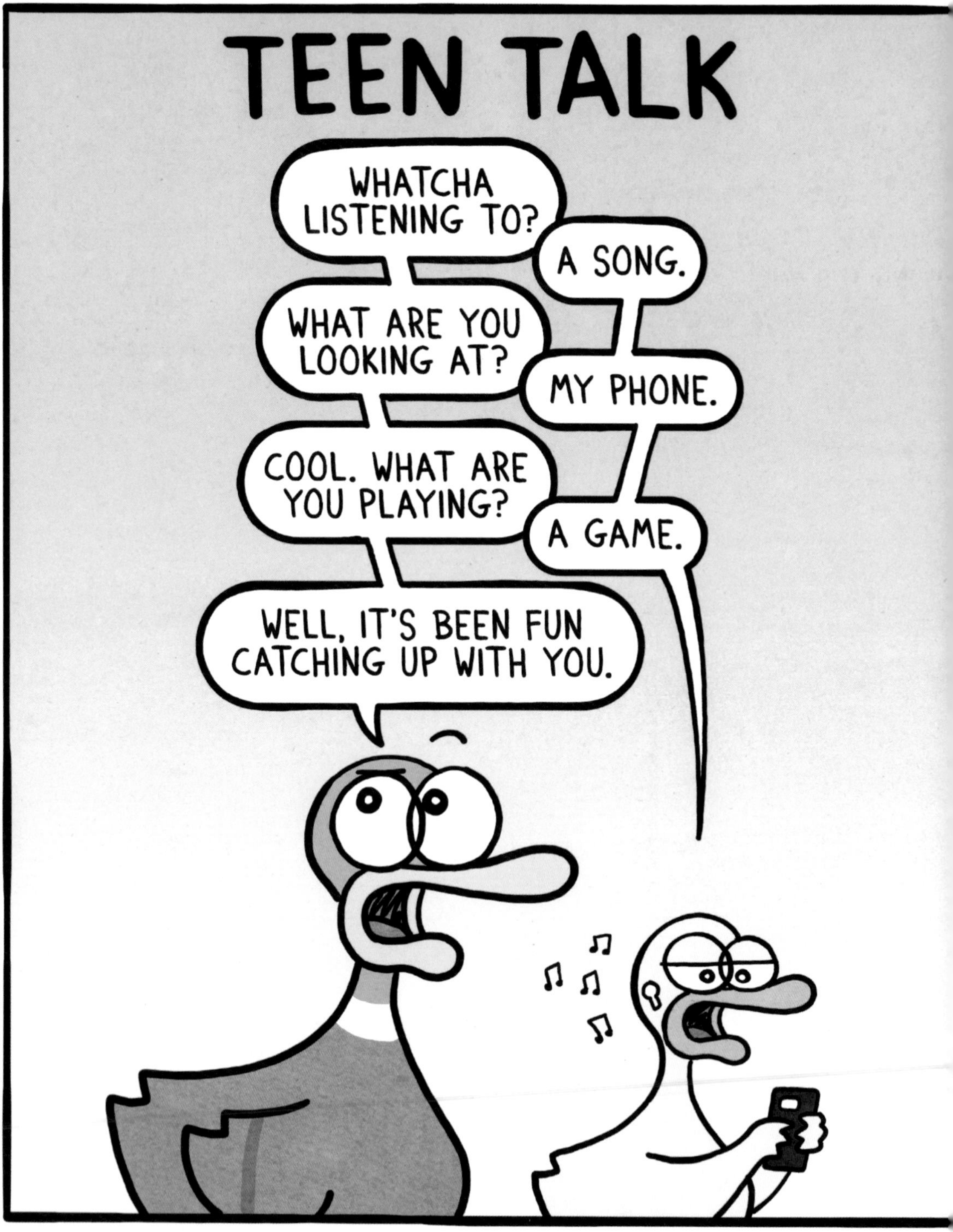
TEEN TALK
WHATCHA LISTENING TO?
A SONG.
WHAT ARE YOU LOOKING AT?
MY PHONE.
COOL. WHAT ARE YOU PLAYING?
A GAME.
WELL, IT'S BEEN FUN CATCHING UP WITH YOU.

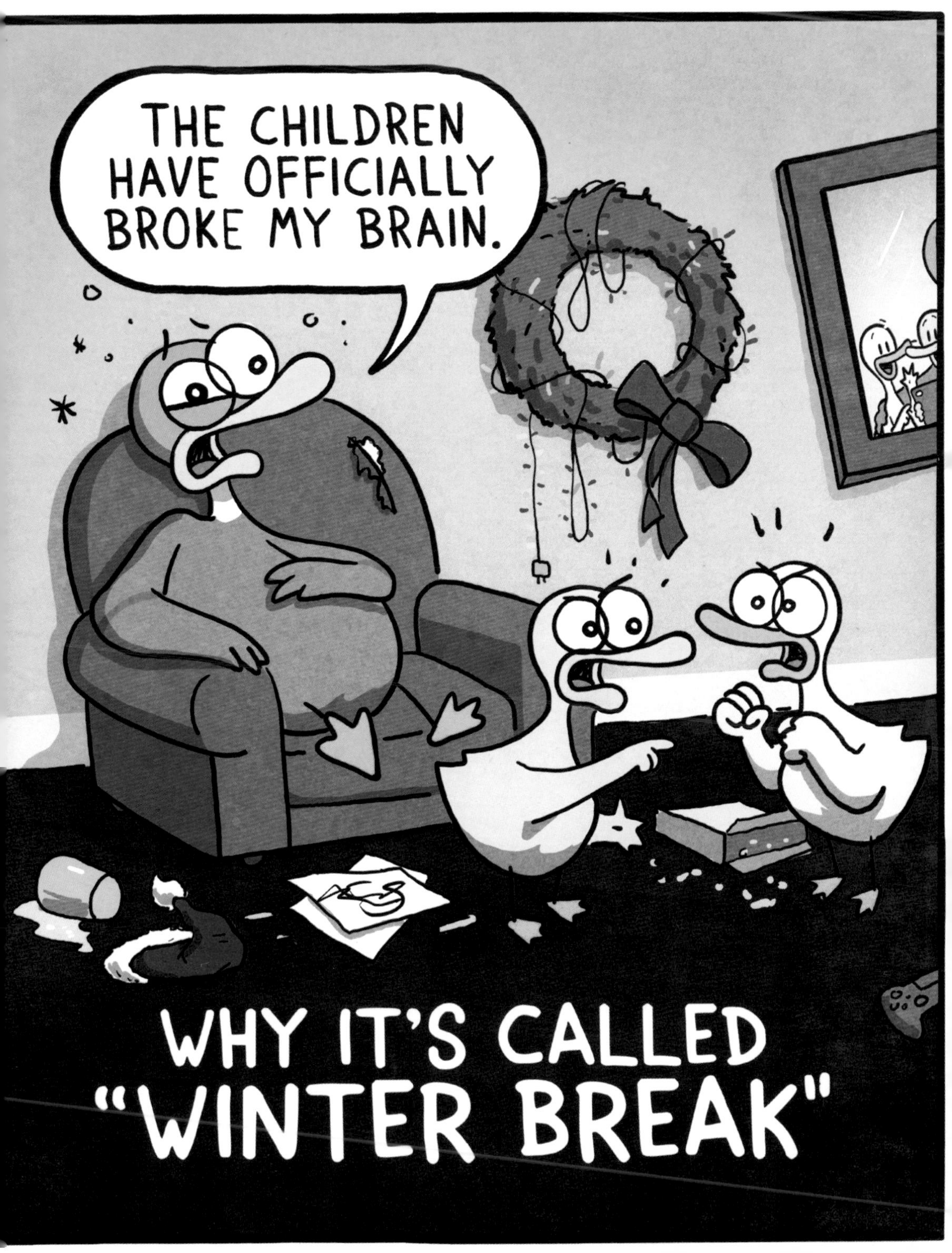
THE CHILDREN HAVE OFFICIALLY BROKE MY BRAIN.
WHY IT'S CALLED "WINTER BREAK"

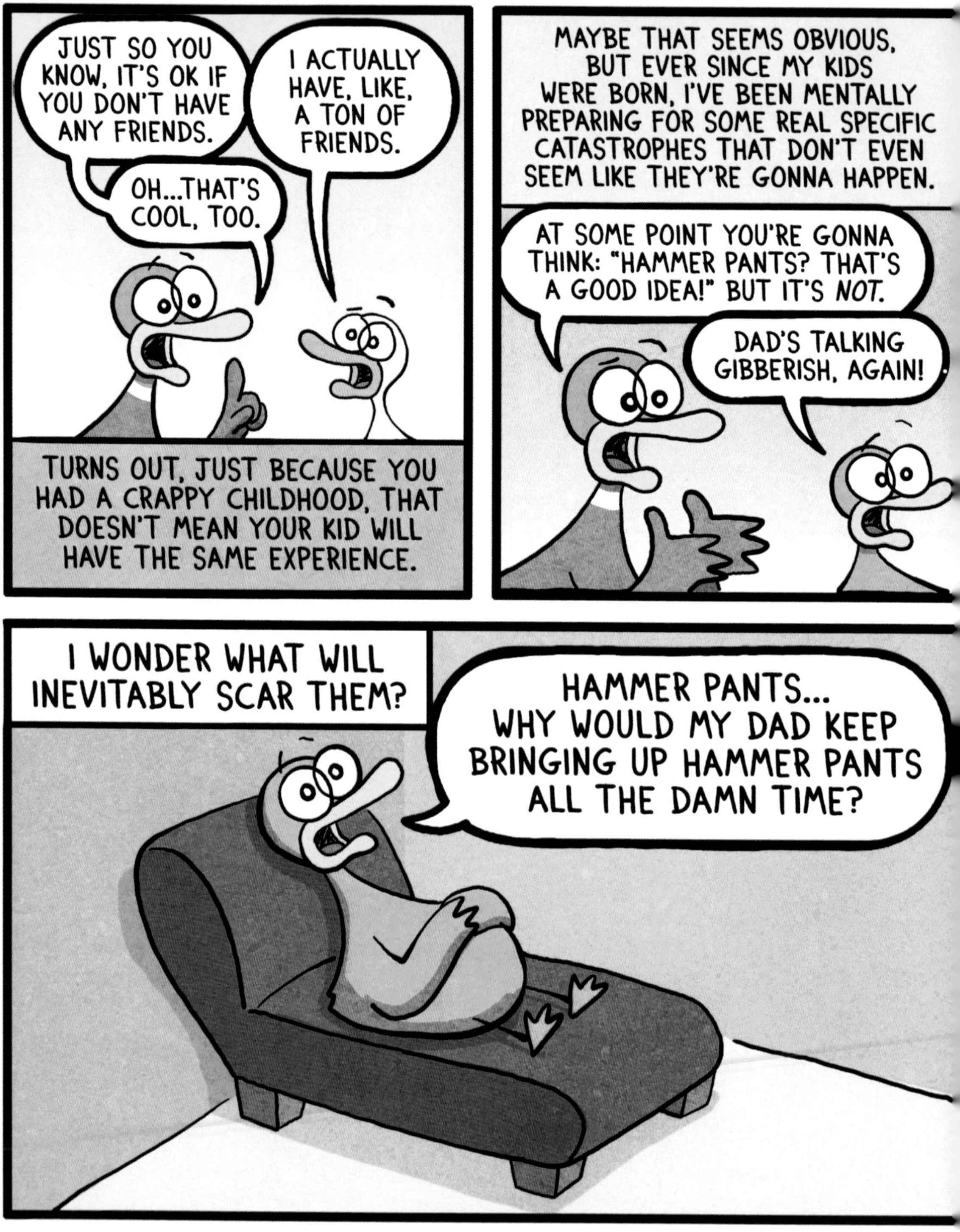
JUST SO YOU KNOW, IT'S OK IF YOU DON'T HAVE ANY FRIENDS.
I ACTUALLY HAVE, LIKE, A TON OF FRIENDS.
OH...THAT'S COOL, TOO.
TURNS OUT, JUST BECAUSE YOU HAD A CRAPPY CHILDHOOD, THAT DOESN'T MEAN YOUR KID WILL HAVE THE SAME EXPERIENCE.
MAYBE THAT SEEMS OBVIOUS, BUT EVER SINCE MY KIDS WERE BORN, I'VE BEEN MENTALLY PREPARING FOR SOME REAL SPECIFIC CATASTROPHES THAT DON'T EVEN SEEM LIKE THEY'RE GONNA HAPPEN.
AT SOME POINT YOU'RE GONNA THINK: "HAMMER PANTS? THAT'S A GOOD IDEA!" BUT IT'S *NOT*.
DAD'S TALKING GIBBERISH, AGAIN!
I WONDER WHAT WILL INEVITABLY SCAR THEM?
HAMMER PANTS... WHY WOULD MY DAD KEEP BRINGING UP HAMMER PANTS ALL THE DAMN TIME?

Prints!

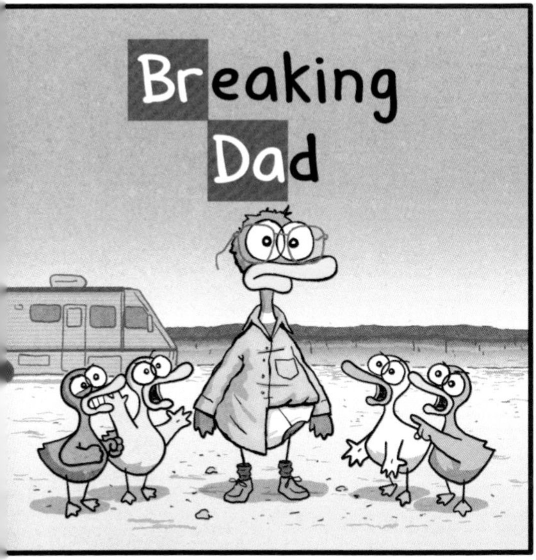
Breaking
Dad

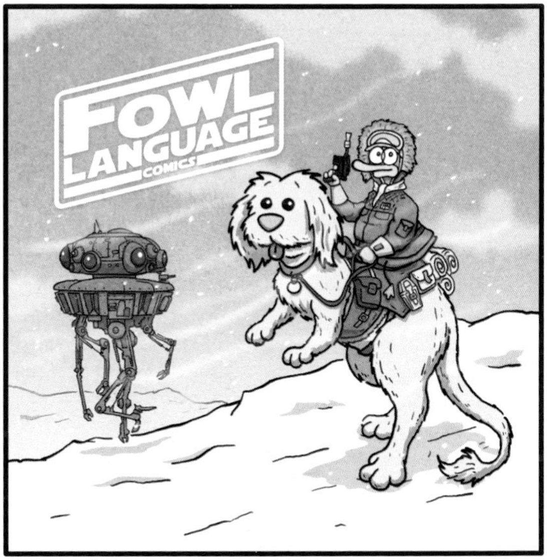
FOWL
LANGUAGE
COMICS

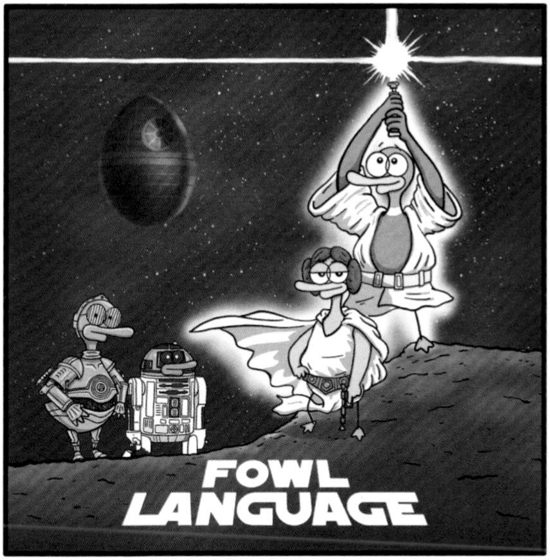
FOWL
LANGUAGE

Just one last note of thanks to everyone who has supported my
work over the years, both on Tinyview.com and on Patreon.
It's been my joy and privledge to share my stuggles, frustrations and more
than a couple mushy moments with you all. Without your help I would have
been out of a job long, long ago.

Much love, Brian

Brian Gordon began drawing FOWL LANGUAGE back in 2013 as a fun (and often profane) way to vent his frustrations over the day-to-day challenges of being a parent to two small children. Over the years, his super-relatable comics have become a viral Internet sensation, shared regularly by millions of overworked parents all over the world! He's since remarried and with two more ducks in his flock, the material just keeps on coming.

Brian's also the creator behind the mystery comic series FRANKIE FEARLESS— you can read both comics (as well as many others) at tinyview.com or on the TinyView app.

And of course, you'll find him on all your favorite social media outlets—and let's face it, he's way more fun to read than your cousin's political posts.